SERVICES FOR TRIAL USE

**AUTHORIZED ALTERNATIVES
TO PRAYER BOOK SERVICES**

1971
THE CHURCH HYMNAL CORPORATION
A Contributing Affiliate of
THE CHURCH PENSION FUND
800 Second Avenue, New York, N.Y. 10017

CERTIFICATE

I certify that the texts
in this edition of
Services for Trial Use
conform to the texts in
Prayer Book Studies 18 through 24
as authorized for trial use
by the General Convention of 1970.
    Charles Mortimer Guilbert
    Custodian of the Standard Book of Common Prayer

The readings from the Scriptures quoted in *The Order for the Burial of the Dead* (Second Service) are from *The New English Bible with the Apocrypha.* © The Delegates of the Oxford University Press and The Syndics of the Cambridge University Press, 1961, 1970. Reprinted by permission.

The three poems quoted in *The Order for the Burial of the Dead* (Second Service) are from *Your Word Is Near* by Huub Oosterhuis. Copyright © 1968 by The Missionary Society of St. Paul the Apostle in the State of New York. Reprinted by permission.

CONTENTS

iii

PREFACE

THE several services contained in this book have been authorized by the 63rd General Convention of the Episcopal Church, in Houston, Texas, for trial use during the triennium 1971–1973.

These forms of worship were prepared by the Standing Liturgical Commission in partial fulfillment of the Plan for Prayer Book Revision adopted by the General Convention in 1967. They are offered for trial use throughout the Church as alternatives to the corresponding services in The Book of Common Prayer, for study and for use in situations of actual worship, with a view to their further development and elaboration. They are not, at this stage, proposed as amendments to, or as substitutes for, the services in the Prayer Book.

The enabling resolutions specify that, "in accordance with Clause (b) of Article X of the Constitution," each Service or Order of Service is authorized "for trial use throughout this Church for a period of three years, as from January 1, 1971, as an alternative at any time or times" to the corresponding Order or Service in The Book of Common Prayer. The official report on the actions taken by the Convention is given in *The Summary of General Convention Actions,* dated November 1970, and prepared by the Secretaries of the House of Deputies and the House of Bishops.

There are two exceptions to the above authorization. One is in respect of The Calendar and The Proper of The Church Year, which are authorized as from the First Sunday in Advent 1970, beginning with the Proper of Year C. Beginning with Advent 1971, Year A is to be used; and from Advent 1972, Year B is to be used. Year C will be used again beginning with Advent 1973, provided that the General Convention of 1973 extends the authorization to use these lections.

The other exception concerns Holy Baptism with the Laying-on-of-Hands. Under the resolution adopted by the General Convention, trial use of this rite is authorized subject to the following specific guidelines:

1) The rite in its entirety may be used by Bishops only, and only in respect of persons who have reached the "present age normal for confirmation";

2) Only the Baptismal section of the rite may be used by priests and other ministers, subject to the consent and direction of the Ordinary, omitting the Laying-on-of-Hands, and the preceding prayer;

3) Children may be admitted to Holy Communion before Confirmation, subject to the direction and guidance of the Ordinary;

4) All Bishops are required to arrange for an intensive study of, and instruction in, Baptism with the Laying-on-of-Hands before the beginning of trial use.

The text of the official report on the General Convention's resolution is reproduced on page 21 of this book, immediately preceding the text of the rite. Because of the decision in paragraph (4) above, calling for an intensive study of the rite as proposed, no attempt has been made to change any part of the rite. It is reproduced exactly as it was presented to the Convention in *Prayer Book Studies* 18. The other services are also reproduced as they first appeared in *Prayer Book Studies* 19 through 24.*

For reasons of economy and convenience, the Introductions to these rites have been omitted from this pew-edition. It must be emphasized, however, that in order to understand the back-

* *Prayer Book Studies* 19, The Church Year; PBS 20, The Ordination of Bishops, Priests, and Deacons; PBS 21, The Holy Eucharist; PBS 22, The Daily Office; PBS 23, The Psalter: Part I; PBS 24, Pastoral Offices. They were prepared by The Standing Liturgical Commission and published by The Church Hymnal Corporation, 800 Second Avenue, New York, N.Y. 10017. Individual copies and complete sets of the Studies may be obtained from The Church Hymnal Corporation.

ground and rationale of the various services, it is essential to consult these Studies. They are indispensable for an intelligent and informed use of the present book.

It is hoped that every parish will have several sets of the Studies available for consultation by interested worshipers and for study by groups.

It will be seen that the services are printed in very different styles of layout and type-face. The reason for this is that the pages which follow are, for the most part, reproduced from the pages of Prayer Book Studies. The Standing Liturgical Commission considers that the format of the services is no less a matter of experimentation than the rites themselves. It hopes that the comments of Church members will help the Commission to decide in which of several styles a future revised Book of Common Prayer should be printed.

The order in which the services are presented in this book is not necessarily the sequence which the future revised Prayer Book will follow. The sequence in the present edition is not, however, without logic. The book begins with the Calendar of the Church Year as the framework which determines most of the liturgical observances. This is taken from *Prayer Book Studies* 19. The Collects and Lectionary from that book appear at the very end.

The Calendar is followed by the first of the major Sacraments, Baptism with the Laying-on-of Hands (*Prayer Book Studies* 18). The second great Sacrament of our Redemption follows: The Holy Eucharist (*Prayer Book Studies* 21). The Psalter: Part I (*Prayer Book Studies* 23) follows immediately. The Psalter is thus located between the Holy Eucharist and the Daily Office, since both make regular use of Psalms. The Daily Office (*Prayer Book Studies* 22) is followed by the Pastoral Offices (*Prayer Book Studies* 24), roughly in the same sequence as in The Book of Common Prayer. The book concludes with the Ordination of Bishops, Priests, and Deacons (*Prayer Book Studies* 20) and the Collects and Lectionary from *Prayer Book Studies* 19.

In several of the services, especially in the Holy Eucharist and the Daily Office, new—and, to many, unfamiliar—texts of the Creeds, the Lord's Prayer, and certain other formularies will be found. Some of them are identified as ICET texts. These initials stand for the International Consultation on English Texts, a group consisting of representatives of the official liturgical or worship commissions of the several major Christian bodies: the Anglican Churches, including the Episcopal Church in the United States, the Church of England, the Episcopal Church of Scotland, the Church of Ireland and the Church in Wales; the Roman Catholic Church, including representatives from England, Ireland, the United States, Canada, and Australia; the Lutheran Churches, including the Lutheran Church in America, the American Lutheran Church, and the Lutheran Church —Missouri Synod; and the (Presbyterian) Church of Scotland, and the English Methodist, Presbyterian, Congregational and Baptist Churches.

The ICET has prepared common versions of the most widely-used liturgical texts, and has recommended them to the respective Churches for trial use. The General Convention, acting on the recommendation of the Standing Liturgical Commission, has authorized the trial use of the texts in all the services which use contemporary English. However, the ICET version of the Nicene Creed is printed in both Eucharistic rites, the traditional and contemporary, thus providing an ecumenical version of the great ecumenical statement of the Church's faith. A detailed note on the ICET may be found on pages 31–34 of *Prayer Book Studies* 21 on The Holy Eucharist, and on pages 38–41 of *Prayer Book Studies* 22 on The Daily Office.

Certain of the services and prayers contained in the present edition appear in two forms: a contemporary and a traditional form. This is true of the Holy Eucharist, where two complete services are given (and also an Order for Celebrating the Holy Eucharist on occasions other than the principal service on Sundays and other Feasts of our Lord) ; the Daily Office, where two forms are given for Morning and Evening Prayer; the Order for the Burial of the Dead; and the Collects for Sundays, Holy Days and special occasions.

This duality of form is a direct result of the comments on, and reactions to, the trial use of *The Liturgy of The Lord's Supper* * received by the Standing Liturgical Commission during the triennium 1967–1970. A substantial minority of those who responded to the Commission's Questionnaires showed a deep-seated attachment to the traditional language of The Book of Common Prayer. The Commission responded to the expressed desire of many Churchmen by preparing revised services in two forms. This was not done, however, with a view to encouraging the formation of partisan groups within the Church, some wedded to one style, some to another. Rather, as the Introduction to The Holy Eucharist points out,** the Commission "offers these services for the whole Church, and not for separate parts of it. This implies a certain responsibility on the part of all types of congregation—from the homogeneous parish in a stable community to an *ad hoc* gathering of Christians in the most uncommon circumstances—to make use of all the orders, to study them thoroughly, to consider them thoughtfully, and to experiment reverently with each of them."

All worshipers are invited to comment on the services contained in this book, through their parish clergy and their Diocesan Liturgical Committees or Commissions. All comments will be given serious consideration, and will be taken into account in the preparation of such revisions of these services as may be necessary, in time for submission to the General Convention of 1973. To all who respond to this invitation, the Standing Liturgical Commission extends its sincere thanks.

THE STANDING LITURGICAL COMMISSION

* *Prayer Book Studies XVII,* "The Liturgy of The Lord's Supper," prepared by The Standing Liturgical Commission and published by The Church Pension Fund, 1967.
** *Prayer Book Studies* 21, pp. 29–30.

THE CALENDAR
OF THE CHURCH YEAR

With Rules of Precedence

THE CALENDAR
OF THE CHURCH YEAR
Observed in This Church

THE CHURCH YEAR consists of two cycles of feasts and holy days: the one is dependent upon the movable date of the Sunday of the Resurrection or Easter Day; the other, upon the fixed date of December 25, the feast of our Lord's Nativity or Christmas Day.

Easter Day is always the first Sunday after the full moon that falls on or after March 21. It cannot occur before March 22 or after April 25.

The sequence of all Sundays of the Church Year depends upon the date of Easter Day. But the Sundays in Advent are always the four Sundays prior to Christmas Day, whether it occurs on a Sunday or a weekday. The date of Easter also determines the beginning of Lent on Ash Wednesday, and the feast of the Ascension on a Thursday forty days after Easter.

1. SUNDAYS

All Sundays of the year are feasts of our Lord Jesus Christ.

Only the following feasts of our Lord Jesus Christ, appointed on fixed days, take precedence of a Sunday:

Christmas Day	The Presentation
The Holy Name	The Transfiguration
The Epiphany	All Saints' Day

All Saints' Day may always be observed on the Sunday following November 1, in addition to its observance on the fixed date.

All other feasts appointed on fixed days in the Calendar, which may occur on a Sunday, are observed on the nearest open day following. But the patronal or dedication feasts of a church may be observed on a Sunday, except those in the seasons of Advent, Lent, and Easter. With the express permission of the Ordinary, and for urgent and sufficient reason, some other special occasion may be observed on a Sunday.

2. HOLY DAYS

The following Holy Days are regularly observed throughout the year. Unless otherwise ordered in the preceding rules concerning Sundays, they have precedence over all other days of commemoration or of special observance:

Feasts of our Lord

Christmas Day	The Visitation
The Holy Name	The Nativity of Saint John
The Epiphany	the Baptist
The Presentation	The Transfiguration
The Annunciation	Holy Cross Day
Ascension Day	All Saints' Day

4

Other Major Feasts

All feasts of Apostles

All feasts of Evangelists

Saint Stephen

The Holy Innocents

Saint Joseph

Saint Mary Magdalene

Saint Mary the Virgin

Saint Michael and All Angels

Saint James, the Brother
   of our Lord

Independence Day

Thanksgiving Day

Fasts

Ash Wednesday   Good Friday

Feasts appointed on fixed days in the Calendar are not observed on the days of Holy Week or of Easter Week. Major feasts falling in these weeks are transferred to the first open day following the Second Sunday of Easter.

Feasts appointed on fixed days in the Calendar do not take precedence of Ash Wednesday or of Ascension Day.

Feasts of our Lord and other major feasts appointed on fixed days, which may fall upon or be transferred to a weekday, may be observed on any open day within the week in which they occur, except Christmas Day, the Epiphany, and All Saints' Day.

3. DAYS OF SPECIAL DEVOTION

The following days are observed by special acts of discipline and self-denial:

Ash Wednesday and the other weekdays of Lent and of Holy Week, except the feast of the Annunciation and other major feasts.

Good Friday and all other Fridays of the year, in commemoration of the Lord's crucifixion, except on Fridays in the Christmas and Easter seasons, and on any major feasts which may occur on a Friday.

5

4. DAYS OF OPTIONAL OBSERVANCE

Subject to the rules of precedence governing Sundays and holy days listed above, the following days may be observed, with the proper prayers and lessons duly authorized by this Church:

> Other commemorations listed in the Calendar
> The Common of Saints
> Special Occasions

Provided, that there is no celebration of the Eucharist for any special occasion on Ash Wednesday, Maundy Thursday, Good Friday, and Holy Saturday; and *provided further,* that no proper appointed for a special occasion is used as a substitute for, or as an addition to the proper appointed on Christmas Day, Easter Day, Ascension Day, and the Day of Pentecost.

The proper appointed for the Sunday serves for celebrations of the Eucharist on the weekdays following, unless otherwise ordered for holy days and special occasions.

The Collect appointed for any Sunday or other feast may be used at the evening service of the day before.

JANUARY

1 A THE HOLY NAME OF OUR LORD JESUS CHRIST

2 b

3 c

4 d

5 e

6 f THE EPIPHANY OF OUR LORD JESUS CHRIST

7 g

8 A

9 b

10 c William Laud, Archbishop of Canterbury, 1645

11 d

12 e

13 f Hilary, Bishop of Poitiers, 367

14 g

15 A

16 b

17 c Antony, Abbot in Egypt, 356

18 d THE CONFESSION OF SAINT PETER THE APOSTLE

19 e Wulfstan, Bishop of Worcester, 1095

20 f Fabian, Bishop and Martyr of Rome, 250

21 g Agnes, Martyr at Rome, 304

22 A Vincent, Deacon of Saragossa, and Martyr, 304

23 b Phillips Brooks, Bishop of Massachusetts, 1893

24 c

25 d THE CONVERSION OF SAINT PAUL THE APOSTLE

26 e Timothy and Titus, Companions of Saint Paul

27 f John Chrysostom, Bishop of Constantinople, 407

28 g Thomas Aquinas, Friar, 1274

29 A

30 b

31 c

FEBRUARY

1 d

2 e THE PRESENTATION OF OUR LORD JESUS CHRIST
     IN THE TEMPLE

3 f Anskar, Archbishop of Hamburg, Missionary
     to Denmark and Sweden, 865

4 g Cornelius the Centurion

5 A The Martyrs of Japan, 1597

6 b

7 c

8 d

9 e

10 f

11 g

12 A

13 b

14 c Cyril, Monk, and Methodius, Bishop, Missionaries
     to the Slavs, 869, 885

15 d Thomas Bray, Priest and Missionary, 1730

16 e

17 f

18 g

19 A

20 b

21 c

22 d

23 e Polycarp, Bishop and Martyr of Smyrna, 156

24 f SAINT MATTHIAS THE APOSTLE

25 g

26 A

27 b George Herbert, Priest, 1633

28 c

29

MARCH

1	d	David, Bishop of Menevia, Wales, c. 544
2	e	Chad, Bishop of Lichfield, 672
3	f	John and Charles Wesley, Priests, 1791, 1788
4	g	
5	A	
6	b	
7	c	Perpetua and her Companions, Martyrs at Carthage, 202
8	d	
9	e	Gregory, Bishop of Nyssa, c. 394
10	f	
11	g	
12	A	Gregory the Great, Bishop of Rome, 604
13	b	
14	c	
15	d	
16	e	
17	f	Patrick, Bishop and Missionary of Ireland, 461
18	g	Cyril, Bishop of Jerusalem, 386
19	A	SAINT JOSEPH
20	b	Cuthbert, Bishop of Lindisfarne, 687
21	c	Thomas Ken, Bishop of Bath and Wells, 1711

14	22	d	James De Koven, Priest, 1879
3	23	e	Gregory the Illuminator, Bishop and Missionary of Armenia, c. 332
	24	f	
11	25	g	THE ANNUNCIATION OF OUR LORD JESUS CHRIST TO THE BLESSED VIRGIN MARY
	26	A	
19	27	b	
8	28	c	
	29	d	John Keble, Priest, 1866
16	30	e	
5	31	f	John Donne, Priest, 1631

APRIL

	1	g	Frederick Denison Maurice, Priest, 1872
13	2	A	James Lloyd Breck, Priest, 1876
2	3	b	Richard, Bishop of Chichester, 1253
	4	c	
10	5	d	
	6	e	
18	7	f	
7	8	g	William Augustus Muhlenberg, Priest, 1877
	9	A	William Law, Priest, 1761
15	10	b	
4	11	c	
	12	d	George Augustus Selwyn, First Missionary Bishop of New Zealand, 1878
12	13	e	
1	14	f	
	15	g	
9	16	A	
17	17	b	
6	18	c	
	19	d	Alphege, Archbishop of Canterbury, and Martyr, 1012
	20	e	
	21	f	Anselm, Archbishop of Canterbury, 1109
	22	g	
	23	A	
	24	b	
	25	c	SAINT MARK THE EVANGELIST
	26	d	
	27	e	
	28	f	
	29	g	Catherine of Siena, 1380
	30	A	

MAY

1 b SAINT PHILIP AND SAINT JAMES, APOSTLES
2 c Athanasius, Bishop of Alexandria, 373
3 d
4 e Monnica, Mother of Augustine of Hippo, 387
5 f
6 g
7 A
8 b
9 c Gregory of Nazianzus, Bishop of Constantinople, 389
10 d
11 e
12 f
13 g
14 A
15 b
16 c
17 d
18 e
19 f Dunstan, Archbishop of Canterbury, 988
20 g Alcuin, Deacon, and Abbot of Tours, 804
21 A
22 b
23 c
24 d Jackson Kemper, First Missionary Bishop
in the United States, 1870
25 e Bede, The Venerable, Priest, and Monk of Jarrow, 735
26 f Augustine, First Archbishop of Canterbury, 605
27 g
28 A
29 b
30 c
31 d THE VISITATION OF THE BLESSED VIRGIN MARY

11

JUNE

1	e	Justin, Martyr at Rome, c. 167
2	f	The Martyrs of Lyons, 177
3	g	The Martyrs of Uganda, 1886
4	A	
5	b	Boniface, Archbishop of Mainz, Missionary to Germany, Martyr, 754
6	c	
7	d	
8	e	
9	f	Columba, Abbot of Iona, 597
10	g	Ephrem of Edessa, Syria, Deacon, 373
11	A	SAINT BARNABAS THE APOSTLE
12	b	
13	c	
14	d	Basil the Great, Bishop of Caesarea, 379
15	e	
16	f	Joseph Butler, Bishop of Durham, 1752
17	g	
18	A	Bernard Mizeki, Martyr in Rhodesia, 1896
19	b	
20	c	
21	d	
22	e	Alban, First Martyr of Britain, c. 304
23	f	
24	g	THE NATIVITY OF SAINT JOHN THE BAPTIST
25	A	
26	b	
27	c	
28	d	Irenaeus, Bishop of Lyons, c. 202
29	e	SAINT PETER AND SAINT PAUL, APOSTLES
30	f	

JULY

1 g
2 A
3 b
4 c INDEPENDENCE DAY
5 d
6 e
7 f
8 g
9 A
10 b
11 c Benedict of Nursia, Abbot of Monte Cassino, c. 540
12 d
13 e
14 f
15 g
16 A
17 b William White, Bishop of Pennsylvania, 1836
18 c
19 d
20 e
21 f
22 g SAINT MARY MAGDALENE
23 A
24 b Thomas a Kempis, Priest, 1471
25 c SAINT JAMES THE APOSTLE
26 d The Parents of the Blessed Virgin Mary
27 e William Reed Huntington, Priest, 1909
28 f
29 g Mary and Martha of Bethany
30 A William Wilberforce, 1833
31 b Joseph of Arimathaea

AUGUST

1 c
2 d
3 e
4 f   Dominic, Friar, 1221
5 g
6 A   THE TRANSFIGURATION OF OUR LORD JESUS CHRIST
7 b   John Mason Neale, Priest, 1866
8 c
9 d
10 e   Laurence, Deacon, and Martyr at Rome, 258
11 f   Clare of Assisi, 1253
12 g
13 A   Hippolytus, Bishop and Martyr, c. 235
14 b   Jeremy Taylor, Bishop of Down, Connor, and Dromore, 1667
15 c   SAINT MARY THE VIRGIN, MOTHER OF OUR LORD JESUS CHRIST
16 d
17 e
18 f   William Porcher DuBose, Priest, 1918
19 g
20 A   Bernard, Abbot of Clairvaux, 1153
21 b
22 c
23 d
24 e   SAINT BARTHOLOMEW THE APOSTLE
25 f   Louis, King of France, 1270
26 g
27 A
28 b   Augustine, Bishop of Hippo, 430
29 c
30 d
31 e   Aidan, Bishop of Lindisfarne, 651

SEPTEMBER

1 f
2 g The Martyrs of New Guinea, 1942
3 A
4 b
5 c
6 d
7 e
8 f
9 g
10 A
11 b
12 c John Henry Hobart, Bishop of New York, 1830
13 d Cyprian, Bishop and Martyr of Carthage, 258
14 e HOLY CROSS DAY
15 f
16 g Ninian, Bishop in Galloway, c. 430
17 A
18 b
19 c Theodore of Tarsus, Archbishop of Canterbury, 690
20 d John Coleridge Patteson, Bishop of Melanesia,
   and his Companions, Martyrs, 1871
21 e SAINT MATTHEW, APOSTLE AND EVANGELIST
22 f
23 g
24 A
25 b Sergius, Abbot of Holy Trinity, Moscow, 1392
26 c Lancelot Andrewes, Bishop of Winchester, 1626
27 d
28 e
29 f SAINT MICHAEL AND ALL ANGELS
30 g Jerome, Priest, and Monk of Bethlehem, 420

pared by The Standing Liturgical Commission and published by The Church Pension Fund, 1967.

** *Prayer Book Studies* 21, pp. 29-30.

OCTOBER

1 A   Remigius, Bishop of Rheims, c. 530
2 b
3 c
4 d   Francis of Assisi, Friar, 1226
5 e
6 f   William Tyndale, Priest, 1536
7 g
8 A
9 b   Robert Grosseteste, Bishop of Lincoln, 1253
10 c
11 d
12 e
13 f
14 g
15 A   Samuel Isaac Joseph Schereschewsky,
        Bishop of Shanghai, 1906
16 b   Hugh Latimer and Nicholas Ridley, Bishops, 1555
17 c   Ignatius, Bishop of Antioch, and Martyr, c. 115
18 d   SAINT LUKE THE EVANGELIST
19 e   Henry Martyn, Priest, and Missionary
        to India and Persia, 1812
20 f
21 g
22 A
23 b   SAINT JAMES OF JERUSALEM, BROTHER OF
        OUR LORD JESUS CHRIST, AND MARTYR, c. 62
24 c
25 d
26 e   Alfred the Great, King of the West Saxons, 899
27 f
28 g   SAINT SIMON AND SAINT JUDE, APOSTLES
29 A   James Hannington, Bishop of Eastern Equatorial Africa,
        and Martyr, 1885
30 b
31 c

16

NOVEMBER

1	d	ALL SAINTS
2	e	Commemoration of All Faithful Departed
3	f	Richard Hooker, Priest, 1600
4	g	
5	A	
6	b	
7	c	Willibrord, Archbishop of Utrecht, Missionary to Frisia, 738
8	d	
9	e	
10	f	Leo the Great, Bishop of Rome, 461
11	g	Martin, Bishop of Tours, 397
12	A	Charles Simeon, Priest, 1836
13	b	
14	c	Consecration of Samuel Seabury, First American Bishop, 1784
15	d	
16	e	Margaret, Queen of Scotland, 1093
17	f	Hugh, Bishop of Lincoln, 1200
18	g	Hilda, Abbess of Whitby, 680
19	A	Elizabeth, Princess of Hungary, 1231
20	b	
21	c	
22	d	
23	e	Clement, Bishop of Rome, c. 100
24	f	
25	g	
26	A	
27	b	
28	c	
29	d	
30	e	SAINT ANDREW THE APOSTLE

DECEMBER

1 f Nicholas Ferrar, Deacon, 1637
2 g Channing Moore Williams, Missionary Bishop
       in China and Japan, 1910
3 A
4 b John of Damascus, Priest, c. 760
5 c Clement of Alexandria, Priest, c. 210
6 d Nicholas, Bishop of Myra, c. 342
7 e Ambrose, Bishop of Milan, 397
8 f
9 g
10 A
11 b
12 c
13 d
14 e
15 f
16 g
17 A
18 b
19 c
20 d
21 e SAINT THOMAS THE APOSTLE
22 f
23 g
24 A
25 b THE NATIVITY OF OUR LORD JESUS CHRIST
26 c SAINT STEPHEN, DEACON AND MARTYR
27 d SAINT JOHN, APOSTLE AND EVANGELIST
28 e THE HOLY INNOCENTS
29 f
30 g
31 A

HOLY BAPTISM
WITH THE
LAYING-ON-OF-HANDS

ENABLING RESOLUTION
CONCERNING
HOLY BAPTISM WITH THE LAYING-ON-OF-HANDS

The 63rd General Convention meeting in Houston, Texas, on October 21, 1970, authorized the trial use of this rite under the following specific guidelines:

1) That the Baptismal Section of the same be authorized for trial use, subject to the direction and guidance of the Ordinary;

2) That children be admitted to Holy Communion before Confirmation, subject to the direction and guidance of the Ordinary;

3) That the Rite entitled, "Holy Baptism with the Laying-on-of-Hands", be authorized for trial use, with a Bishop as the Officiant, provided that no children under the present age normal for confirmation shall receive the Laying-on-of-Hands during the trial-use period;

4) That the document entitled, "Holy Baptism with the Laying-on-of-Hands", be referred to the Anglican Consultative Council at its meeting in Kenya in February-March 1971, for its consideration and counsel;

5) That in the period following the adjournment of this General Convention, the Bishops shall arrange a period of intensive study of, and instruction in, *Prayer Book Studies* 18 in their several Dioceses.

CONCERNING THE SERVICE

NORMALLY, the Bishop will be the chief Minister at this Service; but a Priest may act for him in his absence.

It is appropriate that the chief Minister be assisted by other priests and deacons, if any are present, and by lay persons.

When the Bishop is present, he shall officiate at the Presentation of the Candidates, shall bless the water (and the oil), and shall say the Prayer over the Candidates and lay his hand on the head of each of them.

One or more baptized persons shall serve as Sponsors to present each Candidate. Sponsors are to be instructed about Baptism and their duty to help the Candidate grow in his Christian privileges and responsibilities. Sponsors shall sign the baptismal register as the expression of their assent. Parents may be included among the Sponsors of their own children.

Normally, this Service is to be celebrated as the chief Service on a Sunday or other Feast, and the Proper shall be of the Day. The opening versicles of this Service may always be substituted for the portion of the Liturgy that precedes the Collect of the Day.

Those who have been baptized in this or any other Christian Church, but have not been confirmed, may receive the Laying-on-of-hands at this Service.

NOTE:

Additional Directions and Suggestions will be found on pages 32–33.

HOLY BAPTISM
WITH THE
LAYING-ON-OF-HANDS

A Psalm or Hymn may be sung during the Entrance of the Ministers.

The Bishop or Priest says,

BLESSED BE GOD: Father, Son, and Holy Spirit.
And blessed be his Kingdom, now and forever. Amen.

There is one Body and one Spirit;
There is one hope in God's call to us.

One Lord, one Faith, one Baptism;
One God and Father of all.

> The Lord be with you.
> *And also with you.*
> Let us pray.

The Collect of the Day is then said, or the following Collect:

23

THE COLLECT

GRANT, O LORD, that we who are baptized into the death of Jesus Christ your Son may also live with him in the power of his resurrection; who lives and reigns with you in the unity of the Holy Spirit, one God, for ever and ever. *Amen.*

AT THE MINISTRY OF THE WORD

LESSON	EPISTLE	GOSPEL
Ezekiel 36:24–28	2 Corinthians 5:17–20 or, Romans 8:14–17 or, Romans 6:3–5	Mark 1:9–11 or, John 3:1–8 or, Mark 10:13–16

THE SERMON

After the Sermon, the Ministers, the Candidates, and their Sponsors may go to the font.

THE PRESENTATION AND AFFIRMATIONS

Each Candidate shall be presented to the chief Minister by his Sponsors, as follows:

I present *Name* to receive the Sacrament of Baptism.

Then, if the Candidate is able to answer for himself the chief Minister asks him,

Do you desire to be baptized?

Answer I do.

When all have been presented, the Minister appointed asks the Candidates, their Sponsors, and the Congregation, the following questions, all standing,

Will you obey and follow Jesus Christ as your Savior and Lord?

People That is my desire.

Will you seek and serve Christ in all men, loving your neighbor as yourself?

People I will, with God's help.

Will you strive for justice, peace, and dignity among all men?

People I will, with God's help.

Do you then renounce evil in all its forms?

People I do.

Minister Do you believe in God the Father?

People

I BELIEVE in God, the Father almighty,
   creator of heaven and earth.

Minister Do you believe in Jesus Christ, the Son of God?

People

I believe in Jesus Christ, his only Son, our Lord.
   He was conceived by the power of the Holy Spirit
      and born of the Virgin Mary.
   He suffered under Pontius Pilate,
      was crucified, died, and was buried.
   He descended to the dead.
   On the third day he rose again.
   He ascended into heaven,
      and is seated at the right hand of the Father.
   He will come again to judge the living and the dead.

Minister Do you believe in God the Holy Spirit?
People
I believe in the Holy Spirit,
　the holy catholic Church,
　the communion of saints,
　the forgiveness of sins,
　the resurrection of the body,
　and the life everlasting.

[The version of the Creed which appears here is the common text recommended by the International Consultation on English Texts. See the Preface.]

The Minister then says,

Let us pray for *these persons* who *are* to receive the sacrament of new birth.

A person appointed leads the following Litany:

Redeem *them,* O Lord, from all evil, and rescue *them* from the way of sin and death.
　　　　Lord, hear our prayer.

Open *their hearts* to your grace and truth.
　　　　Lord, hear our prayer.

Keep *them* in the faith and communion of your holy Church.
　　　　Lord, hear our prayer.

Teach *them* to love others in the power of the Spirit.
　　　　Lord, hear our prayer.

Send *them* into the world in witness to your love.
> *Lord, hear our prayer.*

Bring *them* to the fullness of your peace and glory.
> *Lord, hear our prayer.*

THE BLESSING OF THE WATER

Then the Bishop, or in his absence the Priest, shall bless the Water, first addressing the People, and then facing the font.

The Lord be with you.
And also with you.
Let us pray.

WE THANK YOU, HEAVENLY FATHER, for the gift of water. Over it the Holy Spirit moved in the beginning of creation. Through it you led the children of Israel out of the bondage of Egypt into the land of promise. In it your Son Jesus received the Baptism of John and was anointed by the Holy Spirit as the Messiah, the Christ who would lead us by his death and resurrection from the bondage of sin into everlasting life.

We thank you, heavenly Father, for the water of Baptism, in which we are buried with Christ in his death that we may share in his resurrection, and through which we are renewed by the Holy Spirit. In joyful obedience, therefore, to your Son, we make disciples of all nations and baptize them in the Name of the Father, and of the Son, and of the Holy Spirit.

Now sanctify this water, we pray
you, by the power of your Holy
Spirit, that those who here are

Here he is to touch
the water with his
hand.

cleansed from sin may be born again, and continue for
ever in the risen life of Jesus Christ our Savior;

To him, to you, and to the Holy Spirit, be all honor and
glory, now and for ever. *Amen.*

THE BLESSING OF OIL

When Oil of Chrism is to be blessed, the Bishop now says,

Let us pray.

ETERNAL FATHER, whose Son Jesus
Christ was anointed by the Holy
Spirit to be the servant of all men,

Here he is to lay his
hand on the vessel of
oil.

we pray you to consecrate this oil, that those who are
sealed with it may have a share in the ministry of our
great High Priest and King; who lives and reigns with
you and the Holy Spirit, one God, for ever and ever.
Amen.

When there are many Candidates, the People may be seated.

THE BAPTISM AND LAYING-ON-OF-HANDS

One of the Ministers shall dip each Candidate in the water, or pour water on his head, saying,

Name, I BAPTIZE YOU IN THE NAME OF THE FATHER, AND OF THE SON, AND OF THE HOLY SPIRIT. AMEN.

Then, the People standing, the Bishop, or in his absence the Priest, shall say the following prayer over the newly-baptized and other candidates for Confirmation.

Let us pray.

HEAVENLY FATHER, we thank you that by water and the Holy Spirit you have bestowed upon *these* your *servants* the forgiveness of sins, and have raised *them* to the new life of grace. Strengthen and confirm *them,* O Lord, with the riches of your Holy Spirit: an inquiring and discerning spirit, a spirit of purpose and of perseverance, a spirit to know and to love you, and a spirit of joy and wonder in all your works. *Amen.*

The People may be seated.

Here the Bishop, or in his absence the Priest, shall lay his hand on the head of each of them, making on the forehead the sign of the Cross (using Chrism if desired), and saying the following words to each one:

Name, YOU ARE SEALED BY THE HOLY SPIRIT.

When all have been sealed, the Ministers and People, standing, say to them,

We receive you into the Household of God, that you may confess the faith of Christ crucified, and share with us in his eternal priesthood. May the Lord arm you with his heavenly grace, that you may daily increase in his favor all the days of your life. Amen.

Then the Ministers and People exchange the Peace:

The peace of the Lord be always with you.
And with your spirit.

The chief Minister continues either with the Intercession or with the Offertory of the Eucharist. Those who have now been christened may receive Holy Communion.

The following Proper Preface may be used when no other preface is provided:

Because in Jesus Christ our Lord
you have received us as your children,
made us citizens of your kingdom,
and given us the Holy Spirit to
guide us into all truth: Therefore, etc.

If for sufficient reason there is no Communion, the Service continues with

THE LORD'S PRAYER

The Minister then says,

All praise and thanks to you, most merciful Father, for receiving us as your own children and incorporating us into your holy Church, and for making us worthy to share in the inheritance of the Saints in light; through Jesus Christ your Son our Lord, who lives and reigns with you and the Holy Spirit, one God, for ever and ever. *Amen.*

Alms may be received and presented in the usual manner, and the Minister may add other prayers, concluding with this blessing:

Almighty God, the Father of our Lord Jesus Christ, from whom all fatherhood in heaven and earth is named, grant you to be strengthened with might by his Spirit. May Christ dwell in your hearts by faith, that you may be filled with the presence and the power of God. *Amen.*

ADDITIONAL DIRECTIONS AND SUGGESTIONS

THE FONT is to be filled with clean water, either before the Service, or immediately before the Blessing of the Water.

When this Service is not the main Service on a Sunday, the Scripture readings cited in the text may be used; SUBJECT, however, to the rules of precedence governing the observance of the Church Year.

The Lesson from the Old Testament may be read in addition to the Epistle or instead of it. Lay persons shall normally be assigned this function. It may be appropriate for Sponsors to act as readers. The Gospel shall be read by a Deacon or Priest. The Nicene Creed is not used at this Service.

Hymns, Psalms, or Canticles may be used after the Old Testament Lesson and after the Epistle; particularly suitable are Psalms 15, 27, 42, 84, 87, or 122; and Te Deum, Jubilate, Benedictus, and Magnificat.

It is fitting that the Minister who officiates at the Baptismal Affirmations (page 25) be one who has direct pastoral responsibility for the Candidates, whether this minister be Priest, Deacon, Deaconess, or Lay Reader.

The Presentation of the Candidates and the Affirmations shall normally take place at the font. But if, because of the arrangement of the church building, the congregation find it difficult to see the Ministers or to participate in the Affirmations, this part of the Service may take place in the chancel. Thereafter, the Ministers, Candidates, and Sponsors go to the font for the Blessing of the Water.

If the movement to the font is a formal procession, a suitable Psalm, such as Psalm 42, or a Hymn may be sung; alternatively, they may go to the font while the Litany for the Candidates (page 26) is being said or sung.

It is desirable that this Litany be led by a person who is not a Sponsor, from his place in the church.

The Blessing of the Water is the prerogative of the Bishop as the chief sacramental Minister of the Diocese. In his absence, it will normally be done by the Rector or Priest-in-Charge.

The Blessing of Chrism is reserved to the Bishop alone. It is desirable that this be done in the presence of the congregation. Oil blessed by the Bishop for this purpose is left in the church to be used by the Priest when the Bishop is not present.

Any Bishop, Priest, Deacon or Deaconess present may be appointed to assist in administering the Baptism of the Candidates.

It is desirable, especially when a large congregation is present, that the Prayer over the Newly-Baptized (page 29) and the Laying-on-of-hands take place near the Holy Table. If the font is located some distance away, a suitable Psalm, such as Psalm 23, or a Hymn may be sung while the Ministers, Candidates, and Sponsors go to the chancel.

In the absence of the Bishop, the Rector or Priest-in-Charge is the normal officiant at the Prayer over the Newly-Baptized and the Laying-on-of-hands.

The Bishop, when present, should be the principal celebrant at the baptismal Eucharist. For reasonable cause, however, he may delegate this privilege to the Rector or Priest-in-Charge.

It is appropriate that the oblations of bread and wine be brought forward by Sponsors. It is also fitting that the Sponsors accompany the newly-christened persons at the reception of Holy Communion.

CONDITIONAL BAPTISM

If there is reasonable doubt that a person has been baptized with water In the Name of the Father, and of the Son, and of the Holy Spirit, the person shall be baptized in the usual manner, but the form of words shall be,

IF YOU ARE NOT ALREADY BAPTIZED, *Name*,

I BAPTIZE YOU IN THE NAME OF THE FATHER,

AND OF THE SON, AND OF THE HOLY SPIRIT.

AMEN.

THE MINISTRATION OF BAPTISM BY DEACONS

There are times when, in the absence of a Priest, serious pastoral reasons make it necessary for a Deacon or Deaconess to officiate at public Baptism.

It is not appropriate, however, to the Office of Deacon, to bless the water, or to say the Prayer over the Newly-Baptized, or to perform the Laying-on-of-hands.

WHEN OFFICIATING, let a Deacon follow this order:

Begin the Service (page 23) in the usual way, and do and say everything assigned to the Minister as far as the end of the Litany on page 26;

THEN, baptize the Candidate, using the form for Emergency Baptism.

EMERGENCY BAPTISM

In case of emergency, the following form shall be used.

A baptized lay person may administer Baptism according to this form in the absence of a clergyman.

POUR WATER on the head of the one to be baptized.
ADDRESS HIM by his first name.
THEN SAY,

I BAPTIZE YOU IN THE NAME OF THE FATHER,
AND OF THE SON, AND OF THE HOLY SPIRIT. AMEN.

Then make the sign of the Cross on his forehead with your thumb, and say the Lord's Prayer.

OUR FATHER, who art in heaven, Hallowed be thy Name. Thy kingdom come. Thy will be done, On earth as it is in heaven. Give us this day our daily bread. And forgive us our trespasses, As we forgive those who trespass against us. And lead us not into temptation; But deliver us from evil.

For thine is the kingdom, and the power, and the glory, for ever and ever. Amen.

Other prayers, such as the following, may be added.

Heavenly Father, we thank you that by water and the Holy Spirit you have bestowed upon this your servant the forgiveness of sins and have raised *him* to the new life of grace. Strengthen *him*, O Lord, with your presence; enfold *him* in the arms of your mercy, and keep *him* safe for ever. *Amen.*

A person so baptized may receive Holy Communion. He shall, when able (preferably at a public service), make the Baptismal Affirmations and receive the Laying-on-of-hands.

The Holy Eucharist

THE LITURGY FOR

THE PROCLAMATION OF

THE WORD OF GOD

AND CELEBRATION OF

THE HOLY COMMUNION

CONCERNING THE CELEBRATION

The Holy Eucharist is the principal act of Christian worship on the Lord's Day.

At all celebrations of the Liturgy, it is fitting that the presiding Minister, whether bishop or priest, be assisted by other priests, and by deacons and lay persons.

When the Bishop is present, it is his prerogative as the chief sacramental minister of the Diocese to be the principal celebrant at the Lord's Table, and to preach the Gospel.

It is appropriate that other priests present stand with the presiding Minister at the altar, and join with him in the consecration of the gifts, in breaking the Bread, and in distributing Communion.

A deacon, when present, should read the Gospel and lead the Prayer of Intercession. Deacons should also serve at the Lord's Table, preparing and placing on it the elements of bread and wine, and assisting in the ministration of the Sacrament to the People. In the absence of a deacon, his duties may be performed by an assisting priest.

Lay persons appointed by the presiding Minister should normally be assigned the reading of the Lessons which precede the Gospel; and in the absence of a deacon, they may lead the intercession.

The Order for Morning or Evening Prayer may be used in place of all that precedes the Offertory, provided that a Lesson from the Gospel is always included and that the Intercession conforms to the directions on page 93.

Additional Directions and Suggestions for the Ministers will be found on page 124.

THE HOLY EUCHARIST

First Service

A Psalm, Hymn, or Anthem may be sung during the entrance of the Ministers.

The People being assembled, the Priest, standing, says

Almighty God, unto whom all hearts are open, all desires known, and from whom no secrets are hid: Cleanse the thoughts of our hearts by the inspiration of ·thy Holy Spirit, that we may perfectly love thee, and worthily magnify thy holy Name; through Christ our Lord. *Amen.*

Then the Ten Commandments (page 57) may be said, or the following

Hear the words of our Lord Jesus Christ:

Thou shalt love the Lord thy God with all thy heart, and with all thy soul, and with all thy mind. This is the first and great commandment. And the second is like unto it; Thou shalt love thy neighbor as thyself. On these two commandments hang all the Law and the Prophets.

Here is sung or said

Lord, have mercy upon us.		Kyrie eleison.
Christ, have mercy upon us.	or	*Christe eleison.*
Lord, have mercy upon us.		Kyrie eleison.

or this

Holy God,
Holy and Mighty,
Holy Immortal One,
Have mercy upon us.

When appointed, the following Hymn or some other song of praise is sung or said, all standing

GLORY BE TO GOD ON HIGH,
   and on earth peace, good will towards men.
We praise thee, we bless thee,
   we worship thee,
   we glorify thee,
   we give thanks to thee for thy great glory,
O Lord God, heavenly King, God the Father Almighty.

O Lord, the only-begotten Son, Jesus Christ;
O Lord God, Lamb of God, Son of the Father,
   that takest away the sins of the world,
   have mercy upon us.
Thou that takest away the sins of the world,
   receive our prayer.
Thou that sittest at the right hand of God the Father,
   have mercy upon us.

For thou only art holy;
thou only art the Lord;
thou only, O Christ,
   with the Holy Ghost,
   art most high in the glory of God the Father. Amen.

THE PROCLAMATION OF THE WORD OF GOD

The presiding Minister says to the People

> **The Lord be with you.**
> Answer   **And with thy spirit.**
> Priest   **Let us pray.**

The Collect of the Day

The People respond Amen.

The Lessons

The People sit. One or two Lessons, as appointed, are announced and read. [See page 125 for forms for announcing and ending Epistles and other Lessons.]

A Psalm, Hymn, or Anthem may follow each Lesson.

Then, all standing, the Deacon or a priest reads the Gospel, first saying

THE HOLY GOSPEL of our Lord Jesus Christ according to _____.

The People respond   **Glory be to thee, O Lord.**

At the end of the Gospel, the Deacon says

The Gospel of the Lord.

The People respond   **Praise be to thee, O Christ.**

The Sermon

On Sundays and other festivals there follows, all standing

The Nicene Creed*

We believe in one God,
   the Father, the Almighty,
   maker of heaven and earth,
   of all that is seen and unseen.

We believe in one Lord, Jesus Christ,
   the only Son of God,
   eternally begotten of the Father,
   God from God, Light from Light,
   true God from true God,
   begotten, not made, one in Being with the Father.
   Through him all things were made.
For us men and for our salvation
   he came down from heaven:
by the power of the Holy Spirit
   he was born of the Virgin Mary, and became man.
for our sake he was crucified under Pontius Pilate;
   he suffered, died, and was buried.
   On the third day he rose again
     in fulfillment of the Scriptures;
   he ascended into heaven
     and is seated at the right hand of the Father.
He will come again in glory to judge the living and the
     dead,
   and his kingdom will have no end.

---

* This translation of the Creed has been adopted by the International Consultation on English Texts, ICET, and is recommended for experimental use in all Orders of the Eucharist. See the Preface.

We believe in the Holy Spirit, the Lord, the giver of life,
who proceeds from the Father.
With the Father and the Son he is worshiped and
glorified.
He has spoken through the Prophets.
We believe in one holy catholic and apostolic Church.
We acknowledge one baptism for the forgiveness of sins.
We look for the resurrection of the dead,
and the life of the world to come. Amen.

The version of the Creed in the Book of Common Prayer may
be used in place of the preceding.

A confession of sin may be said here (pages 45 or 62).

THE PRAYERS

Intercession is offered according to the following form, or
according to one of those provided on pages 93–112.

The Deacon, or some other person appointed, says

Let us pray for Christ's Church and the world.

After each paragraph of this prayer, the People may make an
appropriate response as directed by the Minister.

Almighty and everliving God, who hast taught us to make
prayers, and supplications, and to give thanks for all men:
Receive these our prayers which we offer unto thy Divine
Majesty, beseeching thee to inspire continually the Universal Church with the spirit of truth, unity, and concord;
and grant that all those who do confess thy holy Name
may agree in the truth of thy holy Word, and live in unity
and godly love.

Give grace, O heavenly Father, to all Bishops and other Ministers, [especially ____], that they may, both by their life and doctrine, set forth thy true and lively Word, and rightly and duly administer thy holy Sacraments.

And to all thy People give thy heavenly grace; and especially to this congregation here present; that, with meek heart and due reverence, they may hear, and receive thy holy Word; truly serving thee in holiness and righteousness all the days of their life.

We beseech thee also, to rule the hearts of those who bear the authority of government in this and every land, [especially ____], and to lead them to wise decisions and right actions for the welfare of mankind, and for the peace of the world.

Grant to all people, Lord, the will and the wisdom to be good stewards of the riches of creation, that we neither selfishly waste nor wantonly destroy thy handiwork.

And we most humbly beseech thee, of thy goodness, O Lord, to comfort and succor all those who, in this transitory life, are in trouble, sorrow, need, sickness, or any other adversity, [especially ____].

And we also bless thy holy Name for all thy servants departed this life in thy faith and fear, [especially ____], beseeching thee to grant them continual growth in thy love and service, and to give us grace so to follow their good examples, that with them we may be partakers of thy heavenly kingdom.

Grant these our prayers, O Father, for Jesus Christ's sake, our only Mediator and Advocate. *Amen.*

If there is no celebration of the Communion, or if a priest is not available, the Service is concluded as directed on page 126.

Confession of Sin

The Deacon or Priest says the following, or the Exhortation on page 59.

Ye who do truly and earnestly repent you of your sins, and are in love and charity with your neighbors, and intend to lead the new life, following the commandments of God, and walking from henceforth in his holy ways; Draw near with faith, and make your humble confession to Almighty God, devoutly kneeling.

The People kneel. A period of silence may be kept; after which one of the Ministers leads the People in this General Confession:

Father almighty, Lord of heaven and earth:
We confess that we have sinned against thee
   in thought, word, and deed.
Have mercy upon us, O God,
   according to thy loving-kindness;
In thy great goodness,
   do away our offences,
   and cleanse us from our sins;
For Jesus Christ's sake. Amen.

or this

Almighty God, Father of our Lord Jesus Christ, Maker of all things, Judge of all men:

We acknowledge and bewail our manifold sins and wickedness, Which we, from time to time, most grievously have committed, By thought, word, and deed, against thy Divine Majesty, Provoking most justly thy wrath and indignation against us.

We do earnestly repent, And are heartily sorry for these our misdoings; The remembrance of them is grievous unto us; The burden of them is intolerable.

45

Have mercy upon us, Have mercy upon us, most merciful Father: for thy Son our Lord Jesus Christ's sake, Forgive us all that is past; And grant that we may ever hereafter, Serve and please thee in newness of life;

To the honor and glory of thy Name; Through Jesus Christ our Lord. Amen.

The Minister may then say

Hear the Word of God to all who truly turn to him:

Come unto me, all ye that travail and are heavy laden, and I will refresh you. [*St. Matthew 11:28*]

God so loved the world, that he gave his only-begotten Son, to the end that all that believe in him should not perish, but have everlasting life. [*St. John 3:16*]

This is a true saying, and worthy of all men to be received, That Christ Jesus came into the world to save sinners. [*1 Timothy 1:15*]

If any man sin, we have an Advocate with the Father, Jesus Christ the righteous; and he is the perfect offering for our sins, and not for ours only, but for the sins of the whole world. [*1 St. John 2:1-2*]

The Bishop, if he is present, or the Priest, stands and says this Absolution:

Almighty God, our heavenly Father, who of his great mercy hath promised forgiveness of sins to all those who with hearty repentance and true faith turn unto him; Have mercy upon you; pardon and deliver you from all your sins; confirm and strengthen you in all goodness; and bring you to everlasting life; through Jesus Christ our Lord. *Amen.*

The Peace

Here (or at one of the other places suggested on page 126, the Priest may say to the People

> The Peace of the Lord be always with you.

Answer   And with thy spirit.

Then the Ministers and People may greet one another in the Name of the Lord.

THE CELEBRATION OF THE HOLY COMMUNION

The Priest, standing at the Holy Table, begins the Offertory with this or some other Sentence of Scripture:

Ascribe to the Lord the honor due his name; bring offerings and come into his courts. (*Psalm 96:8*)

During the Offertory, a Psalm, Hymn, or Anthem may be sung.

Representatives of the Congregation bring the People's offerings of bread and wine, and money or other gifts, to the Deacon or Priest. The People stand while the offerings are presented and placed on the Altar.

The Great Thanksgiving

The People remain standing. The Priest faces them, and sings or says

> The Lord be with you.

People   And with thy spirit.

Priest   Lift up your hearts.

People   We lift them up unto the Lord.

Priest   Let us give thanks unto our Lord God.

People   It is meet and right so to do.

47

Then, facing the Holy Table, the Priest proceeds

It is very meet, right, and our bounden duty, that we should at all times, and in all places, give thanks unto thee, O Lord, Holy Father, Almighty, Everlasting God.

On all Sundays, and on other occasions when a Proper Preface is appointed, it is sung or said here.

Therefore with Angels and Archangels, and with all the company of heaven, we laud and magnify thy glorious Name; evermore praising thee, and saying,

Priest and People

HOLY, HOLY, HOLY, Lord God of Hosts:
Heaven and earth are full of thy glory.
Glory be to thee, O Lord Most High.

Here may be added

Blessed is He that cometh in the Name of the Lord: Hosanna in the highest!

The People may kneel.

Then the Priest continues

All glory be to thee, Almighty God, our heavenly Father, for that thou, of thy tender mercy, didst give thine only Son Jesus Christ to suffer death upon the Cross for our redemption; who made there, by his one oblation of himself once offered, a full, perfect, and sufficient sacrifice for the sins of the whole world; and did institute, and in his holy Gospel command us to continue, a perpetual memory of that his precious death and sacrifice, until his coming again:

At the following words concerning the Bread, the Priest is to hold it, or lay his hand upon it. And at the words concerning the Cup, he is to hold, or lay his hand upon, the Cup and any other vessel containing wine to be consecrated.

For in the night in which he was betrayed, he took bread; and when he had given thanks, he brake it, and gave it to his disciples, saying, "Take, eat: This is my Body which is given for you. Do this in remembrance of me."

Likewise, after supper, he took the cup; and when he had given thanks, he gave it to them, saying, "Drink this, all of you: For this is my Blood of the New Covenant, which is shed for you, and for many, for the remission of sins. Do this, as oft as ye shall drink it, in remembrance of me."

Wherefore, O Lord and heavenly Father, we, thy humble servants, do celebrate and make here before thy Divine Majesty, with these thy holy Gifts, which we now offer unto thee, the memorial thy Son hath commanded us to make; having in remembrance his blessed passion and precious death, his mighty resurrection and glorious ascension; rendering unto thee most hearty thanks for the innumerable benefits procured unto us by the same.

And we most humbly beseech thee, O merciful Father, to hear us; and, of thy almighty goodness, vouchsafe to bless and sanctify, with thy Word and Holy Spirit, these Gifts of bread and wine; that we, receiving them according to thy Son our Savior Jesus Christ's holy institution, may be partakers of his most blessed Body and Blood.

And we earnestly desire thy fatherly goodness, mercifully to accept this our sacrifice of praise and thanksgiving; most humbly beseeching thee to grant that, by the merits and death of thy Son Jesus Christ, and through faith in his blood, we and all thy whole Church, may obtain remission of our sins, and all other benefits of his passion.

And here we offer and present unto thee, O Lord, ourselves, our souls and bodies, to be a reasonable, holy, and living sacrifice unto thee; humbly beseeching thee, that we, and all others who shall be partakers of this Holy Communion, may worthily receive the most precious Body and Blood of thy Son Jesus Christ, be filled with thy grace and heavenly benediction, and made one body with him, that he may dwell in us, and we in him.

And although we are unworthy, through our manifold sins, to offer unto thee any sacrifice; yet we beseech thee to accept this our bounden duty and service; not weighing our merits, but pardoning our offences:

Through Jesus Christ our Lord; by whom, and with whom, in the unity of the Holy Ghost, all honor and glory be unto thee, O Father Almighty, world without end.

Amen.

And now, as our Savior Christ hath taught us, we are bold to say,

People and Priest

Our Father, who art in heaven,
   hallowed be thy Name,
   thy kingdom come,
   thy will be done,
      on earth as it is in heaven.
Give us this day our daily bread.
And forgive us our trespasses,
   as we forgive those who trespass against us.
And lead us not into temptation,
   but deliver us from evil.
For thine is the kingdom, and the power, and the glory,
   for ever and ever. Amen.

The Breaking of the Bread

A period of silence is kept, during which the Priest breaks the consecrated Bread.

Then may be sung or said

(Alleluia.) Christ our Passover is sacrificed for us: *Therefore let us keep the feast.* (*Alleluia.*)

From Ash Wednesday until Easter Eve, Alleluia is omitted; and may be omitted at other times except during Easter Season.

The following prayer may be said:

We do not presume to come to this thy Table, O merciful Lord, trusting in our own righteousness, but in thy manifold and great mercies. We are not worthy so much as to gather up the crumbs under thy Table. But thou art the same Lord whose property is always to have mercy. Grant us therefore, gracious Lord, so to partake of the Body and Blood of thy dear Son Jesus Christ, that we may be cleansed from all our sins, and may evermore dwell in him, and he in us. *Amen.*

The Ministers receive the Sacrament in both kinds, and then immediately deliver it to the People.

The Bread and the Cup are given to the communicants with these words, or with the words on pages 127–128:

The Body of our Lord Jesus Christ, which was given for thee, preserve thy body and soul unto everlasting life. Take and eat this in remembrance that Christ died for thee, and feed on him in thy heart by faith, with thanksgiving.

The Blood of our Lord Jesus Christ, which was shed for thee, preserve thy body and soul unto everlasting life. Drink this in remembrance that Christ's Blood was shed for thee, and be thankful.

During the ministration of Communion, Psalms, Hymns, or Anthems may be sung.

After Communion the Priest says

Let us pray.

He then says this prayer. The People may repeat it with him.

Almighty and everliving God, we most heartily thank thee, For that thou dost feed us in these holy mysteries, With the spiritual food of the most precious Body and Blood of thy Son our Savior Jesus Christ:

And dost assure us thereby of thy favor and goodness toward us; And that we are very members incorporate in the mystical body of thy Son, The blessed company of all faithful people; And are also heirs, through hope, of thine everlasting kingdom.

And we humbly beseech thee, O heavenly Father, So to assist us with thy grace, That we may continue in that holy fellowship, And do all such good works as thou hast prepared for us to walk in:

Through Jesus Christ our Lord, To whom, with thee and the Holy Ghost, be all honor and glory, world without end. *Amen.*

The Bishop, if present, or the Priest, gives the blessing

The Peace of God, which passeth all understanding, keep your hearts and minds in the knowledge and love of God, and of his Son Jesus Christ our Lord: And the Blessing of God Almighty, the Father, the Son, and the Holy Ghost, be amongst you, and remain with you always. *Amen.*

or

The Blessing of God Almighty, the Father, the Son, and the Holy Spirit, be upon you, and remain with you for ever. *Amen.*

The Deacon (or Priest) may then dismiss the People

Go forth into the world,
rejoicing in the power of the Spirit.
Thanks be to God.

or

Go in peace to love and serve the Lord.
Thanks be to God.

or

Let us go forth in the Name of Christ.
Thanks be to God.

OTHER FORMS OF
THE GREAT THANKSGIVING

which may be used in place of the Prayer in the preceding Rite.

I

[From the Liturgy of the Lord's Supper, 1967.]

After the Sursum Corda and Sanctus, the Priest continues

All glory be to thee, Almighty God, Holy Father, Creator of heaven and earth, who didst make us in thine own image: And when we had fallen into sin, thou of thy tender mercy didst give thine only-begotten Son Jesus Christ, to take our nature upon him, and to suffer death upon the Cross for our redemption: Who made there, by his one oblation of himself once offered, a full and perfect sacrifice for the whole world; And instituted and commanded us to continue this perpetual memorial of his precious death and sacrifice, until his coming again.

> At the following words concerning the Bread, the Priest is to hold it, or lay his hand upon it. And at the words concerning the Cup, he is to hold, or lay his hand upon, the Cup and any other vessel containing wine to be consecrated.

For in the night in which he was betrayed, he took bread; and when he had given thanks to thee, he broke it, and gave it to his disciples, and said, "Take, eat: This is my Body which is given for you. Do this in remembrance of me."

In the same way also, after supper, he took the cup; and when he had given thanks, he gave it to them and said, "Drink this, all of you: For this is my Blood of the New Covenant, which is poured out for you and many for the forgiveness of sins. Do this, as often as you drink it, in remembrance of me."

Wherefore, O Lord and Holy Father, we thy people do celebrate here before thy Divine Majesty, with these thy holy Gifts, which we offer unto thee, the memorial of the blessed Passion and precious Death of thy dear Son, his mighty Resurrection and glorious Ascension, looking for his Coming again in power and great glory. And herewith we offer and present unto thee, O Lord, ourselves, which is our bounden duty and service. And we entirely desire thy fatherly goodness mercifully to accept, through the eternal mediation of our Savior Jesus Christ, this our sacrifice of praise and thanksgiving.

We pray thee, gracious Father, of thine almighty power, to bless and sanctify us and these holy Mysteries with thy Life-giving Word and Holy Spirit. Fill with thy grace all who partake of the Body and Blood of our Lord Jesus Christ. Make us one Body, that he may dwell in us and we in him. And grant that with boldness we may confess thy Name in constancy of faith, and at the last Day enter with all thy saints into the joy of thine eternal kingdom:

Through the same Jesus Christ our Lord; by whom, and with whom, and in whom, in the unity of the Holy Spirit all honor and glory be unto thee, O Father Almighty, world without end.

Amen.

II

After the Sursum Corda and Sanctus, the Priest continues

All glory be to thee, Almighty God, our heavenly Father, for that thou, of thy tender mercy, didst give thine only Son Jesus Christ to suffer death upon the Cross for our redemption; who made there by his one oblation of himself once offered, a full, perfect, and sufficient sacrifice for the sins of the whole world; and did institute, and in his holy Gospel command us to continue, a perpetual memory of that his precious death and sacrifice, until his coming again.

At the following words concerning the Bread, the Priest is to hold it, or lay his hand upon it. And at the words concerning the Cup, he is to hold, or lay his hand upon, the Cup and any other vessel containing wine to be consecrated.

For in the night in which he was betrayed, he took bread; and when he had given thanks, he brake it, and gave it to his disciples, saying, "Take, eat: This is my Body, which is given for you. Do this in remembrance of me."

Likewise, after supper, he took the cup; and when he had given thanks, he gave it to them, saying, "Drink this, all of you: For this is my Blood of the New Covenant, which is shed for you, and for many, for the remission of sins. Do this, as oft as ye shall drink it in remembrance of me."

Wherefore, O Lord and heavenly Father, we, thy humble servants, do celebrate and make here before thy Divine Majesty, with these thy holy Gifts, which we now offer unto thee, the memorial thy Son hath commanded us to make; having in remembrance his blessed passion and precious death, his mighty resurrection and glorious ascension; rendering unto thee most hearty thanks for the innumerable benefits procured unto us by the same.

And we most humbly beseech thee, O merciful Father, to hear us; and, of thy almighty goodness, vouchsafe to bless and sanctify, with thy Word and Holy Spirit, these Gifts of bread and wine; that we, receiving them according to thy Son our Savior Jesus Christ's holy institution, may be partakers of his most blessed Body and Blood.

And we earnestly desire thy fatherly goodness, mercifully to accept this our sacrifice of praise and thanksgiving; and to accept us, our souls and bodies, in union with our Savior Jesus Christ, a reasonable, holy, and living sacrifice unto thee; beseeching thee to make us one body with him, that he may dwell in us, and we in him:

Through Jesus Christ our Lord; by whom, and with whom, in the unity of the Holy Ghost, all honor and glory be unto thee, O Father Almighty, world without end.

Amen.

THE DECALOGUE

The Ten Commandments with their responses may be substituted for the Summary of the Law, or may precede it, the People kneeling.

God spake these words, and said:
I am the Lord thy God; Thou shalt have none other gods but me.
Lord, have mercy upon us, and incline our hearts to keep this law.

Thou shalt not make to thyself any graven image, nor the likeness of any thing that is in heaven above, or in the earth beneath, or in the water under the earth; thou shalt not bow down to them, nor worship them.
Lord, have mercy upon us, and incline our hearts to keep this law.

Thou shalt not take the Name of the Lord God in vain.
Lord, have mercy upon us, and incline our hearts to keep this law.

Remember that thou keep holy the Sabbath-day.
Lord, have mercy upon us, and incline our hearts to keep this law.

Honor thy father and thy mother.
Lord, have mercy upon us, and incline our hearts to keep this law.

Thou shalt do no murder.
Lord, have mercy upon us, and incline our hearts to keep this law.

Thou shalt not commit adultery.
Lord, have mercy upon us, and incline our hearts to keep this law.

Thou shalt not steal.
Lord, have mercy upon us, and incline our hearts to keep this law.

Thou shalt not bear false witness against thy neighbor.
Lord, have mercy upon us, and incline our hearts to keep this law.

Thou shalt not covet.
Lord, have mercy upon us, and incline our hearts to keep this law.

The Minister may then proceed directly to the Hymn, "Glory be to God on High", or to the Salutation and Collect of the Day.

AN EXHORTATION

which may be used, in whole or in part, either during the
Liturgy or at other times. In the absence of a deacon or priest,
this Exhortation may be read by a lay person. The People stand
or sit.

Beloved in the Lord:

Our Savior Christ, on the night before he suffered, established the Sacrament of his Body and Blood: as a sign
and pledge of his love, for the continual remembrance
of the sacrifice of his death, and for a spiritual sharing in
his life. For in those holy Mysteries we are made one with
Christ, and Christ with us; we are made one body in him,
and fellow-members one of another.

Having in mind, therefore, his great love for us, and in
obedience to his command, his Church renders to Almighty God our heavenly Father never-ending thanks:

for the creation of the world,
for his continual providence over us,
for his love for all mankind, and

for the redemption of the world by our Savior Christ,
who took upon himself our flesh, and humbled himself
even to death on the Cross, that he might make us the
children of God by the power of the Holy Spirit, and
exalt us to everlasting life.

But if we are to share rightly in the celebration of those
holy Mysteries, and be nourished by that spiritual Food,
we must remember the dignity of that holy Sacrament.
I therefore call upon you to consider how Saint Paul
exhorts all persons to prepare themselves carefully before
eating of that Bread and drinking of that Cup.

For as the benefit is great, if with penitent hearts and living faith we receive the holy Sacrament; so is the danger great, if we receive it improperly, not recognizing the Lord's Body. Judge yourselves therefore, my brothers, lest you be judged by the Lord.

Examine your lives and conduct by the rule of God's commandments, that you may perceive wherein you have offended in what you have done or left undone, whether in thought, word, or deed. And acknowledge your sins before Almighty God, with full purpose of amendment of life, being ready to make restitution for all injuries and wrongs done by you to others; and also being ready to forgive those who have offended you, in order that you yourselves may be forgiven. And then, being reconciled with your brothers, come to the banquet of that most heavenly Food.

And if in your own preparation, you cannot quiet your conscience, but need help and counsel, then go to a discreet and understanding Priest, and open your grief to him: that you may receive the benefit of Absolution and spiritual counsel and advice; to the removal of scruple and doubt, the assurance of pardon, and the strengthening of your faith.

To Christ our Lord who loves us, and washed us in his own blood, and made us a kingdom of priests to serve his God and Father: to him be glory in the Church evermore. Through him let us offer continually the sacrifice of praise which is our bounden duty and service, and, with faith in him, come boldly before the Throne of grace [and humbly confess our sins to Almighty God].

A PENITENTIAL ORDER

This Order may be used immediately before the Liturgy (in which case the Collect for Purity is to be omitted), or as a separate service.

When used separately, a Sermon or the Exhortation on page 59 may follow the Sentences; and then, after the confession of sin, the service may be concluded with suitable prayers, and the Grace.

The Minister begins with this Sentence:

Grace to you and peace from God our Father and the Lord Jesus Christ. [*Philippians 1:2*]

He then adds one or more of the following:

If we say that we have no sin, we deceive ourselves, and the truth is not in us. But if we confess our sins, God, who is faithful and just, will forgive our sins and cleanse us from all unrighteousness. [*1 John 1:8–9*]

Since we have a great high priest who has passed through the heavens, Jesus, the Son of God, let us with confidence draw near to the throne of grace, that we may receive mercy and find grace to help in time of need.
[*Hebrews 4:14*]

Jesus said,
The first commandment is this: "Hear, O Israel: The Lord your God is the only Lord. Love the Lord your God with all your heart, with all your soul, with all your mind, and with all your strength."
The second is this: "Love your neighbor as yourself." There is no other commandment greater than these.
[*Mark 12:29–31*]

Then follows a confession of sin.

Confession of Sin

[For use with the First Service]

The Minister says

Let us confess our sins against God and our neighbor.

A period of silence may be observed.

Minister and People

Most merciful God,
we confess that we have sinned against thee
in thought, word and deed:
we have not loved thee with our whole heart;
we have not loved our neighbors as ourselves.
We pray thee of thy mercy
    forgive what we have been,
    amend what we are,
    direct what we shall be;
that we may delight in thy will,
and walk in thy ways,
through Jesus Christ our Lord. Amen.

Father almighty, Lord of heaven and earth:
We confess that we have sinned against thee
    in thought, word, and deed.
Have mercy upon us, O God,
    according to thy loving-kindness;
In thy great goodness,
    do away our offences,
    and cleanse us from our sins;
for Jesus Christ's sake. Amen.

The Bishop, if present, or the Priest stands and says

The Almighty and merciful Lord grant you Absolution and Remission of all your sins, true repentance, amendment of life, and the grace and consolation of his Holy Spirit. *Amen.*

Confession of Sin

[For use with the Second Service]

The Minister says

Let us confess our sins against God and our neighbor.

A period of silence may be observed.

Minister and People

Most merciful God,
we confess that we have sinned against you
in thought, word and deed:
we have not loved you with our whole heart;
we have not loved our neighbors as ourselves.
We pray you of your mercy
   forgive what we have been,
   amend what we are,
   direct what we shall be;
that we may delight in your will,
and walk in your ways,
through Jesus Christ our Lord. Amen.

The Bishop, if present, or the Priest stands and says

Almighty God have mercy on you, forgive you all your sins, through our Lord Jesus Christ; strengthen you in all goodness, and by the power of the Holy Spirit, keep you in eternal life. *Amen.*

CONCERNING THE CELEBRATION

The Holy Eucharist is the principal act of Christian worship on the Lord's Day.

At all celebrations of the Liturgy, it is fitting that the presiding Minister, whether bishop or priest, be assisted by other priests, and by deacons and lay persons.

When the Bishop is present, it is his prerogative as the chief sacramental minister of the Diocese to be the principal celebrant at the Lord's Table, and to preach the Gospel.

It is appropriate that other priests present stand with the presiding Minister at the altar, and join with him in the consecration of the gifts, in breaking the Bread, and in distributing Communion.

A deacon, when present, should read the Gospel and lead the prayer of Intercession. Deacons should also serve at the Lord's Table, preparing and placing on it the elements of bread and wine, and assisting in the ministration of the Sacrament to the People. In the absence of a deacon, his duties may be performed by an assisting priest.

Lay persons appointed by the presiding Minister should normally be assigned the reading of the Lessons which precede the Gospel; and in the absence of a deacon, they may lead the intercession.

The Order for Morning or Evening Prayer may be used in place of all that precedes the Offertory, provided that a Lesson from the Gospel is always included and that the Intercession conforms tothe directions on page 93.

Additional Directions and Suggestions for the Ministers will be found on page 124.

THE HOLY EUCHARIST

Second Service

A Psalm, Hymn, or Anthem may be sung during the entrance of the Ministers.

The People being assembled, and all standing, the Priest says

Blessed be God: Father, Son, and Holy Spirit.

People

And blessed be his Kingdom, now and for ever. Amen.

From Easter Day through the Day of Pentecost, in place of the above, he says

Alleluia! Christ is risen.
People   **The Lord is risen indeed. Alleluia!**

The Priest may say

Almighty God, to you all hearts are open, all desires known, and from you no secrets are hid: Cleanse the thoughts of our hearts by the inspiration of your Holy Spirit, that we may perfectly love you, and worthily magnify your holy Name; through Christ our Lord. *Amen.*

When appointed, the following Hymn* or some other song of praise is sung or said, all standing

GLORY TO GOD IN THE HIGHEST,
and peace to his people on earth.
Lord God, heavenly King,
almighty God and Father,
we worship you, we give you thanks,
we praise you for your glory.
Lord Jesus Christ, only Son of the Father,
Lord God, Lamb of God,
you take away the sin of the world:
have mercy on us;
you are seated at the right hand of the Father:
receive our prayer.
For you alone are the Holy One,
you alone are the Lord,
you alone are the Most High,
Jesus Christ,
with the Holy Spirit,
in the glory of God the Father. Amen.

On other occasions the following is used

Lord, have mercy.		Kyrie eleison.
Christ, have mercy.	or	*Christe eleison.*
Lord, have mercy.		Kyrie eleison.

or this
Holy God,
Holy and Mighty,
Holy Immortal One,
Have mercy upon us.

* An ICET text. See the Preface.

THE PROCLAMATION OF THE WORD OF GOD

The presiding Minister says to the People

The Lord be with you.
Answer   **And also with you.**
Priest   **Let us pray.**

The Collect of the Day

The People respond Amen.

The Lessons

The People sit. One or two Lessons, as appointed, are announced and read. [See page 125 for forms for announcing and ending Epistles and other Lessons.]

A Psalm, Hymn, or Anthem may follow each Lesson.

Then, all standing, the Deacon or a priest reads the Gospel, first saying

THE HOLY GOSPEL of our Lord Jesus Christ according to _____.

The People respond   **Glory to you, Lord Christ.**

At the end of the Gospel, the Deacon says

The Gospel of the Lord.

The People respond   **Praise to you, Lord Christ.**

The Sermon

On Sundays and other festivals there follows, all standing

The Nicene Creed

We believe in one God,
   the Father, the Almighty,
   maker of heaven and earth,
   of all that is seen and unseen.

We believe in one Lord, Jesus Christ,
   the only Son of God,
   eternally begotten of the Father,
   God from God, Light from Light,
   true God from true God,
   begotten, not made, one in Being with the Father.
   Through him all things were made.
   For us men and for our salvation
      he came down from heaven:
   by the power of the Holy Spirit
      he was born of the Virgin Mary, and became man.
   For our sake he was crucified under Pontius Pilate;
      he suffered, died, and was buried.
      On the third day he rose again
         in fulfillment of the Scriptures;
      he ascended into heaven
         and is seated at the right hand of the Father.
   He will come again in glory to judge the living and the
      dead,
   and his kingdom will have no end.

We believe in the Holy Spirit, the Lord, the giver of life,
   who proceeds from the Father.
   With the Father and the Son he is worshiped and
      glorified.
   He has spoken through the Prophets.

We believe in one holy catholic and apostolic Church.
We acknowledge one baptism for the forgiveness of sins.
We look for the resurrection of the dead,
    and the life of the world to come. Amen.

A confession of sin may be said here, or after the Intercession.

Confession of Sin

The Minister says

Let us confess our sins against God and our neighbor.

A period of silence may be observed.

Minister and People

Most merciful God,
we confess that we have sinned against you
in thought, word and deed:
we have not loved you with our whole heart;
we have not loved our neighbors as ourselves.
We pray you of your mercy
    forgive what we have been,
    amend what we are,
    direct what we shall be;
that we may delight in your will,
and walk in your ways,
    through Jesus Christ our Lord. Amen.

The Bishop, if present, or the Priest stands and says

Almighty God have mercy on you, forgive you all your
sins, through Lord Jesus Christ; strengthen you in all
goodness, and by the power of the Holy Spirit, keep you
in eternal life. *Amen.*

THE PRAYERS

Here Prayer is offered with intercession for

The Universal Church and all its members
The Nation and all in authority
The welfare of the world
The concerns of the local community
Those who suffer and those in any trouble
The departed (with commemoration of a saint when appropriate)

See pages 93–112 for various forms of Intercession.

The Peace

Here (or at one of the other places suggested on page 126), the Priest may say to the People

The Peace of the Lord be always with you.
Answer   **And also with you.**

Then the Ministers and People may greet one another in the Name of the Lord.

If there is no celebration of the Communion, or if a priest is not available, the Service is concluded as directed on page 126.

THE CELEBRATION OF THE HOLY COMMUNION

The Priest, standing at the Holy Table, begins the Offertory with this or some other Sentence of Scripture:

Ascribe to the Lord the honor due his Name; bring offerings and come into his courts. [*Psalm 96:8*]

During the Offertory, a Psalm, Hymn, or Anthem may be sung.

Representatives of the Congregation bring the People's offerings of bread and wine, and money or other gifts, to the Deacon or Priest. The People stand while the offerings are presented and placed on the Altar.

The Great Thanksgiving

The People remain standing. The Priest faces them, and sings or says

Priest The Lord be with you.
People And also with you.
Priest Lift up your hearts.
People We lift them up to the Lord.
Priest Let us give thanks to the Lord our God.
People It is right to give him thanks and praise.

Then, facing the Holy Table, the Priest proceeds

It is right, and a good and joyful thing, always and everywhere to give thanks to you, Father Almighty, Creator of heaven and earth:

On all Sundays, and on other occasions when a Proper Preface is appointed, it is sung or said here.

Therefore we praise you,
joining our voices with angels and archangels
and with all the company of heaven,
who for ever sing this hymn
to proclaim the glory of your Name:

Priest and People

Holy, holy, holy Lord, God of power and might,
heaven and earth are full of your glory.
Hosanna in the highest.
Blessed is he who comes in the name of the Lord.
Hosanna in the highest.

The People may kneel.

Then the Priest continues

Holy and gracious Father,
in your infinite love you made us for yourself;
and when we fell into sin
and became subject to evil and death,
you, in your mercy, sent Jesus Christ,
your only and eternal Son,
to share our human nature,
to live and die as one of us
to reconcile us to you,
the God and Father of all.

He stretched out his arms upon the Cross,
and offered himself, in obedience to your will,
a perfect sacrifice for all mankind.

At the following words concerning the Bread, the Priest is to
hold it, or lay his hand upon it. And at the words concerning
the Cup, he is to hold, or lay his hand upon, the Cup and any
other vessel containing wine to be consecrated.

On the night he was handed over to suffering and death,
our Lord Jesus Christ took bread;
and when he had given thanks to you,
he broke it, and gave it to his disciples,
and said, "Take this and eat it:
This is my Body, which is given for you.
Do this for the remembrance of me."

After supper he took the cup of wine;
and when he had given thanks, he gave it to them,
and said, "Drink this, all of you:

This is my Blood of the new Covenant,
which is shed for you and for many
for the forgiveness of sins.
Whenever you drink it, do this for the remembrance of
me."

Priest and People

Christ has died,
Christ is risen,
Christ will come again.

The Priest continues

We celebrate the memorial of our redemption, O Father,
in this sacrifice of praise and thanksgiving,
and we offer you these Gifts.
Sanctify them by your Holy Spirit
to be for your people the Body and Blood of your Son,
the holy food and drink of new and unending life in him.
Sanctify us also
that we may faithfully receive this holy Sacrament,
and serve you in unity, constancy, and peace;
and at the last day bring us with all your saints
into the joy of your eternal kingdom.

All this we ask through your Son Jesus Christ:
By him, and with him, and in him,
in the unity of the Holy Spirit
all honor and glory is yours, Almighty Father,
now and for ever.

Amen.

As our Savior Christ has taught us, we now pray,

People and Priest

Our Father in heaven,
    holy be your Name,
    your kingdom come,
    your will be done,
        on earth as in heaven.
Give us today our daily bread.
Forgive us our sins
    as we forgive those who sin against us.
Do not bring us to the test
    but deliver us from evil.

For the kingdom, the power, and the glory are yours
    now and for ever. Amen.

The Breaking of the Bread

A period of silence is kept, during which the Priest breaks the consecrated Bread.

Then may be sung or said

(Alleluia.) Christ our Passover is sacrificed for us:
Therefore let us keep the feast. (Alleluia.)

From Ash Wednesday until Easter Eve, Alleluia is omitted; and may be omitted at other times except during Easter Season.

Facing the People, the Priest says the following Sentence of Invitation:

The Gifts of God for the People of God.

He may add: Take them in remembrance that Christ
gives himself for you, and feed on him in
your hearts by faith, with thanksgiving.

74

The Ministers receive the Sacrament in both kinds, and then immediately deliver it to the People.

The Bread and the Cup are given with these words, to which the communicant may respond, *Amen*.

The Body [Blood] of our Lord Jesus Christ keep you in everlasting life.

or this

The Body of Christ, the Bread of heaven.
The Blood of Christ, the Cup of salvation.

During the ministration of Communion, Psalms, Hymns, or Anthems may be sung.

After Communion, the Priest says

Let us pray.

People and Priest

Eternal God, Heavenly Father,
you have accepted us as living members of your Son
our Savior Jesus Christ,
and you have fed us with spiritual food
in the Sacrament of his Body and Blood.
Send us now into the world in peace,
and grant us strength and courage
to love and serve you
with gladness and singleness of heart. Amen.

or this

Almighty and everliving God,
you have fed us with the spiritual food
of the most precious Body and Blood
of your Son, our Savior Jesus Christ;

You have assured us, in these holy Mysteries,
    that we are living members
    of the Body of your Son,
    and heirs of your eternal kingdom.

And now, Father, send us out
    to do the work you have given us to do,
To love and serve you
    as faithful witnesses of Christ our Lord.

To him, to you, and to the Holy Spirit,
    be honor and glory now and for ever. Amen.

The Bishop, if present, or the Priest, may bless the People.

The Deacon (or Priest) may dismiss them with these words:

Go forth into the world,
rejoicing in the power of the Spirit.
Thanks be to God.

or

Go in peace to love and serve the Lord.
Thanks be to God.

or

Let us go forth in the Name of Christ.
Thanks be to God.

ANOTHER FORM OF
THE GREAT THANKSGIVING

[Based on the Liturgy of the Lord's Supper, 1967]

After the Sursum Corda and the Sanctus, the Priest continues

All glory is yours, Almighty God, Holy Father:
You made us in your own image;
and when we had fallen into sin,
you gave your only-begotten Son Jesus Christ,
to take our nature upon him,
and to suffer death upon the Cross for our redemption.
He made there, by his one oblation of himself,
a full and perfect sacrifice for the whole world;
And instituted and commanded us to continue
this memorial of his precious death and sacrifice,
until his coming again.

At the following words concerning the Bread, the Priest is to
hold it, or lay his hand upon it. And at the words concerning
the Cup, he is to hold, or lay his hand upon, the Cup and any
other vessel containing wine to be consecrated.

For in the night in which he was betrayed, he took bread;
and when he had given thanks to you,
he broke it, and gave it to his disciples, and said,
"Take, eat: This is my Body which is given for you.
Do this in remembrance of me."

After supper, he took the cup;
and when he had given thanks, he gave it to them and said,
"Drink this, all of you: For this is my Blood of the New
      Covenant
which is poured out for you and for many
for the forgiveness of sins.
Do this, as often as you drink it, in remembrance of me."

77

Therefore, O Lord and Holy Father, we your people
celebrate here before your Divine Majesty,
with these holy Gifts which we offer to you,
the memorial of the blessed Passion
and precious Death of your dear Son,
his mighty Resurrection and glorious Ascension,
looking for his Coming again in power and great glory.
And with these Gifts, O Lord, we offer to you ourselves,
for this is our duty and service.
And we pray you, in your goodness and mercy, to accept,
through the eternal mediation of our Savior Jesus Christ,
this our sacrifice of praise and thanksgiving.

Gracious Father, in your almighty power,
bless and sanctify us and these holy Mysteries
with your Life-giving Word and Holy Spirit;
fill with your grace all who partake
of the Body and Blood of our Lord Jesus Christ;
make us one Body that he may dwell in us and we in him.
And grant that with boldness
we may confess your Name in constancy of faith,
and at the last Day enter with all your Saints
into the joy of your eternal kingdom:

Through Jesus Christ our Lord,
by whom, and with whom, and in whom,
in the unity of the Holy Spirit
all honor and glory is yours,
O Father Almighty,
now and for ever.

Amen.

An Order For Celebrating
The Holy Eucharist

*which may be used on occasions other than
the principal service on sundays and other
feasts of our lord*

ORDER OF THE CELEBRATION

This order requires for its effective use careful preparation by all the worshippers so that all may understand what takes place and their own part in the celebration.

The use of silence, movement, and music will depend on the nature of the particular occasion.

THE PEOPLE AND PRIEST

gather in the lord's name

proclaim and respond to the word of god

> *the proclamation and response may include, in addition to a reading from the gospel, other readings, song, talk, dance, instrumental music, other art forms, silence.*

pray for the world and the church

exchange the peace

prepare the table

some of those present prepare the table; the bread, the cup of wine, and other offerings, are placed upon it.

make eucharist

the great thanksgiving is said by the priest in the name of the gathering, using one of the eucharistic prayers provided. In the course of the prayer, he takes the bread and cup into his hands, or places his hand upon them.

the people respond—amen!

break the bread

eat and drink together

the body and blood of the lord are shared in a reverent manner; after all have received, any of the sacrament that remains is then consumed.

When a common meal or agapé accompanies the celebration, it follows here.

Eucharistic Prayers

In making Eucharist, the Priest uses one of the Eucharistic Prayers from the First or Second Service, or one of the following.

A

After a suitable invitation by the Priest, and a response by the People, the Priest gives thanks as follows:

We give thanks to you, O God our Creator;
You are worthy of praise from every creature you have made.
For in these last days you have sent your only Son
to be the Savior and Redeemer of the world.
In him, you have forgiven our sins,
and made us worthy to stand before you.
In him, you have brought us out of darkness into light
out of error into truth,
out of death into life.

On the night he was handed over to suffering and death,
our Lord Jesus Christ took bread;
and when he had given thanks to you,
he broke it, and gave it to his disciples,
and said, "Take this and eat it:
This is my Body, which is given for you.
Do this for the remembrance of me."

After supper he took the cup of wine,
and when he had given thanks, he gave it to them,
and said, "Drink this, all of you:
This is my Blood of the new Covenant,
which is shed for you and for many
for the forgiveness of sins.
Whenever you drink it, do this for the remembrance of me."

Remembering his death and resurrection,
we offer in thanksgiving this Bread and this Cup.
And we pray you to send your Holy Spirit
upon this Offering and upon your People,
to change us, and to make us one in your kingdom.
To you be praise and honor and worship
through your Son Jesus Christ
with the Holy Spirit
for ever and ever.

Amen.

B

After a suitable invitation by the Priest, and a response by the People, the Priest gives thanks as follows:

We give you thanks, O Father,
for the goodness and love
which you have made known to us in creation,
in the calling of Israel,
in the words of the prophets,
and, above all, in Jesus your Son:

Who, on the night before he died for us,
took bread and gave thanks;
he broke it and gave it to his disciples, and said:
"This is my body which is for you:
do this for my memorial."
In the same way,
he took the cup after supper and said:
"This cup is the new Covenant in my Blood.
Whenever you drink it,
do this for my memorial."

Remembering now his suffering and death,
and celebrating his resurrection,
and looking for his coming again
to fulfill all things according to your will,
we ask you, Father,
through the power of the Holy Spirit,
to accept and bless these Gifts.
Make us one with your Son in his sacrifice,
that his life may be renewed in us.

And therefore, Father, through Jesus your Son,
in whom we have been accepted and made your children,
by your life-giving Spirit
we offer our grateful praise and say:

People and Priest

Our Father . . .

C

In the following Prayer, the italicized lines are spoken by the People.

The Lord be with you.
And also with you.

Lift up your hearts.
We lift them up to the Lord.

Let us give thanks to the Lord our God.
Let us praise him for his goodness now and for ever.

God of all power, Ruler of the Universe,
you are worthy of glory and praise.
Glory to you for ever and ever.

At your command all things came to be,
the vast expanse of interstellar space,

galaxies, suns, the planets in their courses,
and this fragile earth, our island home:
By your will they were created and have their being.

From the primal elements you brought forth the race of
   man,
and blessed us with memory, reason, and skill;
you made us the rulers of creation.
But we turned against you, and betrayed your trust;
and we turned against one another.
Have mercy, Lord, for we are sinners in your sight.

Again and again, you called us to return.
Through prophets and sages you revealed your righteous
   Law;
and in the fullness of time, you sent your only Son,
born of a woman, to fulfill your Law,
to open for us the way of freedom and peace.
By his blood, he reconciled us.
By his wounds, we are healed.

[And, therefore, we praise you,
  joining with the heavenly chorus,
  with prophets, apostles, and martyrs,
  and with men of every generation
    who have looked to you in hope:
  to proclaim with them your glory,
  in their unending hymn:

Priest and People

Holy, holy, holy Lord, God of power and might,
heaven and earth are full of your glory.
   Hosanna in the highest.
Blessed is he who comes in the name of the Lord.
   Hosanna in the highest.]

The Priest continues

And so, Father, we who have been redeemed by him,
and made a new people by water and the Spirit,
now bring before you these gifts.
Sanctify them by your Holy Spirit
to be for us the Body and Blood
of Jesus Christ our Lord.

On the night he was betrayed,
he took bread, said the blessing,
broke the bread, and gave it to his friends,
and said, "Take this and eat it.
This is my Body, which is given for you.
Do this for the remembrance of me."

In the same way, after supper, he took the cup,
and said "Drink of this, all of you.
This is my Blood of the new Covenant,
which is poured out for you and for all mankind
for the forgiveness of sins.
Whenever you drink it, do this for the remembrance of me."

Priest and People

When we eat this Bread
and drink this Cup,
we show forth your death, Lord Christ,
until you come in glory.

Priest

Lord God of our Fathers,
God of Abraham, Isaac, and Jacob,
God and Father of our Lord Jesus Christ:
open our eyes to see your hand at work in the world
about us.

Deliver us from the presumption of coming to this Table
for solace only, and not for strength;
for pardon only, and not for renewal.
Let the grace of this Holy Communion
make us one body, one spirit in Christ,
that we may worthily serve the world in his name.
Risen Lord, be known to us in the breaking of the Bread.

Accept these prayers and praises, Father,
through Jesus Christ, our great High Priest,
to whom with you and the Holy Spirit,
your Church gives honor, glory, and worship,
from generation to generation.

Amen.

D

Priest   The grace of our Lord Jesus Christ and the love
of God and the fellowship of the Holy Spirit be
with you all.

or   The Lord be with you.

People   And also with you.

Priest   Lift up your hearts.
People   We lift them up to the Lord.

Priest   Let us give thanks to the Lord our God.
People   It is right to give him thanks and praise.

The Priest begins the Prayer with these or similar words:

Father, we thank you and we praise you . . .

He gives thanks for God's work in Creation
and his revelation of himself to men.

He may recall before God the particular occasion
being celebrated.

He may incorporate or adapt the Proper Preface of the day.

[If the Sanctus is to be included he leads into it with these or
similar words:

And so we join the saints and angels
in proclaiming your glory as we sing (say),

Holy, holy, holy Lord . . .]

Here he praises God for the salvation of the world through
Jesus Christ our Lord.

He then continues with these words

And so, Father, we bring you these gifts.
Sanctify them by your Holy Spirit
to be for your People the Body and Blood
of Jesus Christ our Lord.

On the night he was betrayed,
he took bread, said the blessing,
broke the bread, and gave it to his friends,
and said, "Take this and eat it.
This is my Body, which is given for you.
Do this for the remembrance of me."

In the same way, after the supper, he took the cup,
and said "Drink of this, all of you.
This is my Blood of the new Covenant,
which is poured out for you and for all men
for the forgiveness of sins.
Whenever you drink it, do this for the remembrance of me."

Father, we now celebrate the memorial of your Son.
By means of this holy Bread and Cup,
we show forth the sacrifice of his death
and proclaim his resurrection
until he comes again.

Gather us by this Holy Communion
into one Body in your Son Jesus Christ.
Make us a living sacrifice of praise.

By him, and with him, and in him,
in the unity of the Holy Spirit
all honor and glory is yours,
Almighty Father,
now and for ever.

Amen.

Forms of Intercession

FORMS OF INTERCESSION

Prayer is offered with intercession for

The Universal Church and all its members

The Nation and all in authority

The welfare of the world

The concerns of the local community

Those who suffer and those in any trouble

The departed (with commemoration of a saint when appropriate)

If a confession of sin is not said at the service, a form of Intercession containing a penitential petition should be chosen. [For example: I, V, or VII.]

The Priest may introduce the Prayers with a sentence of invitation related to the Season or the Proper of the Day.

When a briefer form of Prayer is desired, some or all of the petitions marked with an asterisk may be omitted.

I

Deacon or other leader

With all our heart and with all our mind, let us pray to the Lord, saying, "Lord, have mercy".

* For the peace from above, for the loving kindness of God, and for the salvation of our souls,
let us pray to the Lord.

Lord, have mercy.

For the peace of the world, for the welfare of the holy Church of God, and for the unity of all mankind,
let us pray to the Lord.

Lord, have mercy.

93

For our Bishop, and for all the clergy and people,
let us pray to the Lord.

Lord, have mercy.

For our President, for the leaders of the nations, and for
all in authority,
let us pray to the Lord.

Lord, have mercy.

For this city (*town, village, . . .*), for every city and community, and for those who live in them,
let us pray to the Lord.

Lord, have mercy.

* For seasonable weather, and for an abundance of the
fruits of the earth,
let us pray to the Lord.

Lord, have mercy.

* For the good earth which God has given us, and for the
wisdom and will to conserve it,
let us pray to the Lord.

Lord, have mercy.

* For those who travel on land, on water, in the air, or
through outer space,
let us pray to the Lord.

Lord, have mercy.

For the aged and infirm, for widows and orphans, and for
the sick and the suffering,
let us pray to the Lord.

Lord, have mercy.

For the poor and the oppressed, for prisoners and captives,
and for all who remember and care for them,
let us pray to the Lord.

Lord, have mercy.

For all who have died in the hope of the resurrection, and
for all the departed,
let us pray to the Lord.

Lord, have mercy.

* For deliverance from all danger, violence, oppression,
and degradation,
let us pray to the Lord.

Lord, have mercy.

* For the absolution and remission of our sins and offenses,
let us pray to the Lord.

Lord, have mercy.

* That we may end our lives in faith and hope, without
suffering and without reproach,
let us pray to the Lord.

Lord, have mercy.

* Defend us, deliver us, and in *thy* compassion protect us,
O Lord, by *thy* grace.

Lord, have mercy.

In the Communion of Saints, let us commend ourselves,
and one another, and all our life, to Christ our God.

To thee, O Lord our God.

A brief silence is then observed.

95

The Priest concludes with the following or some other prayer:

Lord Jesus Christ: *who hast* given us grace at this time with one accord to make our common supplication; and *hast* promised that when two or three are agreed together in *thy* Name *thou wilt* grant their requests; Fulfill now, O Lord, our desires and petitions, as may be best for us; granting us in this world knowledge of *thy* truth, and in the world to come life everlasting; through *thy* mercy, O Christ, to whom with the Father and the Holy Spirit be honor and glory for ever and ever. *Amen.*

II

In the course of the silence after each bidding, the People offer their own prayers, either silently or aloud.

I ask your prayers for God's people throughout the world: for our Bishop(s) ___; for this gathering; and for all ministers and people.
Pray, brothers, for the Church.

Silence

I ask your prayers for peace among men; for goodwill among nations; and for the well-being of all people.
Pray, brothers, for justice and peace.

Silence

I ask your prayers for the poor, the sick, the hungry, the oppressed, and those in prison.
Pray, brothers, for those in any need or trouble.

Silence

I ask your prayers for all who seek God, or a deeper knowledge of him.
Pray, brothers, that they may find and be found of him.

Silence

I ask your prayers for the departed [especially _____].
Pray, brothers, for those who have died.

Silence

Members of the congregation may ask the prayers or the thanksgiving of those present.

* I ask your prayers for . . .

* I ask your thanksgiving for . . .
Give thanks, brothers, for God's great goodness.

Silence

Praise God for those in every generation in whom Christ has been honored [especially _____ whom we remember today]. And pray that we may have grace to glorify Christ in our own day.

Silence

The Priest adds a concluding collect.

III
(Traditional Form)

After the Priest's invitation to prayer, the Leader and People pray responsively.

Father, we pray for thy holy Catholic Church:
That we all may be one.

Grant that every member of the Church may truly and humbly serve thee:
That thy Name may be glorified by all people.

We pray for all Bishops, Priests and Deacons:
That they may be faithful stewards of thy holy mysteries.

We pray for all who govern and hold authority in the nations of the world:
That there may be peace and justice among men.

May we seek to do thy will in all that we undertake:
That we may be blest in all our works.

Have compassion on those who suffer from any grief or trouble:
That they may be delivered from their distress.

Grant rest eternal to the departed:
Let light perpetual shine upon them.

We praise thee for all thy saints who have entered into joy:
May we also come to share in thy heavenly kingdom.

Let us pray in silence for our own needs and those of others.

Silence

The Priest concludes with this or some other collect:

Almighty God, the fountain of all wisdom, who knowest our necessities before we ask, and our ignorance in asking: We beseech thee to have compassion upon our infirmities; and those things which for our unworthiness we dare not, and for our blindness cannot ask, mercifully give us for the sake of thy Son Jesus Christ our Lord. *Amen.*

III
(Contemporary Form)

After the Priest's invitation to prayer, the Leader and People pray responsively.

Father, we pray for your holy Catholic Church:
That we all may be one.

Grant that every member of the Church may truly and humbly serve you:
That your Name may be glorified by all people.

We pray for all Bishops, Priests and Deacons:
That they may be faithful ministers of your Word and Sacraments.

We pray for all who govern and hold authority in the nations of the world:
That there may be peace and justice among men.

Give us courage to do your will in all that we undertake:
That we may be blest in all our works.

Have compassion on those who suffer from any grief or trouble:
That they may be delivered from their distress.

Give to the departed eternal rest:
Let your light shine upon them for ever.

We praise you for all your saints who have entered into joy:
May we also come to share in your heavenly kingdom.

Let us pray in silence for our own needs and those of others.

Silence

The Priest concludes with this or some other collect:

Almighty God, to whom our needs are known before we ask, help us to ask only what accords with your will; and those good things which we dare not, or in our blindness cannot ask, grant us for the sake of your Son, Jesus Christ our Lord. *Amen.*

IV

The Leader may expand any paragraph with specific petitions. A short period of silence follows each paragraph. The periods of silence may be concluded as follows:

Lord, in your mercy
Hear our prayer.

Let us pray for the whole Church of God in Christ Jesus, and for all men according to their needs.

Silence

Grant, Almighty God, that we who confess your Name may be united in your truth, live together in your love, and show forth your glory in the world.

Silence

Direct this and every nation into the ways of justice and peace, that we may honor all men, and seek the common good.

Silence

Save and comfort those who suffer, that they may hold to you through good and ill, and trust in your unfailing love.

Silence

Remember, Lord, those who have died in the peace of Christ, and those whose faith is known to you alone, and deal with us and them according to your great mercy.

Silence

Grant these our prayers, O merciful Father, for the sake of your Son, our Savior Jesus Christ. *Amen.*

V

Deacon or other leader

In peace, let us pray to the Lord, saying

"Lord, have mercy"
or   "Kyrie eleison".

For the peace of the world, that a spirit of respect and forbearance may grow among nations and peoples, we pray to you, O Lord.

Here and after every petition the People respond:

Kyrie eleison.
or   *Lord, have mercy.*

For the holy Church of God, that it may be filled with truth and love, and be found without fault at the Day of your Coming, we pray to you, O Lord.

For *N.* our Presiding Bishop, for *N. (N.)* our own Bishop(s), for all Bishops and other Ministers, and for all the holy People of God,
we pray to you, O Lord.

* For all who fear God and believe in his Christ, that our divisions may cease and all may be one as you, Lord, and the Father are one,
  we pray to you, O Lord.

* For the mission of the Church, that in faithful witness it may preach the Gospel to the ends of the earth,
  we pray to you, O Lord.

* For those who do not yet believe, and for those who have lost their faith, that they may receive the light of the Gospel,
  we pray to you, O Lord.

For those in positions of public trust, [especially _____], that they may serve justice, and promote the dignity and freedom of all men,
we pray to you, O Lord.

* For a blessing upon the labors of men, and for the right use of the riches of creation, that mankind may be freed from famine and disaster,
  we pray to you, O Lord.

For the poor, the persecuted, the sick, and all who suffer; for refugees, prisoners, and all who are in danger: that they may be relieved and protected,
we pray to you, O Lord.

For this Congregation; for those who are present, and for those who are absent, that we may be delivered from hardness of heart, and show forth your glory in all that we do,
we pray to you, O Lord.

* For our enemies and those who wish us harm; and for all whom we have injured or offended,
we pray to you, O Lord.

* For ourselves; for the forgiveness of our sins, and for the grace of the Holy Spirit to amend our lives,
we pray to you, O Lord,

For all who have commended themselves to our prayers: for our families, friends, and neighbors; that being freed from anxiety, they may live in joy, peace, and health,
we pray to you, O Lord.

* For _____,
we pray to you, O Lord.

For all who have died in the faith of Christ, that, with all the saints, they may have rest in that place where there is no pain or grief, but life eternal,
we pray to you, O Lord.

Rejoicing in the fellowship of [the ever-blessed Virgin Mary, (blessed N.) and] all the saints, let us commend ourselves, and one another, and all our life to Christ our God.

To you, O Lord our God.

Silence

103

The Priest says this doxology:

For yours is the Majesty, O Father, Son, and Holy Spirit;
yours is the kingdom and the power and the glory,
now and for ever. *Amen.*

or else he concludes with this or some other prayer:

O Lord our God, accept the fervent prayers of your people;
in the multitude of your mercies, look with compassion
upon us and all who turn to you for help: For you are
gracious, O lover of men; and to you we give glory, Father,
Son, and Holy Spirit, now and for ever. *Amen.*

VI

The specific petitions that are indented may be adapted by
addition or omission, as appropriate, at the discretion of the
Minister. The collects which follow each period of silent prayer
are customarily said by the Priest. Each collect is printed twice:
first in contemporary and then in traditional language.

Deacon or other leader

Let us pray for all men everywhere according to their
need, and for the people of God in every place.

Let us pray for the holy Catholic Church of Christ
throughout the world; especially,

   For its unity in witness and service
   For all Bishops and other Ministers
      and the people whom they serve
   For N., our Bishop, and all the people of this Diocese
   For all Christians in this community
   For those preparing to be baptized (particularly, . . .)

that God will confirm his church in faith, increase it in love, and preserve it in peace.

Silence

Almighty and everlasting God, by whose Spirit the whole company of your faithful people is governed and sanctified: Receive our prayers which we now offer before you for all members of your holy Church, that in their vocation and ministry they may truly and devoutly serve you, to the glory of your Name; through our Lord and Savior Jesus Christ. *Amen.*

Almighty and everlasting God, by whose Spirit the whole body of the Church is governed and sanctified: Receive our supplications and prayers, which we offer before thee for all members of thy holy Church, that every member of the same, in his vocation and ministry, may truly and godly serve thee; through our Lord and Savior Jesus Christ. *Amen.*

Let us pray for all nations and peoples of the earth, and for those in authority among them; especially,

> For *N.,* the President of the United States
> For the Congress and the Supreme Court
> For the Members and representatives of the United
>   Nations
> For all who serve the common good of men

that by God's help they may seek justice and truth, and live in peace and concord.

Silence

Almighty God, from whom all thoughts of truth and peace proceed: We pray you to kindle in the hearts of all men the true love of peace; and guide with your pure and

105

peaceable wisdom those who take counsel for the nations of the earth, that in tranquillity your kingdom may go forward, until the earth is filled with the knowledge of your love; through Jesus Christ our Lord. *Amen.*

Almighty God, from whom all thoughts of truth and peace proceed: Kindle, we pray thee, in the hearts of all men the true love of peace; and guide with thy pure and peaceable wisdom those who take counsel for the nations of the earth; that in tranquillity thy kingdom may go forward, till the earth is filled with the knowledge of thy love; through Jesus Christ our Lord. *Amen.*

Let us pray for all who suffer, and are afflicted in body or in mind; especially,

> For the hungry and the homeless, the destitute and the oppressed
> For the sick, the wounded, and the crippled
> For those in loneliness, fear, and anguish
> For those who face temptation, doubt, and despair
> For prisoners and captives, and those in mortal danger
> For the sorrowful and bereaved

that God in his mercy will comfort and relieve them, and grant them the knowledge of his love, and stir up in us the will and patience to minister to their needs.

Silence

Gracious God, you see all the suffering, injustice, and misery which abound in this world. We implore you to look mercifully upon the poor, the oppressed, and all who are burdened with pain and sorrow. Fill our hearts with your compassion, and give us strength to serve them in their need, for the sake of him who suffered for us, our Savior Jesus Christ. *Amen.*

Gracious God, who seest all the suffering, injustice, and misery which abound in this world: We beseech thee to look mercifully upon the poor, the oppressed, and all who are burdened with pain and sorrow. Fill our hearts with thy compassion, and give us strength to serve them in their need, for the sake of him who suffered for us, our Savior Jesus Christ. *Amen.*

Let us pray for all who, whether in ignorance or in disbelief, have not received the gospel of Christ; especially,

> For those who have never heard the word of Christ
> For those who have lost their faith
> For those hardened by sin or indifference
> For the contemptuous and the scornful
> For those who are enemies of the Cross of Christ,
>   and persecutors of his disciples

that God will open their hearts to the truth, and lead them to faith and obedience.

Silence

Merciful God, who made all men and hate nothing that you have made; nor do you desire the death of a sinner, but rather that he should be converted and live: Have mercy upon all who know you not as you are revealed in the Gospel of your Son. Take from them all ignorance, hardness of heart, and contempt of your Word. Bring all men home, good Lord, to your fold, so that they may be one flock under the one shepherd, your Son Jesus Christ our Lord. *Amen.*

Merciful God, who hast made all men, and hatest nothing that thou hast made, nor desirest the death of a sinner, but rather that he should be converted and live: Have mercy upon all who know thee not as thou art revealed in the Gospel of thy Son. Take from them all ignorance, hardness of heart, and contempt of thy Word; and so bring them home, blessed Lord, to thy fold, that they may be made one flock under one shepherd, Jesus Christ our Lord. *Amen.*

Let us commit ourselves to our God, and pray for the grace of a holy life, that, with all who have departed this world and have died in the faith, we may be accounted worthy to enter into the fullness of the joy of our Lord, and receive the crown of life in the day of resurrection.

Silence

O God of unchangeable power and eternal light: Look favorably on your whole Church, that wonderful and sacred mystery. By the tranquil operation of your providence, carry out the work of man's salvation. Let the whole world see and know that things which were cast down are being raised up, and things which had grown old are being made new, and that all things are being renewed to the perfection of him through whom all things were made, your Son our Lord Jesus Christ, who lives and reigns with you, in the unity of the Holy Spirit, one God, for ever and ever. *Amen.*

O God of unchangeable power and eternal light: Look favorably upon thy whole Church, that wonderful and sacred mystery; and by the tranquil operation of thy providence, carry out the work of man's salvation. Let the whole world see and know that things which were cast down are being raised up, and things which had grown old are being made new, and that all things are being renewed unto the perfection of him through whom all things were made, thy Son our Lord Jesus Christ, who liveth and reigneth with thee in the unity of the Holy Spirit, one God, for ever and ever. *Amen.*

VII

The Leader and People pray responsively

In peace, we pray to you, Lord God:

For all people in their daily life and work;
For our families, friends, and neighbors, and for those who are alone.

For this community, the nation, and the world;
For all who work for justice, freedom, and peace.

For the just and proper use of your creation;
For the victims of hunger, fear, injustice and oppression.

For all who are in danger, sorrow, or any kind of trouble;
For those who minister to the sick, the friendless, and the needy.

For the peace and unity of the Church of God;
For all who proclaim the Gospel, and all who seek the Truth.

For Bishops and other Ministers, [especially for *N.* our Presiding Bishop, and *N.(N.)* our Bishop(s)];
For all who serve God in his Church.

For the special needs and concerns of this congregation.

Those present may add their own petitions.

Hear us, Lord;
For your mercy is great.

We thank you, Lord, for all the blessings of this life.

The People may add their own thanksgivings

We will exalt you, O God our King;
And praise your Name for ever and ever.

We pray for all who have died, [especially _____], that
they may have a place in your eternal kingdom.

Lord, let your loving-kindness be upon them;
Who put their trust in you.

* We pray to you also for the forgiveness of our sins.

Leader and People

Have mercy upon us, most merciful Father:
In your compassion forgive us our sins,
known and unknown, things done and left undone:
And so uphold us by your Spirit
that we may live and serve you in newness of life,
to the honor and glory of your Name.

The Priest concludes the prayers with a suitable collect.

Concerning the Collect at the Prayers

When a Collect concludes the Intercession, a suitable one is
selected, such as:

(a) a collect appropriate to the Season or occasion being celebrated;
(b) a collect expressive of some special need in the life of the
local congregation;
(c) a collect for the mission of the Church;
(d) a general collect such as the following:

Lord, hear the prayers of your people; and what we have
asked faithfully, grant that we may obtain effectually, to
the glory of your Name; through Jesus Christ our Lord.
Amen.

Heavenly Father, you have promised to hear what we ask
in the Name of your Son: We pray you, accept and fulfill
our petitions, not as we ask in our ignorance, nor as we
deserve in our sinfulness, but as you know and love us in
your Son, Jesus Christ our Lord. *Amen.*

Almighty and eternal God, ruler of all things in heaven
and earth: Mercifully accept the prayers of your people,
and strengthen us to do your will; through Jesus Christ
our Lord. *Amen.*

Hasten, O Father, the coming of your Kingdom; and grant
that we your servants, who now live by faith, may with
joy behold your Son at his coming in glorious majesty;
even Jesus Christ, our only Mediator and Advocate. *Amen.*

SUGGESTED OFFERTORY SENTENCES

One of the following, or some other appropriate Sentence of Scripture, may be used in place of the Offertory Sentence provided in the text of the Service.

Walk in love, as Christ loved us and gave himself for us, an offering and sacrifice to God. (*Ephesians 5:2*)

I pray you brethren, by the mercies of God, to present yourselves as a living sacrifice, holy and acceptable to God, which is your spiritual worship. (*Romans 12:1*)

HOLY EUCHARIST

Lord Jesus Christ, you said to your Apostles, "Peace I give to you; my own peace I leave with you": Regard not our sins, but the faith of your Church, and give to us the peace and unity of that heavenly City where, with the Father and the Holy Spirit, you live and reign now and for ever. *Amen.*

O God, you have brought us near to an innumerable company of angels, and to the spirits of just men made perfect: Grant us during our earthly pilgrimage to abide in their fellowship, and in our heavenly country to become partakers of their joy; through Jesus Christ our Lord. *Amen.*

God grant to the living—grace;
to the departed—rest;
to the church, the nation, and all mankind—
    peace and concord;
and to us and all his servants—life everlasting. *Amen.*

SUGGESTED OFFERTORY SENTENCES

One of the following, or some other appropriate Sentence of Scripture, may be used in place of the Offertory Sentence provided in the text of the Service.

Walk in love, as Christ loved us and gave himself for us, an offering and sacrifice to God. (*Ephesians 5:2*)

I pray you brethren, by the mercies of God, to present yourselves as a living sacrifice, holy and acceptable to God, which is your spiritual worship. (*Romans 12:1*)

If you are offering your gift at the altar, and there remember that your brother has something against you, leave your gift there before the altar and go; first be reconciled to your brother, and then come and offer your gift. (*Matthew 5:23–24*)

Thine, O Lord, is the greatness, and the power, and the glory, and the victory, and the majesty. For all that is in the heaven and in the earth is thine. Thine is the kingdom, O Lord, and thou art exalted as head above all. (*1 Chronicles 29:11*)

Yours, O Lord, is the greatness, the power, the glory, the victory, and the majesty. For everything in the heaven and on earth is yours. Yours, O Lord, is the kingdom, and you are exalted as head over all. (*1 Chronicles 29:11*)

Worthy art thou, our Lord and God, to receive glory and honor and power; for thou hast created all things, and by thy will they exist and were created. (*Revelation 4:11*)

O Lord our God: you are worthy to receive glory and honor and power; because you have created all things; and by your will they were created and have their being. (*Revelation 4:11*)

or this Bidding

Let us with gladness present the offerings and oblations of our life and labor unto the Lord.

The Lord be with you. And al-so with you.

Lift up your hearts. We lift them up to the Lord.

Let us give thanks to the Lord our God.

It is right to give him thanks and praise.

The Lord be with you. And also with you.
The Lord be with you. And with thy spirit.

Lift up your hearts. We lift them up to the Lord.
Lift up your hearts. We lift them up un-to the Lord.

Let us give thanks to the Lord our God.
Let us give thanks unto our Lord God.

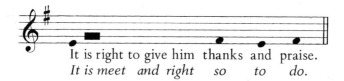

It is right to give him thanks and praise.
It is meet and right so to do.

Proper Prefaces

ADVENT

From the First Sunday in Advent until Christmas Day, except on Saints' Days.

Traditional wording

Because thou didst send thy well-beloved Son to redeem us from sin and death, and to make us, in him, sons and heirs of everlasting life: that when he shall come again in power and great triumph to judge the world, we may without shame or fear rejoice to behold his appearing:

Contemporary wording

Because you sent your well-beloved Son to redeem us from sin and death, and to make us, in him, sons and heirs of everlasting life: that when he shall come again in power and great triumph to judge the world, we may without shame or fear rejoice to behold his appearing:

CHRISTMAS

From Christmas Day until the Epiphany.

Traditional wording

Because thou didst give Jesus Christ, thine only Son, to be born for us; who, by the mighty power of the Holy Spirit, was made perfect Man of the flesh of the Virgin Mary his mother: that we, being delivered from the bondage of sin, might receive power to become the sons of God:

Contemporary wording

Because you gave Jesus Christ, your only Son, to be born for us; who, by the mighty power of the Holy Spirit, was made perfect Man of the flesh of the Virgin Mary his mother: that we, being delivered from the bondage of sin, might receive power to become the sons of God:

EPIPHANY

From the Epiphany until Ash Wednesday, except on Saints' Days.

Through Jesus Christ our Lord; who, in the substance of our human nature, manifested his glory: that he might bring us out of darkness into his own marvelous light:

THE INCARNATION

On the Feasts of the Presentation, Annunciation, Visitation, and Transfiguration.

Traditional wording

Because in the Mystery of the Word made flesh, thou hast caused a new light to shine in our hearts, to give the knowledge of thy glory in the face of thy Son Jesus Christ our Lord:

Contemporary wording

Because in the Mystery of the Word made flesh, you have caused a new light to shine in our hearts, to give the knowledge of your glory in the face of your Son Jesus Christ our Lord:

LENT

From Ash Wednesday until Palm Sunday, except upon the Annunciation, and major Saints' Days.

Through Jesus Christ our Lord; who was in every way tempted as we are, yet did not sin; by whose grace we are able to triumph over every evil, and to live no longer unto ourselves, but unto him who died for us and rose again:

HOLY WEEK

From Palm Sunday through Maundy Thursday, and on Holy Cross Day.

Through Jesus Christ our Lord; who for our sins was lifted up upon the Cross, that he might draw all men to himself; who by his suffering and death became the way of eternal salvation to all who obey him:

EASTER

From Easter Day until Ascension Day, except on major Holy Days.

Traditional wording

But chiefly are we bound to praise thee for the glorious Resurrection of thy Son Jesus Christ our Lord, for he is the Paschal Lamb who by his death hath overcome death, and by his rising to life again hath opened to us the way of everlasting life:

Contemporary wording

But chiefly are we bound to praise you for the glorious Resurrection of your Son Jesus Christ our Lord, for he is the Paschal Lamb who by his death has overcome death, and by his rising to life again has opened to us the way of everlasting life:

ASCENSION

From Ascension Day until the Day of Pentecost, except on major Holy Days.

Through thy (*your*) dearly beloved Son Jesus Christ our Lord; who, after his glorious Resurrection, openly appeared to all his Apostles, and in their sight was taken into heaven, to prepare a place for us: that where he is, there we might also be, and reign with him in glory:

PENTECOST

On the day of Pentecost, and on the Feasts of the Apostles.

Through Jesus Christ our Lord; according to whose true promise the Holy Spirit came down from heaven upon the disciples, to teach them and to lead them into all truth; giving them boldness with fervent zeal to preach the Gospel to all nations:

TRINITY SUNDAY

Traditional wording

Whom with thy co-eternal Son and Holy Spirit we worship as one God, one Lord, in Trinity of Persons and in Unity of Being; and we celebrate the one and equal glory of thee, O Father, and of the Son, and of the Holy Spirit:

Contemporary wording

Whom with your co-eternal Son and Holy Spirit we wor-
ship as one God, one Lord, in Trinity of Persons and in
Unity of Being; and we celebrate the one and equal glory,
O Father, of you, and of the Son, and of the Holy Spirit:

THE LORD'S DAY

For use on the Sundays after Pentecost, but not on the succeed-
ing weekdays.

Traditional wording

Creator of the light and source of life; who hast made us
in thine image and called us to new life in Jesus Christ
our Lord:

Contemporary wording

For you are the source of light and life; you made us in
your image and called us to new life in Jesus Christ our
Lord:

or this

Through Jesus Christ our Lord, who on this day overcame
death and the grave, and by his glorious resurrection
opened to us the way of everlasting life:

or this

Traditional wording

Who by water and the Holy Spirit hast made us a new people in Jesus Christ our Lord, to set forth thy glory in all the world:

Contemporary wording

For by water and the Holy Spirit you have made us a new people in Jesus Christ our Lord, to set forth your glory in all the world:

ALL SAINTS

On All Saints' Day and upon certain other Saints' Days.

Traditional wording

Who, in the multitude of thy saints, hast compassed us about with so great a cloud of witnesses: that we, rejoicing in their fellowship, may run with patience the race that is set before us; and, together with them, may receive the crown of glory that fadeth not away:

Contemporary wording

For in the multitude of your saints, you have compassed us about with so great a cloud of witnesses: that we, rejoicing in their fellowship, may run with patience the race that is set before us; and, together with them, may receive the crown of glory that never fades away:

APOSTLES AND ORDINATIONS

On Feasts of the Apostles, and at the time of conferring Holy Orders.

Through the great Shepherd of thy (*your*) flock, Jesus Christ our Lord; who after his Resurrection sent forth his Apostles to preach the Gospel, and to teach all nations; and promised to be with them always, even unto the end of the ages:

BAPTISM

For use at Baptism when there is no other Preface appointed.

Because in Jesus Christ our Lord thou hast (*you have*) received us as *your* children, made us citizens of *your* kingdom, and given us the Holy Spirit to guide us into all truth:

MARRIAGE

Traditional wording

Because thou hast ordained the solemn covenant of love between husband and wife as a witness of the union of thy son Jesus Christ with the holy fellowship of all faithful people:

Contemporary wording

Because you have ordained the solemn covenant of love between husband and wife as a witness of the union of your son Jesus Christ with the holy fellowship of all faithful people:

COMMEMORATION OF THE DEAD

Through Jesus Christ our Lord; who brought to light the living hope of a blessed resurrection: that in our grief we may rejoice in full assurance of our change into the likeness of his glory:

ADDITIONAL DIRECTIONS AND SUGGESTIONS

The Holy Table is spread with a clean white cloth during the celebration.

A Psalm, or part of a Psalm, may be sung or said at the places indicated in the Services. The addition of Gloria Patri is optional.

On occasion, and when appropriate, instrumental music may be used in place of a Psalm, Hymn, or Anthem.

The Beginning of the Service

When the Litany is sung or said immediately before the Eucharist, the Prayer of Intercession may be omitted. The Litany may be concluded with the Kyries, in which case the Eucharist begins with the Salutation and Collect of the Day.

In the First Service, the Priest may preface the Collect for Purity with an Opening Sentence from Morning or Evening Prayer.

The Decalogue (page 57) with its responses may be used before the Summary of the Law and Kyries, or in place of them.

The Kyrie eleison, or "Lord, have mercy", may be sung or said in three-fold, six-fold, or nine-fold form. The Trisagion, "Holy God", may be sung or said three times.

Gloria in excelsis is sung or said from Christmas Day through the Feast of the Epiphany; on Sundays from Easter Day through the Day of Pentecost, and on Ascension Day; and at other times as desired; but it is not used on the Sundays or ordinary weekdays of Advent or Lent. Te Deum laudamus is not used on the Sundays or ordinary weekdays of Lent.

The Collect of the Day is said by the Bishop or Priest presiding at the celebration. With few exceptions, there is only one Collect at this point.

Concerning the Lessons

It is desirable that the Lessons which precede the Gospel be read from a lectern.

Lessons are announced in the following manner:

"A Reading from [*Name of Book*]",
or "The Word of God, written in [*Name of Book*]",

(A citation in the following words may be added:
   "chapter _____ , beginning at the _____ verse.")

After each Lesson, the reader may say,
"Here ends the Lesson (Reading, Epistle)."

It is desirable that the Gospel be read from the pulpit or a lectern or from the midst of the Congregation.

When a significant portion of the Congregation is composed of persons whose native tongue is other than English, the Gospel may be read in that language by a reader appointed by the Priest, either in place of, or in addition to, the Gospel in English.

A Hymn may be sung before or after the Sermon.

The Nicene Creed may be omitted, except on Sundays and major Feasts.

Directions concerning the Prayer of Intercession will be found on page 93.

The Confession of Sin

A confession of sin is a normal part of the Service, but may be omitted on appropriate occasions. It may be said before

the Liturgy begins; or before or after the Prayer of Intercession. When a confession is used, the Peace should not precede
it. When the Confession is omitted, a form of Intercession
containing a penitential petition should be chosen.

When there is no Communion

If there is no Communion, all that is appointed through the
Prayer of Intercession may be said. (The Confession of Sin
under such circumstances should be said before the Service
begins or before the Intercession). A Hymn or Anthem may
then be sung, and the offerings of the People received. The
Service may then conclude with the Lord's Prayer; and with
either the Grace or a Blessing, or with the exchange of the
Peace.

In the absence of a priest, all that is described above (except
for the Absolution and Blessing) may be said by a deacon, or
if there is no deacon, by a lay-reader specially licensed by
the Bishop.

At the Peace and Offertory

The greeting, "The Peace of the Lord be always with you",
is addressed to the entire assembly. In the exchange between
individuals which may follow, any appropriate words of
greeting may be used.

The greeting of Peace may take place:
1. Before the Offertory Sentence.
2. Before the Prayer of Intercession.
3. Before the ministration of the Sacrament (before or
   after the Sentence of Invitation.)

Necessary announcements may be made after the Creed, or
before the Offertory (before or after the Peace), or at the
end of the Service, as convenient.

It is appropriate that the Deacon and other assisting ministers
make ready the Table for the celebration, preparing and

placing upon it the bread and cup of wine. (In preparing the chalice it is customary to add a little water.)

Alternative Acclamations at the Great Thanksgiving

One of the following alternative acclamations may be used in the course of the Great Thanksgiving:

A.   We remember his death;
     We proclaim his resurrection;
     We await his coming in glory.

B.   When we eat this Bread and drink this Cup,
     we proclaim your death, Lord Christ,
     until you come in glory.

At the Breaking of the Bread

At the Breaking of the Bread, in place of "Christ our Passover", some other appropriate Anthem may be used.

If the number of communicants requires the use of additional chalices, it is convenient that Wine which had been consecrated in a flagon be poured into them at the time of the Breaking of the Bread.

At the Ministration of the Sacrament

In the First Service, at the ministration of the Sacrament, the following procedure may be used:

1. Before receiving Communion himself, the Priest says to the People:

    The Body and Blood of our Lord Jesus Christ, given for you, preserve your bodies and souls unto everlasting life. Take this in remembrance that Christ died for you, and feed on him in your hearts by faith, with thanksgiving.

2. The Gifts are then ministered with these words:

    The Body [Blood] of our Lord Jesus Christ. (*Amen.*)

or he may use this Invitation:

The Gifts of God for the People of God.

or this Invitation:

The Gifts of God for the People of God: Take them in remembrance that Christ gives himself for you, and feed on him in your hearts by faith, with thanksgiving.

While the People are coming forward to receive Communion, the presiding Minister receives the Sacrament in both kinds. The bishops, priests, and deacons at the Holy Table then communicate, and after them the People.

Opportunity shall always be given to every communicant to receive the consecrated Bread and Wine separately. But the Sacrament may be received in both kinds simultaneously, in a manner approved by the Bishop.

When the presiding Minister is assisted by a deacon or another priest, it is customary for the President to minister the consecrated Bread and the assistant the Chalice. When several deacons or priests are present, some may minister the Bread, others the Wine, as the President may appoint.

The Consecration of Additional Elements

If the Consecrated Bread or Wine does not suffice for the number of communicants, the Priest is to consecrate more of either or both, by saying,

HEAR US, O HEAVENLY FATHER, AND WITH THY (YOUR) WORD AND HOLY SPIRIT BLESS AND SANCTIFY THIS BREAD [WINE] THAT IT, ALSO, MAY BE THE SACRAMENT OF THE PRECIOUS BODY [BLOOD] OF THY (YOUR) SON JESUS CHRIST OUR LORD, WHO TOOK BREAD [THE CUP] AND SAID, "THIS IS MY BODY [BLOOD]". *Amen.*

or else he may consecrate more of both kinds, saying again the Prayer of Consecration, beginning with the words which follow the Sanctus, and ending with the Invocation.

The Ministration of Communion by a Deacon

When there is no priest available, a deacon may be appointed to distribute Holy Communion from the reserved Sacrament in the following manner:

After the Intercession (and the receiving of the People's offerings), the Deacon reverently places the holy Sacrament on the altar.

The Lord's Prayer is then said, the Deacon first saying, "Let us pray in the words which our Savior Christ has (*hath*) taught us."

And then, omitting the breaking of the Bread, he proceeds with what follows in the Liturgy (page 51 or 74) as far as the end of the Prayer after Communion, after which he dismisses the People.

The Conclusion of the Service

If any of the consecrated Bread or Wine remain, apart from any which may be required for the Communion of the sick or of others who for weighty cause could not be present at the celebration, the Priest (or Deacon) and other communicants shall reverently eat and drink the same, either immediately after the Communion of the People or after the Dismissal.

A hymn of praise may be sung before or after the Prayer after Communion.

From Easter Day through the Day of Pentecost, Alleluia may be added to any of the Dismissals in the following manner:

"Go in peace to love and serve the Lord. Alleluia, alleluia. *Thanks be to God. Alleluia, alleluia.*"

The Music of the Liturgy

In the Second Service, the texts of the Kyrie eleison, Gloria in excelsis, Nicene Creed, and Sanctus given in the Book of Common Prayer may be substituted for the ICET versions when a musical setting composed for the Prayer Book wording is being used.

Musicians are encouraged to write new music for the Services, and especially for the ICET and other new texts.

THE PSALTER
PART I

A SELECTION OF THE MOST FREQUENTLY
APPOINTED PSALMS

CONTENTS OF THE PSALTER: PART I

During the triennium 1967–1970, The Standing Liturgical Commission produced revised texts of the most frequently appointed Psalms. During the triennium 1970–1973, it intends to produce revised texts of the remaining Psalms.

The following 71 Psalms are included in this edition:

1, 2, 8,
11, 12, 15, 18, 19,
20, 22, 23, 24, 25, 27, 28, 29,
31, 33, 34, 36,
40, 42, 43, 46, 48,
50, 51,
65, 66, 67,
70, 72,
80, 84, 85, 86,
90, 91, 92, 93, 95, 96, 97, 98, 99,
100, 102, 103, 104, 108,
110, 111, 112, 113, 114, 116, 117, 118,
121, 122, 124, 126,
130, 133, 134, 139,
142, 145, 147, 148,
150.

CONCERNING
THE RECITATION OF THE PSALMS

The Psalter is a body of liturgical poetry. It is designed for vocal, congregational use, whether by singing or reading. There are several traditional methods of psalmody. The exclusive use of a single method makes the recitation of the Psalter needlessly monotonous. The traditional methods, each of which can be elaborate or simple, are the following:

Direct recitation denotes the reading or chanting of a whole Psalm, or portion of a Psalm, in unison. It is particularly appropriate for the Psalm verses suggested in the eucharistic lectionary for use at the Entrance of the Ministers and between the Lessons, when the verses are recited rather than sung, and may often be found the most satisfactory method of chanting them.

Antiphonal recitation is the verse-by-verse alternation between groups of singers or readers; *e.g.,* between choir and congregation, or between one side of the congregation and the other. The alternate recitation concludes either with the *Gloria Patri* or a refrain (called the Antiphon) recited in unison. This is probably the most satisfying method for reciting the Psalms in Morning and Evening Prayer.

Responsorial recitation is the name given to a method of psalmody in which the verses of a Psalm are sung by a solo voice, with the choir and congregation singing a refrain after each verse or group of verses. This was the traditional method of singing the *Venite,* and the restoration of Invitatory Antiphons for the *Venite* makes possible a recovery of this ancient form of sacred song in the daily Office. It was also an ancient manner of chanting the Psalms between the Lessons in the Eucharist, and it is increasingly favored by modern composers.

Responsive recitation is the method most frequently in use in Episcopal churches at the present time: the Minister alternating with the congregation, verse by verse. Despite the long tradition of this use in Anglicanism, there is increasing evidence of dissatisfaction with it on the grounds of artificiality and monotony.

The version of the Psalter which follows is printed as poetry—in lines of verse. Most Psalm verses are in two sections, which has brought it about that chants, both Anglican and plainsong, are predominantly in two sections as well: a reciting note, followed by an inflection; then a new reciting note, and a final cadence. The 1928 Prayer Book Psalter marked the division within verses by an asterisk; in this version, an indentation serves the same purpose; but the elimination of the asterisk or other sign of internal division makes possible the singing of the Psalms to the three-section or four-section chants now being composed.

Psalm 1

1 How blest is the man who has not walked in the counsel of
the wicked,
nor loitered in the way of sinners;
nor sat in the seats of the scornful!

2 His delight is in the law of the LORD,
and he meditates on his law day and night.

3 He is like a tree planted near streams of water,
bearing its fruit in due season and with leaves that
do not wither;
and everything he does shall prosper.

4 It is not so with the wicked;
they are like the chaff which the wind blows away.

5 Therefore the wicked shall not stand when judgment comes,
nor the sinner when the righteous assemble.

6 For the LORD knows the way of the righteous;
but the way of the wicked is doomed.

Psalm 2

1 Why are the nations in an uproar,
and the peoples muttering empty threats?

2 Why do the kings of the earth rise up in revolt,
and the princes plot together,
against the LORD and against his anointed?

3 "Let us break their yoke," they say;
"Let us cast off their bonds from us."

4 He whose throne is in heaven is laughing;
our Lord has them in derision.

5   Then he speaks to them in his wrath;
        and his rage fills them with terror.

6   "I myself have set up my King
        upon my holy hill of Zion."

7   Let me recite the decree of the LORD:
        he said to me, You are my Son;
        this day have I begotten you.

8   Ask of me, and I will give you the nations for
                        your inheritance,
        and the ends of the earth for your possession.

9   You shall crush them with an iron rod,
        and shatter them like a piece of pottery.

10   Now, therefore, you kings, be wise;
        be warned, you rulers of the earth.

11   Submit to the LORD with fear,
        and with trembling bow before him;

12   Lest he be angry and you perish;
        for his wrath is quickly kindled.

13   How blest are they all
        who take refuge in him!

Psalm 8

1 O LORD our Governor,
how exalted is your Name in all the world!

2 Above the heavens your majesty is praised in song,
out of the mouths of infants and children.

3 You have set up a stronghold against your adversaries,
to quell the enemy and the avenger.

4 When I consider your heavens, the work of your fingers,
the moon and the stars you have set in their courses,

5 What is man that you should be mindful of him?
the sons of men that you should seek them out?

6 You have made man but little lower than the angels;
you adorn him with glory and honor;

7 You give him mastery over the works of your hands;
you put all things under his feet:

8 All sheep and oxen;
even the wild beasts of the field;

9 The birds of the air, the fish of the sea,
and whatsoever walks in the paths of the sea.

10 O LORD our Governor,
how exalted is your Name in all the world!

Psalm 11

1 In the Lord have I taken refuge:
    how then can you say to me,
    "Fly away like a bird to the hilltop."?

2 For see how the wicked bend the bow,
  and fit their arrows to the string,
    to shoot from ambush at the true of heart.

3 When the foundations are being destroyed,
    what can the righteous do?

4 The LORD is in his holy temple;
    the LORD's throne is in heaven.

5 His eyes behold the inhabited world;
    his piercing eye weighs the worth of men.

6 The LORD weighs the righteous as well as the wicked;
    but him who delights in violence he abhors.

7 Upon the ungodly he shall rain coals of fire
                and burning sulphur;
    a scorching wind shall be their lot.

8 For the LORD is righteous;
  he delights in righteous deeds;
    and the upright shall see his face.

Psalm 12

1 Help me, LORD, for there is not one godly man left;
   for the faithful have vanished from the children of men.

2 Every man speaks falsely with his neighbor;
   with a smooth tongue they speak from a double heart.

3 O that the LORD would cut off all smooth tongues,
   and close the lips that utter proud boasts!

4 Those who say, "With our tongue will we prevail;
   our lips are our own;
   who is lord over us?"

5 "Because the needy are oppressed,
and the poor cry out in misery,
   I will up," says the LORD,
   "and will give them the help they long for."

6 The words of the LORD are pure words,
like silver refined from ore in a furnace,
   and purified seven times over.

7 O LORD, watch over us,
   and save us from this generation for ever.

8 The wicked prowl on every side;
   and that which is worthless is highly prized by the
      children of men.

Psalm 15

1   LORD, who may dwell in your tabernacle?
    or who may abide upon your holy hill?

2   "He who leads a blameless life,
  and does what is right,
    and speaks the truth from his heart."

3   There is no guile upon his tongue;
  he does no evil to his friend;
    he does not heap contempt upon his neighbor.

4   In his sight the wicked is rejected,
    but he honors those who fear the LORD;

5   He has sworn to do no wrong,
    and does not go back on his word.

6   He does not give his money in hope of gain,
    nor does he take a bribe against the innocent.

7   Whoever does these things
    shall stand fast for ever.

Psalm 18

1 I love you, O LORD my strength;
   O LORD my stronghold, my crag, and my haven.

2 My God, my rock in whom I put my trust;
   My shield, the horn of my salvation, and my refuge.
      You are worthy of praise.

3 I will call upon the LORD,
   and so shall I be saved from my enemies.

4 The breakers of death rolled over me,
   and the torrents of oblivion made me afraid.

5 The cords of hell entangled me,
   and the snares of death were set for me.

6 I called upon the LORD in my anguish;
   and cried out to my God for help.

7 He heard my voice from his palace in the heavens;
   my cry came to his ears.

8 The earth reeled and rocked;
   the roots of the mountains shook;
      they reeled because of his anger.

9 Smoke rose from his nostrils,
   and a consuming fire out of his mouth;
      hot burning coals blazed out from him.

10 He parted the heavens and came down,
    a storm-cloud under his feet.

11 He mounted a cherub and flew;
    he swooped on the wings of the wind.

12 He wrapped darkness about him;
    he made dark waters and thick clouds his pavilion.

13 From the brightness of his presence, through his clouds,
    there burst hailstones and coals of fire.

14 The LORD thundered out of heaven;
    the Most High uttered his voice.

15 He loosed his arrows in showers;
    he hurled volleys of thunderbolts.

16 The beds of the seas were uncovered,
and the foundations of the world laid bare;
    at your battle-cry, O LORD;
    at the blast of the breath of your nostrils.

17 He reached down from on high and grasped me;
    he drew me out of great waters.

18 He delivered me from my strong enemies,
and from those who hated me;
    for they were too mighty for me.

19 They confronted me in the day of my disaster;
    but the LORD was like a shepherd's staff to me.

20 He brought me out into a place of liberty;
    he set me free, because he delighted in me.

21 The LORD rewarded me because of my righteous dealing;
    because my hands were clean, he recompensed me:

22 For I have kept the ways of the LORD,
    and have not offended against my God;

23 For all his judgments are before my eyes,
    and his decrees I have not put away from me;

24   For I have been blameless with him,
      and have kept myself from iniquity;

25   Therefore the LORD rewarded me according to my
            righteous dealing;
      because of the cleanness of my hands in his sight.

26   With the faithful you show yourself faithful;
      with the upright you deal forthrightly.

27   With the pure you show yourself pure;
      but with the crooked you are wily.

28   For you will save a lowly people;
      but you will humble the haughty eyes.

29   For you, O LORD, are my lamp;
      my God, you make my darkness bright.

30   For with you I will break down an enclosure.
      with the help of my God I will scale any wall.

31   This God, his ways are perfect;
      the words of the LORD are tried in the fire;
      he is a shield to all who trust in him.

32   For who is God, but the LORD?
      who is the Rock, except our God?

33   It is God who girds me about with strength,
      and makes my way secure.

34   He makes me sure-footed like a deer,
      and lets me stand firm on the heights;

35   He trains my hands for battle,
      and my arms for bending even a bow of bronze.

36 You have given me your shield of victory;
   your right hand also sustains me;
   your loving care makes me great.

37 You lengthen my stride beneath me,
   and my ankles do not give way.

38 I pursue my enemies and overtake them;
   I will not turn back till I have destroyed them.

39 I strike them down and they cannot rise;
   they fall defeated at my feet.

40 You have girded me with strength for the battle;
   you have cast down my adversaries beneath me;
   you have put my enemies to flight.

41 I destroy those who hate me;
   they cry out, but there is none to help them;
   they cry to the LORD, but he does not answer.

42 I beat them small, like dust before the wind;
   I trample them like mud in the streets.

43 You deliver me from the strife of the peoples;
   you put me at the head of the nations.

44 A people I have not known shall serve me;
   no sooner shall they hear than they shall obey me;
   aliens shall cringe before me.

45 The alien people shall lose heart;
   they shall come trembling out of their strongholds.

46 The LORD lives! Blessed is my Rock!
   Exalted is the God of my help!

47 He is the God who gave me victory,
   and cast down the peoples beneath me.

48   You rescued me from the fury of my enemies;
       you exalted me above those who rose against me;
          you saved me from the man of violence.

49   Therefore will I extol you among the nations, O LORD,
       and sing praises to your Name.

50   He multiplies the victories of his king;
       he shows loving-kindness to his anointed,
          to David and his descendants for ever.

Psalm 19

1   The heavens declare the glory of God;
       and the firmament shows his handiwork.

2   One day tells its tale to another;
       and one night imparts knowledge to another.

3   There are no words, there is no language,
       in which their voices are not heard.

4   Their sound has gone out into all lands;
       and their message to the ends of the world.

5   In the deep has he set a pavilion for the sun;
       it comes forth, like a bridegroom out of his chamber;
          it rejoices, like a champion, to run its course.

6   It goes forth from the uttermost edge of the heavens,
       and runs about to the end of it again;
       and nothing is hidden from its burning heat.

7　The　Law of the Lord is perfect,
　　　　　　　and revives the soul;
　　　the testimony of the Lord is sure,
　　　　　　　and gives wisdom to the innocent.

8　The statutes of the Lord are just,
　　　　　　　and rejoice the heart;
　　　the commandment of the Lord is clear,
　　　　　　　and gives light to the eyes.

9　The fear of the Lord is clean,
　　　　　　　and endures forever;
　　　the judgments of the Lord are true,
　　　　　　　and righteous altogether.

10　More to be desired are they than gold;
　　　　　　　more than much fine gold;
　　　sweeter far than honey,
　　　　　　　than honey in the comb.

11　By them also is your servant enlightened;
　　　and in keeping them there is a great reward.

12　Who can tell how often he offends?
　　　Cleanse me from my secret faults.

13　Above all, keep your servant from presumptuous sins;
　　　let them not get dominion over me;
　　　　then shall I be whole and sound,
　　　　and innocent of the great offence.

14　Let the words of my mouth and the meditation of my
　　　　　　　heart be acceptable in your sight,
　　　O Lord, my strength and my redeemer.

Psalm 20

1 The LORD answer you in the day of trouble;
   the Name of the God of Jacob defend you;

2 Send you help from his holy place,
   and strengthen you out of Zion;

3 Remember all your offerings,
   and accept your burnt-sacrifices;

4 Grant you your heart's desire,
   and prosper all your plans.

5 We will shout for joy at your victory,
   and triumph in the Name of our God.
      May the LORD grant all your requests.

6 Now I know that the LORD gives victory to his anointed;
   he will answer him out of his holy heaven,
      with the victorious strength of his right hand.

7 Some put their trust in chariots,
   and some in horses;
      but we will call upon the Name of the LORD our God.

8 They collapse and fall down;
   but we will arise and stand upright.

9 O LORD, give victory to the King,
   and answer us when we call.

Psalm 22

1 My God, my God, why have you forsaken me?
   and are so far from my cry,
   and from the words of my distress?

2 O my God, I cry in the daytime, but you do not answer;
   by night also, but I find no rest.

3 Yet you are the Holy One,
   enthroned upon the praises of Israel,

4 Our fathers put their trust in you;
   they trusted, and you delivered them.

5 They cried out to you, and were delivered;
   they trusted in you, and were not put to shame.

6 But as for me, I am a worm, and no man.
   scorned by men, and despised by the people.

7 All who see me laugh me to scorn;
   they curl their lips and wag their heads, saying,

8 "He trusted in the LORD; let him deliver him;
   let him rescue him, if he delights in him."

9 Yet you are he who took me out of the womb,
   and made me trustful on my mother's breast.

10 I have been cast upon you ever since I was born;
   you were my God when I was still in my
                          mother's womb.

11 Be not far from me, for trouble is near,
   and there is none to help.

12 Many young bulls encircle me;
   strong bulls of Bashan surround me.

13 They open wide their jaws at me,
> like a ravening and a roaring lion.

14 I am poured out like water,
> and all my bones are out of joint;
>> my heart within my breast is melting wax.

15 My mouth is dried out like a pot-sherd;
> my tongue sticks to the roof of my mouth;
>> and you have laid me in the dust of the grave.

16 Packs of dogs close me in,
> and gangs of evil-doers circle around me;
>> they pierce my hands and my feet;
>> I can count all my bones.

17 They stare and gloat over me;
>> they divide my garments among them;
>> they cast lots for my clothing.

18 Be not far away, O LORD;
>> you are my strength; hasten to help me.

19 Save me from the sword,
>> my life from the power of the dog.

20 Save me from the lion's mouth,
>> and from the horns of wild oxen—
> O God, you have answered me.

21 I will declare your Name to my brethren;
>> in the midst of the congregation I will praise you.

22 Praise the LORD, you that fear him!
>> all you of Jacob's line, give glory!
>> stand in awe of him, O offspring of Israel!

23   For he does not despise nor abhor the poor in his poverty;
neither does he hide his face from him:
but when he cries to him he hears him.

24   My praise is of him in the great assembly;
I will perform my vows in the presence of those who
worship him.

25   The poor shall eat and be satisfied,
and those who seek the LORD shall praise him.
"May your heart live for ever!"

26   All the ends of the earth shall remember and turn to
the LORD;
and all the families of the nations shall bow before him.

27   For kingship is the LORD's;
he rules over the nations.

28   To him alone all who sleep in the earth bow down
in worship;
all who go down to the dust fall before him.

29   My soul shall live for him;
my descendants shall serve him;
they shall be known as the LORD's for ever.

30   They shall come and make known to a people yet unborn
the saving deeds that he has done.

Psalm 23

1 The Lord is my shepherd;
    nothing, therefore, shall I lack.

2 He makes me lie down in green pastures;
    and leads me beside still waters.

3 He revives my soul,
    and guides me along safe pathways for his Name's sake.

4 Though I walk through the valley of the shadow of death,
    I shall fear no evil;
        for you are with me;
        your rod and your staff, they comfort me,

5 You spread a table before me,
    in the presence of those who trouble me;
        you have anointed my head with oil,
        and my cup is full.

6 Surely your goodness and mercy shall follow me all the days
                of my life;
    and I will dwell in the house of the Lord for ever.

Psalm 24

1 The earth is the LORD's, and all that is in it;
   the world, and all who dwell therein.

2 For he it is who founded it upon the seas,
   and made it firm upon the rivers of the deep.

3 "Who can ascend the hill of the LORD?
   and who can stand in his holy place?"

4 "He who has clean hands and a pure heart;
   who has not pledged himself to falsehood,
   nor sworn by what is a fraud.

5 "He shall receive a blessing from the LORD,
   and a just reward from the God of his salvation."

6 Such is the generation of those who seek him,
   of those who seek out your face, O God of Jacob.

7 Lift up your heads, O gates,
   lift them high, O ancient doors,
   and the King of Glory shall come in.

8 "Who is this King of Glory?"
   "The LORD, strong and mighty;
   The LORD, mighty in battle."

9 Lift up your heads, O gates,
   lift them high, O ancient doors,
   and the King of Glory shall come in.

10 "Who is he, this King of Glory?"
   "The LORD of hosts,
   he is the King of Glory."

Psalm 25

1   To you, O LORD, I lift up my soul;
    my God, I put my trust in you;
      let me not be humiliated,
      nor let my enemies triumph over me.

2   Let none who look to you be put to shame;
      let them be put to shame who deal treacherously
          without a cause.

3   Show me your ways, O LORD,
      and teach me your paths.

4   Lead me in your truth, and teach me;
    for you are the God of my salvation;
      in you have I trusted all the day long.

5   Remember, O LORD, your compassion and love,
      for they are from everlasting.

6   Remember not the sins of my youth and my transgressions;
      remember me according to your love,
      and for the sake of your goodness, O LORD.

7   Gracious and upright is the LORD;
      therefore, he teaches sinners in his way.

8   He guides the humble in doing right,
      and teaches his way to the lowly.

9   All the paths of the LORD are love and faithfulness
      to those who keep his covenant and his testimonies.

10   For your Name's sake, O LORD,
      forgive my wickedness, for it is great.

11   Who is the man who fears the LORD?
      him will he teach the way that he should choose.

12 He shall dwell in prosperity,
      and his children shall inherit the land.

13 The LORD is a friend to those who fear him,
      and will show them his covenant.

14 My eyes are ever looking to the LORD,
      for he shall pluck my feet out of the net.

15 Turn to me and have pity on me,
      for I am left alone and in misery.

16 The sorrows of my heart have increased;
      bring me out of my troubles.

17 Look upon my adversity and misery,
      and forgive me all my sin.

18 Look upon my enemies, for they are many,
      and they bear a violent hatred against me.

19 Protect my life, and deliver me;
      let me not be put to shame,
      for I have trusted in you.

20 Let integrity and uprightness preserve me,
      for my hope has been in you.

21 Deliver Israel, O God,
      out of all his troubles.

Psalm 27

1 The LORD is my light and my salvation;
whom then shall I fear?
  the LORD is the strength of my life;
  of whom then shall I be afraid?

2 When evildoers came upon me to eat up my flesh,
  it was they, my foes and my adversaries, who
    stumbled and fell.

3 Though an army should encamp against me,
yet shall not my heart be afraid;
  and though war should rise up against me,
  yet will I put my trust in him.

4 For one thing have I asked the Lord;
for one thing I seek:
  that I may dwell in the house of the LORD all the days
    of my life;

5 To behold the fair beauty of the LORD,
  and to seek him in his temple.

6 For in the day of trouble he shall keep me safe
    in his shelter;
  he shall hide me in the secrecy of his dwelling,
  and set me up upon a rock of stone.

7 Even now he lifts up my head
  above my enemies round about me.

8 Therefore, I will offer in his dwelling an oblation,
with sounds of great gladness;
  I will sing and make music to the LORD.

9 Hearken to my voice, O LORD, when I call;
  have mercy on me and answer me.

10   My heart speaks for you and says,
"Seek my face."
>Your face, LORD, will I seek.

11   Hide not your face from me;
>nor turn away your servant in displeasure.

12   You have been my helper;
>cast me not away; do not forsake me,
>O God of my salvation.

13   Though my father and my mother forsake me,
>the LORD will sustain me.

14   Teach me your way, O LORD;
>and lead me by the right way,
>because of my enemies.

15   Deliver me not into the will of my adversaries;
>for false witnesses have risen up against me,
>and such as speak malice.

16   What if I had not believed
that I should see the goodness of the LORD
>in the land of the living!

17   O tarry, and await the LORD's pleasure;
be strong, and he shall comfort your heart;
>and wait patiently for the LORD.

Psalm 28

1 O LORD, I call to you;
   my Rock, do not be deaf to me;
      lest, if you do not hear me,
      I become like those who go down to the Pit.

2 Hear the voice of my prayer when I cry out to you,
      when I lift up my hands to your holy of holies.

3 Do not snatch me away with the wicked,
   or with the evil doers,
      who speak peaceably with their neighbors,
      while strife is in their hearts.

4 Repay them according to their deeds,
      and according to the wickedness of their actions.

5 According to the work of their hands repay them,
      and give them their just deserts.

6 For they have no understanding of the LORD's doings,
   nor of the operation of his hands;
      therefore he will break them down and not
         build them up.

7 Blessed is the LORD!
      for he has heard the voice of my prayer.

8 The LORD is my strength and my shield;
   my heart trusts in him, and I have been helped;
      therefore my heart dances for joy,
      and in my song will I praise him.

9 The LORD is the strength of his people,
   a safe refuge for his anointed.

10 Save your people, and bless your inheritance;
      shepherd them, and carry them for ever.

Psalm 29

1 Ascribe to the LORD, you gods,
   ascribe to the LORD glory and strength.

2 Ascribe to the LORD the glory due his Name;
   worship the LORD in the beauty of holiness.

3 The voice of the LORD is upon the waters;
   the God of Glory thunders;
      the LORD is upon the mighty waters.

4 The voice of the LORD is a powerful voice;
   the voice of the LORD is a voice of splendor.

5 The voice of the LORD breaks the cedar-trees;
   the LORD breaks the cedars of Lebanon;

6 He makes Lebanon skip like a bull-calf,
   and Mount Hermon like a young wild ox.

7 The voice of the LORD splits the flames of fire;
   the voice of the LORD shakes the wilderness;
      the LORD shakes the wilderness of Kadesh.

8 The voice of the LORD makes the oak-trees writhe,
   and strips the forests bare.

9 And in his temple,
   all are crying, "Glory!"

10 The LORD sits enthroned above the flood;
   the LORD sits enthroned as King for evermore.

11 The LORD shall give strength to his people;
   the LORD shall give his people the blessing of peace.

Psalm 31

1 In you, O LORD, have I taken refuge;
   let me never be put to shame;
      deliver me in your righteousness.

2 Incline your ear to me,
      make haste to deliver me.

3 Be my strong rock, a castle to keep me safe;
   for you are my crag and my stronghold;
      for the sake of your Name, lead me and guide me.

4 Take me out of the net that they have secretly set for me;
      for you are my tower of strength.

5 Into your hands I commend my spirit;
      for you have redeemed me,
      O LORD, O God of truth.

6 I hate those who cling to worthless idols,
      and I put my trust in the LORD.

7 I will rejoice and be glad because of your mercy;
      for you have seen my affliction;
      you know my distress.

8 You have not shut me up in the power of the enemy;
      you have set my feet in an open place.

9 Have mercy on me, O LORD; for I am in trouble;
      my eye is consumed with sorrow;
      my throat, also, and my belly.

10 For my life is wasted with grief,
and my years with sighing;
my strength fails me because of affliction,
and my bones are consumed.

11 I have become a reproach to all my enemies,
and even to my neighbors,
and a dismay to my acquaintances;
when they see me in the street they avoid me.

12 I am forgotten like a dead man, out of mind;
I am as useless as a broken pot.

13 For I have heard the whispering of the crowd
(terror all around!);
they put their heads together against me:
they plot to take my life.

14 But as for me, I have trusted in you, O Lord:
I have said, "You are my God."

15 My times are in your hand;
rescue me from the hand of my enemies,
and from those who persecute me.

16 Make your face to shine upon your servant;
in your loving-kindness, save me.

17 Lord, let me not be ashamed for having called upon you;
rather, let the wicked be put to shame;
let them be silent in the grave.

18 Let the lying lips be dumb which insolently speak
                          against the righteous,
      disdainfully, and with contempt.

19 How great is your goodness, O LORD,
      which you have laid up for those who fear you;
          which you have done, in the sight of all men,
          for those who put their trust in you!

20 You hide them in the covert of your presence from the
                          slanderings of men;
          you keep them in your shelter from the strife of tongues.

21 Blessed be the LORD!
          for he has been wonderfully kind to me in a beseiged city.

22 Yet I said, when I was alarmed,
      "I have been cut out of the sight of your eyes."
          Nevertheless, you heard the sound of my entreaty,
          when I cried out to you.

23 Love the Lord; all you who worship him;
          the LORD protects the faithful,
              but repays to the full those who act haughtily.

24 Be strong, and let your heart take courage,
          all you who wait for the LORD.

Psalm 33

1   Rejoice in the LORD, O you righteous;
    to sing praises is becoming to the upright.

2   Praise the LORD with the harp;
    play to him upon the psaltery and lyre.

3   Sing for him a new song;
    sound a fanfare with all your skill upon the trumpet.

4   For the word of the LORD is right,
    and all his works are sure.

5   He loves righteousness and justice;
    the loving-kindness of the LORD fills the whole earth.

6   By the word of the LORD were the heavens made,
    by the breath of his mouth all the heavenly hosts.

7   He gathers up the waters of the ocean as in a water-skin,
    and stores up the depths of the sea.

8   Let all the earth fear the LORD;
    let all who dwell in the world stand in awe of him.

9   For he spoke and it came to pass;
    he commanded and it stood fast.

10   The LORD brings the will of the nations to naught;
    he thwarts the designs of the peoples.

11   But the LORD's will stands fast for ever,
    and the designs of his heart from age to age.

12   Happy is the nation whose God is the LORD!
    happy the people he has chosen to be his own!

13 The LORD looks down from heaven,
    and beholds all the children of men.

14 From where he sits enthroned he turns his gaze
    on all who dwell on the earth.

15 He who fashions all the hearts of them,
    he it is who understands all their works.

16 There is no king that can be saved by a mighty army;
    a strong man is not delivered by his great strength.

17 The horse is a vain hope for deliverance;
    for all its strength it cannot save.

18 Behold, the eye of the LORD is upon those who fear him,
    on those who wait upon his love.

19 To pluck their lives from death,
    and to keep them in the time of famine.

20 Our soul waits for the LORD;
    he is our help and our shield.

21 Indeed, our heart rejoices in him,
    for in his holy Name we put our trust.

22 Let your loving-kindness, O LORD, be upon us,
    as we have put our trust in you.

Psalm 34

1 I will bless the LORD at all times;
 his praise shall ever be in my mouth.

2 I will glory in the LORD;
 let the humble hear and rejoice.

3 Magnify the LORD with me,
 and let us exalt his Name together.

4 I sought the LORD, and he answered me,
 and delivered me out of all my terror.

5 Look upon him, and be radiant,
 and let not your faces be ashamed.

6 This poor man called, and the LORD heard him,
 and saved him from all his troubles.

7 The angel of the LORD encompasses those who fear him,
 and he will deliver them.

8 Taste and see that the LORD is good;
 happy is the man who trusts in him.

9 Fear the LORD, you saints of his,
 for those who fear him lack nothing.

10 The young lions lack, and suffer hunger;
 but those who seek the LORD shall lack nothing
  that is good.

11 Come, children, and listen to me;
 I will teach you the fear of the LORD.

12 Who is the man who loves life;
   who desires long life to enjoy prosperity?

13 Keep your tongue from evil-speaking,
   and your lips from lying words.

14 Turn from evil, and do good;
   seek peace, and pursue it.

15 The eyes of the LORD are upon the righteous,
   and his ears are open to their cry.

16 The face of the LORD is against those who do evil,
   to root out the remembrance of them from the earth.

17 The righteous cry, and the LORD hears them,
   and delivers them from all their troubles.

18 The LORD is near to the broken-hearted,
   and will save those who spirits are crushed.

19 Many are the troubles of the righteous;
   but the LORD will deliver him from them all.

20 He will keep safe all his bones;
   not one of them shall be broken.

21 Evil shall slay the wicked,
   and those who hate the righteous will be punished.

22 The LORD ransoms the life of his servants,
   and none will be punished who trust in him.

Psalm 36

1 There is a voice of rebellion deep in the heart of the wicked;
   there is no fear of God before his eyes.

2 He flatters himself in his own eyes;
   but to find out his sin is to hate it.

3 The words of his mouth are wicked and deceitful;
   he has left off acting wisely and doing good.

4 He thinks up wickedness upon his bed,
   and has set himself in no good way;
     he does not abhor that which is evil.

5 Your love, O God, reaches the heavens,
   and your faithfulness the clouds.

6 Your righteousness is like the strong mountains,
   your justice like the great deep;
     you save both man and beast, O LORD.

7 How priceless is your love, O God!
     the sons of men take refuge under the shadow
         of your wings.

8 They feast upon the abundance of your house;
   you give them drink from the river of your delights.

9 For with you is the well of life,
   and in your light we see light.

10 Continue your loving-kindness to those who know you,
     and your favor to those who are true of heart.

11 Let not the foot of the proud come near me,
     nor the hand of the wicked push me aside.

12 See how they are fallen, those who work wickedness!
     they are cast down, and shall not be able to rise.

Psalm 40

1 I waited patiently upon the LORD;
    he stooped to me and heard my cry.

2 He lifted me out of the desolate pit,
    out of the muck and mire;
        he set my feet upon a high cliff,
        and made my footing sure.

3 He put a new song in my mouth,
    a song of praise to our God;
        many shall see, and stand in awe,
        and shall put their trust in the LORD.

4 Happy is the man who trusts in the LORD!
    he does not resort to evil spirits,
        or turn to false gods.

5 Great things are they that you have done, O LORD my God,
    your miracles and your plans for us!
        there is none who can be compared with you.

6 O that I could make them known and tell them!
    but they are more than I can count.

7 In sacrifice and offering you take no pleasure
    (you have given me ears to hear you);

8 Burnt-offering and sin-offering you have not required;
    and so I said, "Behold, I come."

9 In the roll of the book it is written concerning me:
    "I love to do your will, O my God;
        your law is deep in my heart."

10 I proclaimed righteousness in the great congregation;
    behold, I did not restrain my lips;
        and that, O LORD, you know.

11   Your righteousness have I not hidden in my heart;
I have spoken of your faithfulness and your deliverance;
     I have not concealed your love and faithfulness from the
        great congregation.

12   You are the LORD; do not withhold your
        compassion from me;
     let your love and your faithfulness keep me safe for ever.

13   For innumerable troubles have crowded upon me;
my sins have overtaken me and I cannot see;
     they are more in number than the hairs of my head,
     and my heart fails me.

14   Be pleased, O LORD, to deliver me;
     O LORD, make haste to help me.

15   Let them be ashamed and altogether dismayed
who seek after my life to destroy it;
     let them draw back and be disgraced
     who take pleasure in my misfortune.

16   Let them be desolate, because they are ashamed,
     who say to me, "You had it coming to you."

17   Let all who seek you rejoice in you and be glad;
     let those who love your salvation continually say,
     "Great is the LORD!"

18   Though I am poor and afflicted,
     the Lord will have regard for me.

19   You are my helper and my deliverer;
     do not tarry, O my God.

Psalm 42

1 As the deer longs for the water-brooks,
  so longs my soul for you, O God,

2 My soul is athirst for God, athirst for the living God;
  when shall I come to appear before the presence of God?

3 My tears have been my food day and night,
  while all day long they say to me, "Where is now
    your God?"

4 I pour out my soul, when I think on these things:
  how I went with the multitude and led them into the
    house of God,

5 With the voice of praise and thanksgiving,
  among such as keep holy-day.

6 Why are you so full of heaviness, O my soul?
  and why are you so disquieted within me?

7 O put your trust in God;
  for I will yet give thanks to him,
  who is the help of my countenance, and my God.

8 My soul is heavy within me;
  therefore, I will remember you from the land of Jordan,
  and from the peak of Mizar among the heights of Hermon.

9 One deep calls to another in the noise of your cataracts;
  all your rapids and floods have gone over me.

10 The LORD grants his loving-kindness in the day-time;
  in the night-season his song is with me,
  a prayer to the God of my life.

11 I will say to the God of my strength, "Why have you
forgotten me?
and why do I go so heavily while the enemy
oppresses me?"

12 My bones are smitten asunder;
while my enemies mock me to my face;

13 While all day long they mock me, saying,
"Where is now your God?"

14 Why are you so full of heaviness, O my soul?
and why are you so disquieted within me?"

15 O put your trust in God;
for I will yet give thanks to him,
who is the help of my countenance, and my God.

Psalm 43

1   Give judgment for me, O God;
    and defend my cause against an ungodly people;
        deliver me from deceitful and wicked men.

2   For you are the God of my strength;
    why have you put me from you?
        and why do I go so heavily while the enemy
            oppresses me?

3   Send out your light and your truth, that they may lead me;
        and bring me to your holy hill,
        and to your dwelling.

4   That I may go to the altar of God,
        to the God of my joy and gladness;
        and on the harp will I give thanks to you,
            O God my God.

5   Why are you so full of heaviness, O my soul?
        and why are you so disquieted within me?

6   Put your trust in God;
        for I will yet give thanks to him,
        who is the help of my countenance and my God.

Psalm 46

1 God is our refuge and strength;
     a very present help in trouble.

2 Therefore we will not fear, though the earth be moved;
     and though the mountains be toppled into the depths
          of the sea;

3 Though its waters rage and foam;
     and though the mountains tremble at the tumult
          of the same.

4 There is a river, whose streams make glad the city of God,
     the holy habitation of the Most High.

5 God is in the midst of her; she shall not be overthrown;
     God shall help her, and that right early.

6 The nations make much ado, and the kingdoms are shaken;
     God has spoken, and the earth shall melt away.

7 The LORD of hosts is with us;
     the God of Jacob is our stronghold.

8 Come now and look upon the works of the LORD,
     what awesome things he has done on earth.

9 It is he who makes war to cease in all the world;
     he breaks the bow, and shatters the spear asunder,
     and burns the chariots with fire.

10 "Be still, then, and know that I am God;
      I will be exalted among the nations;
      I will be exalted in the earth."

11 The LORD of hosts is with us;
      the God of Jacob is our stronghold.

Psalm 48

1 Great is the LORD, and highly to be praised;
   in the city of the LORD is his holy hill.

2 Beautiful and lofty, the joy of all the earth,
   is the hill of Zion,
        the very center of the world,
        and the city of the great King.

3 God is in her citadels;
        he is known to be her sure refuge.

4 Behold, the kings of the earth assembled,
        and marched forward together.

5 They looked, and were astounded;
        they retreated, and fled in terror.

6 Trembling siezed them there;
        they writhed like a woman in child-birth,
        like ships of the sea when the east wind shatters them.

7 As we have heard, so have we seen,
        in the city of the LORD of hosts, in the city of our God:
        God has established her for ever.

8 We have meditated on your loving-kindness, O God,
        in the midst of your temple.

9 Your praise, like your Name, reaches to the world's end;
        your right hand is full of justice.

10 Let Mount Zion be glad;
        let the cities of Judah rejoice,
            because of your judgments.

11   Make the circuit of Zion
     walk round about her;
        count the number of her towers.

12   Consider well her bulwarks,
     examine her citadels,
        that you may tell those who come after.

13   This God is our God for ever and ever;
        he shall be our guide for evermore.

Psalm 50

1   The LORD, the God of gods, has spoken;
        he has called the earth from the rising of the sun to
           its setting.

2   Out of Zion, perfect in its beauty,
     God reveals himself in glory.

3   Our God shall come and shall not keep silence;
     before him there is a consuming flame,
     and round about him a raging storm.

4   He calls the heavens and the earth from above
     to witness the judgment of his people.

5   "Gather before me my loyal followers,
     those who have made a covenant with me,
     and sealed it with sacrifice."

6   Let the heavens declare the rightness of his cause;
     for God himself is judge.

7   Hear, O my people, and I will speak:
O Israel, I will bear witness against you;
   for I am God, your God.

8   I do not accuse you because of your sacrifices;
   your offerings are always before me.

9   I will take no bull-calf from your stalls;
   nor he-goats out of your pens;

10   For all the beasts of the forest are mine,
   the cattle in their thousands upon the hills;

11   I know every bird in the sky,
   and the creatures of the fields are in my sight.

12   If I were hungry, I would not tell you;
   for the whole world is mine and all that is in it.

13   Do you think I eat bulls' flesh,
   or drink the blood of goats?

14   Offer to God a sacrifice of thanksgiving,
   and make good your vows to the Most High.

15   Call upon me in the day of trouble;
   I will deliver you and you shall honor me.

16   But to the wicked man God says,
Why do you recite my statutes,
   and take my covenant upon your lips,

17   When you refuse discipline,
   and toss my words behind your back?

18 When you see a thief, you make him your friend,
   and you cast in your lot with adulterers.

19 You have loosed your lips for evil,
   and harnessed your tongue to a lie.

20 You are always speaking evil of your brother;
   and slandering your own mother's son.

21 These things you have done, and I kept still,
   and you thought that I am like you.

22 I have made my accusation;
   I have put my case in order before your eyes.

23 Consider this well, you who forget God,
   lest I rend you and there be none to deliver you.

24 Whoever offers me the sacrifice of thanksgiving,
                      he honors me;
   but to him who keeps himself in my way will I show
                      the salvation of God.

Psalm 51

1 Have mercy on me, O God, according to your
loving-kindness;
in your great compassion blot out my offences.

2 Wash me through and through from my wickedness,
and cleanse me from my sin.

3 For I know my transgressions only too well,
and my sin is ever before me.

4 Against you only have I sinned,
and done what is evil in your sight.

5 And so you are justified when you speak,
and upright in your judgment.

6 Indeed, I have been wicked from my birth,
a sinner from my mother's womb.

7 For behold, you look for truth in the inward parts,
and shall make me understand wisdom secretly.

8 Take away my sin, and I shall be pure;
wash me, and I shall be cleaner than snow.

9 Make me hear of joy and gladness,
that the body you have broken may rejoice.

10 Hide your face from my sins,
and blot out all my iniquities.

11 Create in me a clean heart, O God,
and renew a right spirit within me.

12 Cast me not away from your presence,
and take not your holy Spirit from me.

13 Give me the joy of your saving help again,
      and sustain me with your bountiful spirit.

14 I shall teach your ways to the wicked,
      and sinners shall return to you.

15 Deliver me from death, O God,
      and my tongue shall sing of your righteousness,
      O God of my salvation.

16 Open my lips, O LORD,
      and my mouth shall show forth your praise.

17 Had you desired it, I would have offered sacrifice;
      but you take no delight in burnt-offerings.

18 The sacrifice of God is a troubled spirit;
      a broken and contrite heart, O God, you will not despise.

19 Be favorable and gracious to Zion,
      and build the walls of Jerusalem.

20 Then you will be pleased with the appointed sacrifices,
    with burnt-offerings and oblations;
      then shall they offer young bullocks upon your altar.

Psalm 65

1   You are to be praised, O God, in Zion;
     to you shall vows be performed.

2   To you that hear prayer shall all men come,
     because of their transgressions.

3   Our sins are stronger than we are;
     but you will blot them out.

4   How blest is the man you choose,
   whom you draw to your courts to dwell there!
     we shall be satisfied by the beauty of your house,
     by the holiness of your temple.

5   Awesome things will you show us in your righteousness,
   O God of our salvation,
     O Hope of all the ends of the earth,
     and of the seas that are far away.

6   You make fast the mountains by your power,
     they are girded about with might.

7   You still the roaring of the seas,
     the roaring of their waves,
     and the clamor of the peoples.

8   Those who dwell at the ends of the earth
   shall tremble at your marvelous signs;
     you make the dawn and the dusk to sing for joy.

9   You visit the earth and water it abundantly;
      you make it very plenteous:
      the river of God is full of water.

10   You prepare the grain,
      for so you provide for the earth.

11   You thoroughly drench the furrows
   and smooth out the ridges;
      with heavy rain you soften the ground;
      and bless its increase.

12   You crown the year with your goodness,
      and your paths overflow with plenty.

13   May the fields of the wilderness be rich for grazing,
      and the hills be clothed with joy.

14   May the meadows cover themselves with flocks,
   and the valleys cloak themselves with grain;
      let them shout for joy and sing.

Psalm 66

1   Be joyful in God, all you lands;
    sing the glory of his Name;
    sing the glory of his praise.

2   Say to God, "How awesome are your deeds!
    because of your great strength your enemies
        cringe before you.

3   All the earth bows down before you,
    sings to you, sings out your Name."

4   Come now, and see the works of God,
    how wonderful he is in his doing toward the
        children of men.

5   He turned the sea into dry land,
    so that they went through the water on foot;
    there we rejoiced in him.

6   In his might he rules for ever;
    his eyes keep watch over the nations;
    let no rebel rise up against him.

7   Bless our God, you peoples;
    make the voice of his praise to be heard.

8   Who holds our souls in life,
    and will not allow our feet to slip.

9   For you, O God, have proved us;
    you tried us just as silver is tried.

10   You brought us into the snare;
       you laid heavy burdens upon our backs.

11   You let men ride over our heads;
      we went through fire and water;
         but you brought us out into a place of refreshment.

12   I will enter your house with burnt-offerings;
      and will pay you my vows,
         which I promised with my lips, and spoke
              with my mouth,
         when I was in trouble.

13   I will offer you sacrifices of fat beasts,
      with the smoke of rams;
         I will give you oxen and goats.

14   Come and listen, all you who fear God,
        and I will tell you what he has done for me.

15   I called out to him with my mouth,
        and his praise was on my tongue.

16   If I had found evil in my heart
        the LORD would not have heard me;

17   But in truth God has heard me;
        he has attended to the voice of my prayer.

18   Blessed be God, who has not rejected my prayer,
        nor withheld his love from me.

Psalm 67

1 God be merciful to us, and bless us,
show us the light of his countenance, and come to us.

2 Let your ways be known upon earth,
your saving health among all nations.

3 Let the peoples praise you, O God;
let all the peoples praise you.

4 Let the nations be glad and sing for joy;
for you judge the peoples with equity,
and guide all the nations upon earth.

5 Let the peoples praise you, O God;
let all the peoples praise you.

6 The earth has brought forth her increase;
may God, our own God, give us his blessing.

7 May God give us his blessing;
and may all the ends of the earth stand in awe of him.

Psalm 70

1 Be pleased, O God, to deliver me;
  O LORD, make haste to help me.

2 Let those who seek my life be ashamed,
  and altogether dismayed;
    let those who take pleasure in my misfortune
    draw back and be disgraced.

3 Let those who say to me, "You had it coming to you."
  turn back because they are ashamed.

4 Let all who seek you rejoice in you and be glad;
    let those who love your salvation continually say,
    "Great is the LORD!"

5 But as for me, I am poor and needy;
  come to me speedily, O God.

6 You are my helper and my deliverer;
  O LORD, do not tarry.

Psalm 72

1 Give the king your justice, O God,
    and your righteousness to the king's son;

2 That he may rule your people righteously,
    and the poor with justice.

3 May the mountains bring prosperity to the people,
    and the little hills bring righteousness.

4 May he defend the needy among the people;
    may he rescue the poor,
    and crush the oppressor.

5 May he live as long as the sun and the moon endure,
    from one generation to another.

6 May he come down like rain upon the mown field;
    like showers may he water the earth.

7 In his time may the righteous flourish;
    may there be abundance of peace,
    till the moon shall be no more.

8 May he rule from sea to sea,
    and from the River to the ends of the earth.

9 May his foes bow down before him,
    and his enemies lick the dust.

10 May the kings of Tarshish and of the isles pay tribute,
    and the kings of Arabia and Saba offer gifts.

11 May all kings bow down to him,
    and all the nations do him service.

12   For he shall deliver the poor who cries out in distress,
        and the oppressed who has no helper.

13   He shall have pity on the lowly and poor;
        he shall preserve the lives of the needy.

14   He shall redeem their lives from oppression and violence,
        and dear shall their blood be in his sight.

15   Long may he live!
    and may there be given to him of the gold of Arabia;
        may prayer be made for him continually,
        and may they bless him all the day long.

16   May there be abundance of grain on the earth,
    growing thick even on the hilltops;
        may its fruit flourish like Lebanon,
        and its grain like grass upon the earth.

17   May his name endure forever,
    and be established as long as the sun endures;
        through him may all the nations bless themselves, and
        call him blessed.

18   Blessed be the LORD God, the God of Israel,
        who alone does wondrous deeds!

19   And blessed be his glorious Name forever!
    and may all the earth be filled with his glory.
    Amen. Amen.

Psalm 80

1 Hear, O Shepherd of Israel, leading Joseph like a flock;
    shine forth, you that are enthroned upon the cherubim.

2 In the presence of Ephraim, Benjamin, and Manasseh,
    stir up your strength, and come and help us.

3 Restore us, O God of hosts;
    show the light of your countenance
    and we shall be saved.

4 O LORD God of hosts,
    how long will you be angered with
            the prayers of your people?

5 You have fed them with the bread of tears;
    you have given them bowls of tears to drink.

6 You have made us the derision of our neighbors,
    and our enemies laugh us to scorn.

7 Restore us, O God of hosts;
    show the light of your countenance
    and we shall be saved.

8 You have brought a vine out of Egypt;
    you cast out the nations, and planted it.

9 You prepared the ground for it;
    it took root and filled the land.

10 The mountains were covered by its shadow,
    and the towering cedar-trees by its boughs.

11 You stretched out its tendrils to the sea
    and its branches to the River.

187

12   Why have you broken down its wall,
       so that all who pass by pluck off its grapes?

13   The wild boar of the forest has ravaged it,
       and the wild beasts of the field have grazed upon it.

14   Turn now, O God of hosts,
    look down from heaven, and behold, and tend this vine;
       preserve what your right hand has planted.

15   They burn it with fire like rubbish;
       at the rebuke of your countenance let them perish.

16   Let your hand be upon the man whom you favor,
       the son of man you have made so strong for yourself.

17   And so we will never turn away from you;
       give us life, that we may call upon your Name.

18   Restore us, O LORD God of hosts;
       show the light of your countenance
    and we shall be saved.

Psalm 84

1   How dear to me is your dwelling, O LORD of hosts!
    My soul has a desire and longing for the courts of
       the LORD;
    my heart and my flesh rejoice in the living God.

2   The sparrow has found her a house,
    and the swallow a nest, where she may lay her young;
      upon your altars, O LORD of hosts,
       my King and my God.

3 How blest are they who dwell in your house!
  they will always be praising you.

4 How blest are the men whose strength is in you!
  whose hearts are set on the pilgrims' way.

5 They who go through the desolate valley
  will find it a place of springs;
    for the early rains have covered it with pools of water,

6 They will climb from height to height;
  the God of gods will reveal himself in Zion.

7 LORD God of hosts, hear my prayer;
  hearken, O God of Jacob.

8 Behold our defender, O God;
  and look upon the face of your anointed.

9 For one day in your courts
  is better than a thousand in my own room;
    and to stand at the threshold of the house of my God
    than to dwell in the tents of the wicked.

10 For the LORD God is a sun and a shield;
  he will give grace and glory;
    and no good thing will the LORD withhold
    from those who walk with integrity.

11 LORD God of hosts,
  how blest is the man who puts his trust in you!

Psalm 85

1   You have been gracious to your land, O LORD;
    you have restored the good fortune of Jacob.

2   You have forgiven the iniquity of your people,
    and blotted out all their sins.

3   You have withdrawn all your fury;
    and turned yourself from your wrathful indignation.

4   Restore us, then, O God our Savior;
    let your anger depart from us.

5   Will you be displeased with us forever?
    will you prolong your anger from age to age?

6   Will you not give us life again,
    so that your people may rejoice in you?

7   Show us your mercy, O LORD,
    and grant us your salvation.

8   I will hearken to what the LORD God is saying;
    for he is speaking peace to his faithful people,
    and to those who turn their hearts to him.

9   Truly, his salvation is very near to those who fear him,
    so that his glory may dwell in our land.

10 Mercy and truth have met together;
    righteousness and peace have kissed each other.

11 Truth shall spring up from the earth,
    and righteousness shall look down from heaven.

12 The LORD will grant prosperity indeed,
    and our land shall yield her increase.

13 Righteousness shall go before him,
    and peace shall be a pathway for his feet.

Psalm 86

1 Bow down your ear, O LORD, and answer me,
   for I am poor and in misery.

2 Keep watch over my life, for I am faithful;
   save your servant who puts his trust in you.

3 You are my God;
   be merciful to me,
   for I call upon you all the day long.

4 Gladden the soul of your servant,
   for to you, O LORD, I lift up my soul.

5 For you, O LORD, are good and forgiving,
   and great is your love toward all who call upon you.

6 Give ear, O LORD, to my prayers,
   and attend to the voice of my supplication.

7 In the time of my trouble I will call upon you,
   for you will answer me.

8 Among the gods there is none like you, O LORD,
   nor anything like your works.

9 All nations you have made will come and
                     worship you, O LORD,
   and glorify your Name.

10 For you are great;
   you do marvelous things;
      you alone are God.

11 Teach me your way, O LORD,
   and I will walk in your truth;
      knit my heart to you, that I may fear your Name.

12   I will thank you, O LORD my God, with all my heart,
     and glorify your Name for evermore.

13   For great is your love toward me;
     you have delivered me from the nethermost Pit.

14   The arrogant rise up against me, O God,
     and a band of violent men seeks my life;
      they have not set you before their eyes.

15   But you, O LORD, are compassionate and gracious,
     slow to anger, and full of kindness and truth.

16   Turn to me, and have mercy upon me;
     give your strength to your servant,
     and save the son of your handmaid.

17   Show me a sign of your favor,
     so that those who hate me may see it and be ashamed;
      because you, O LORD, have helped me and comforted me.

Psalm 90

1   Lord, you have been our refuge
     from one generation to another.

2   Before the mountains were brought forth,
     or the land and the earth were born;
     from age to age you are God.

3   You turn man back to the dust, and say,
     "Go back, O mortal man."

4   For a thousand years in your sight are like yesterday
       when it is past,
     and like a watch in the night.

5   You sweep men away like a dream;
        they fade away suddenly like the grass.

6   In the morning it is green and flourishes;
        in the evening it is dried up and withered.

7   For we consume away in your displeasure;
        we are afraid at your wrathful indignation.

8   You have set our iniquities before you;
        and our secret sins in the light of your countenance.

9   When you are angry, all our days are gone;
        we bring our years to an end like a sigh.

10 The span of our life is seventy years;
        perhaps by strength even eighty;
            yet the sum of them is but labor and sorrow,
            for they pass away quickly and we are gone.

11 Who regards the power of your wrath?
        who rightly fears your indignation?

12 So teach us to number our days,
        that we may apply our hearts to wisdom.

13 Return, O LORD; how long will you tarry?
        Be gracious to your servants.

14 Satisfy us by your loving-kindness in the morning;
        so shall we rejoice and be glad all the days of our life.

15 Make us glad by the measure of the days that you afflicted us,
        and the years in which we suffered adversity.

16 Show your servants your works,
        and your splendor to their children.

17 May the graciousness of the Lord our God be upon us;
        prosper the work of our hands;
        prosper our handiwork.

Psalm 91

1 He who dwells in the shelter of the Most High,
    abides under the shadow of the Almighty.

2 He shall say to the LORD,
  "You are my refuge and my stronghold,
    my God in whom I put my trust."

3 He shall deliver you from the snare of the hunter,
    and from the deadly pestilence.

4 He shall cover you with his pinions,
  and you shall find refuge under his wings;
    his faithfulness shall be a shield and buckler.

5 You shall not be afraid of any terror by night,
    nor of the arrow that flies by day;

6 Of the plague that stalks in the darkness,
    nor of the sickness that lays waste at mid-day.

7 A thousand shall fall at your side,
  and ten thousand at your right hand;
    but it shall not come near you.

8 Your eyes have only to behold,
    to see the reward of the wicked.

9 Because you have made the LORD your refuge,
  and the Most High your habitation,
    there shall no evil happen to you,
      neither shall any plague come near your dwelling.

10   For he shall give his angels charge over you,
      to keep you in all your ways.

11   They shall bear you in their hands,
      lest you dash your foot against a stone.

12   You shall tread upon the lion and adder;
      you shall trample the young lion and the serpent
         under your feet.

13   Because he is bound to me in love,
         therefore will I deliver him;
     I will protect him, because he knows my Name.

14   He shall call upon me, and I will answer him;
      I am with him in trouble;
      I will rescue him and bring him to honor.

15   With long life will I satisfy him,
      and show him my salvation.

Psalm 92

1   It is a good thing to give thanks to the LORD;
      and to sing praises to your Name, O Most High;

2   To tell of your loving-kindness early in the morning,
      and of your faithfulness in the night season;

3   On the psaltery and on the lyre,
      and to the melody of the harp.

4   For you have made me glad by your acts, O LORD;
      and I shout for joy because of the works of your hands.

5   LORD, how great are your works!
      your thoughts are very deep.

6   The dullard does not know,
    nor does the fool understand,
        that though the ungodly grow like weeds,
        and all the workers of wickedness flourish,

7   They flourish only to be destroyed for ever;
        but you, O LORD, are exalted for evermore.

8   For lo, your enemies, O LORD,
    lo, your enemies shall perish,
        and all the workers of wickedness shall be scattered.

9   But my horn you have exalted like the horns of wild oxen;
        I am anointed with fresh oil.

10 My eyes also gloat over my enemies;
        and my ears have heard the last of the wicked
            who rise up against me.

11 The righteous shall flourish like a palm-tree;
        and shall spread abroad like a cedar of Lebanon.

12 Such as are planted in the house of the LORD
        shall flourish in the courts of our God;

13 They shall still bear fruit in old age;
        they shall be green and succulent;

14 That they may show how upright the LORD is,
        my Rock, in whom there is no fault.

Psalm 93

1 The LORD is King;
   he has put on splendid apparel;
      the LORD has put on his apparel,
      and girded himself with strength.

2 He has made the whole world so sure,
      that it cannot be moved.

3 Ever since the world began, your throne has been established;
      you are from everlasting.

4 The waters have lifted up, O LORD,
   the waters have lifted up their voice;
      the waters have lifted up their pounding waves.

5 Mightier than the sound of many waters,
   mightier than the breakers of the sea,
      mightier is the LORD who dwells on high.

6 Your testimonies are very sure,
      and holiness adorns your house, O LORD,
      for ever and for ever.

Psalm 95

1 Come, let us sing to the LORD;
>   let us shout for joy to the Rock of our salvation.

2 Let us come before his presence with thanksgiving;
>   and raise a loud shout to him with psalms.

3 For the LORD is a great God;
>   and a great King above all gods.

4 In his hand are the caverns of the earth;
>   and the heights of the hills are his also.

5 The sea is his, for he made it;
>   and his hands have molded the dry land.

6 Come, let us bow down, and bend the knee,
>   and kneel before the LORD our Maker.

7 For he is our God;
>   and we are the people of his pasture,
>>   and the sheep of his hand.
>   O that today you would hearken to his voice!

8 Harden not your hearts,
>   as your fathers did in the wilderness,
>>   at Meribah, and on that day at Massah,
>   when they tempted me:

9 They put me to the test,
>   though they had seen my works.

10 Forty years long I detested that generation, and said,
>   "This people waver in their hearts,
>   for they do not know my ways."

11 So I swore in my wrath,
>   "They shall not enter into my rest."

Psalm 96

1   Sing to the LORD a new song;
      sing to the LORD, all the whole earth.

2   Sing to the LORD, and bless his Name;
      proclaim the good news of his salvation from day to day.

3   Declare his glory among the nations;
      and his wonders among all peoples.

4   For great is the LORD, and greatly to be praised;
      he is more to be feared than all gods.

5   As for all the gods of the nations, they are but idols;
      but it is the LORD who made the heavens.

6   O the majesty and magnificence of his presence!
      O the power and the splendor of his sanctuary!

7   Ascribe to the LORD, you families of the peoples;
      ascribe to the LORD honor and power.

8   Ascribe to the LORD the honor proper to his Name;
      bring offerings, and come into his courts.

9   Worship the LORD in the beauty of holiness;
      let the whole earth tremble before him.

10   Tell it out among the nations: "The LORD is King!"
      the world, also, has he made so firm
            that it cannot be moved;
      and he will judge the peoples with equity.

11   Let the heavens rejoice, and let the earth be glad;
      let the sea make a noise, and all that is in it;
        let the field be joyful and all that therein is.

12   Then shall all the trees of the wood shout for joy
      before the LORD when he comes,
      when he comes to judge the earth.

13   He will judge the world with righteousness
      and the peoples with his truth.

Psalm 97

1 The LORD is King;
   let the earth rejoice;
     let the multitude of the isles be glad.

2 Clouds and darkness are round about him;
     righteousness and justice are the foundation of his throne.

3 A fire goes before him,
     and burns up his enemies on every side.

4 His lightnings light up the world;
     the earth sees it and is afraid.

5 The mountains melt like wax at the presence of the LORD,
     at the presence of the Lord of the whole earth.

6 The heavens declare his righteousness,
     and all the peoples see his glory.

7 Confounded be all who worship carved images,
   and delight in false gods!
     Bow down before him, all you gods.

8 Zion hears and is glad,
   and the cities of Judah rejoice;
     because of your judgments, O LORD.

9 For you are the LORD,
   most high over all the earth;
     you are exalted far above all gods.

10 The LORD loves those who hate evil;
     he preserves the lives of his saints,
       and delivers them from the hand of the wicked.

11 Light has sprung up for the righteous,
     and joyful gladness for such as are true-hearted.

12 Rejoice in the LORD, O you righteous,
     and give thanks to his holy Name.

Psalm 98

1   Sing to the LORD a new song;
      for he has done marvelous things.

2   With his right hand and his holy arm
      has he got for himself the victory.

3   The LORD has made known his victory;
      his righteousness has he openly showed
                in the sight of the nations.

4   He remembers his mercy and faithfulness
                to the house of Israel;
      and all the ends of the earth have seen
                the victory of our God.

5   Shout with joy to the Lord, all you lands;
      lift up your voice, rejoice, and sing.

6   Sing to the LORD with the harp;
      with the harp and the voice of song.

7   With trumpets and the sound of the horn,
      shout with joy before the King, the LORD.

8   Let the sea make a noise, and all that is in it;
      the lands, and those who dwell therein.

9   Let the rivers clap their hands;
      and let the hills ring out with joy before the LORD,
      when he comes to judge the earth.

10 In righteousness shall he judge the world,
      and the peoples with equity.

Psalm 99

1   The LORD is King,
    let the people tremble;
       he is enthroned upon the cherubim,
       let the earth shake.

2   The LORD is great in Zion;
       he is high above all peoples.

3   Let them confess his Name,
    which is great and awesome;
       he is the Holy One.

4   "O mighty King, Lover of justice,
    you have established equity;
       you have executed justice and righteousness in Jacob."

5   Magnify the LORD our God,
    and fall down before his footstool;
       he is the Holy One.

6   Moses and Aaron among his priests,
    and Samuel among those who call upon his Name;
       they called upon the LORD, and he answered them.

7   He spoke to them out of the pillar of cloud;
    they kept his testimonies,
    and the decree that he gave them.

8   O LORD our God, you answered them indeed;
    you were a God who forgave them,
    yet punished them for their evil deeds.

9   Magnify the LORD our God,
    and worship him upon his holy hill;
       for the LORD our God is the Holy One.

Psalm 100

1 Be joyful in the LORD, all you lands;
    serve the LORD with gladness,
    and come before his presence with a song.

2 Know this: The LORD himself is God;
    he himself has made us, and we are his;
    we are his people and the sheep of his pasture.

3 Enter his gates with thanksgiving;
    go into his courts with praise;
    give thanks to him and call upon his Name.

4 For the LORD is good;
    his mercy is everlasting;
    and his faithfulness endures from age to age.

Psalm 102

1 LORD, hear my prayer,
    and let my cry come before you;
    hide not your face from me,
    in the day of my trouble.

2 Incline your ear to me;
    when I call, make haste to answer me.

3 For my days drift away like smoke,
    and my bones are hot as burning coals.

4 My heart is smitten like grass and withered,
    so that I forget to eat my bread.

5 Because of the voice of my groaning,
    I am but skin and bones.

6 I have become like a vulture in the wilderness,
    like an owl among the ruins.

7 I lie awake and groan;
    I am like a sparrow, lonely on a house-top.

8 My enemies revile me all day long;
    and those who conspire against me are satisfied.

9 For I have eaten ashes for bread,
    and mingled my drink with weeping,
      because of your indignation and wrath;
    for you have lifted me up and thrown me away.

10 My days pass away like a shadow;
    and I wither like the grass.

11 But you, O LORD, endure for ever,
    and your Name from age to age.

12 You shall arise and have compassion on Zion;
    for it is time to have mercy upon her;
    indeed, the appointed time has come.

13 For your servants love her very rubble,
    and are moved to pity even for her dust.

14 The nations shall fear your Name, O LORD,
    and all the kings of the earth your glory.

15 For the LORD will build up Zion,
    and his glory will appear.

16 He will look with favor on the prayer of the homeless;
    he will not despise their plea.

17 Let this be written for a future generation,
    so that a people yet unborn may praise the LORD.

18 For the LORD looked down from his holy place on high;
    from the heavens he beheld the earth;

19   That he might hear the groan of the captive,
      and set free those condemned to die;

20   That men may declare in Zion the Name of the LORD,
      and his praise in Jerusalem;

21   When the peoples are gathered together,
      and the kingdoms also, to serve the LORD.

22   He has brought down my strength before my time;
      he has shortened the number of my days;

23   And I said, O my God,
      do not take me away in the midst of my days;
      your years endure throughout all generations.

24   In the beginning, O LORD, you laid the foundations
          of the earth,
      and the heavens are the work of your hands;

25   They shall perish, but you will endure;
      they all shall wear out like a garment;
      like clothing you will change them,
          and they shall be changed;

26   But you are always the same;
      and your years will never end.

27   The children of your servants shall continue;
      and their offspring shall stand fast in your sight.

Psalm 103

1   Bless the LORD, O my soul;
      and all that is within me, bless his holy Name.

2   Bless the LORD, O my soul;
      and forget not all his benefits.

3   He forgives all my sins,
      and heals all my infirmities;

4   He redeems my life from the grave,
      and crowns me with mercy and loving-kindness;

5   He satisfies me with good things,
      and my youth is renewed like an eagle's.

6   The LORD executes righteousness,
      and judgment for all who are oppressed.

7   He made his ways known to Moses;
      and his works to the children of Israel.

8   The LORD is full of compassion and mercy,
      slow to anger and of great kindness.

9   He will not always accuse us,
      nor will he keep his anger forever.

10   He has not dealt with us according to our sins,
      nor rewarded us according to our wickedness.

11   For as the heavens are high over the earth,
      so is his mercy great over those who fear him.

12   Far as the east is from the west,
      so far has he removed our sins from us.

13 As a father cares for his children,
  so does the LORD care for those who fear him.

14 For he himself knows whereof we are made;
  he remembers that we are but dust.

15 The days of man are like the grass:
  he flourishes like a flower of the field;

16 When the wind goes over it, it is gone;
  and its place shall know it no more.

17 But the merciful goodness of the LORD endures for ever
    on those who fear him,
  and his righteousness on children's children;

18 On those who keep his covenant;
  and remember his commandments and do them.

19 The LORD has set his throne in heaven;
  and his kingship has dominion over all.

20 Bless the LORD, you angels of his,
  you mighty ones who do his bidding.
  and hearken to the voice of his word.

21 Bless the LORD, all you his hosts,
  you ministers of his who do his will.

22 Bless the LORD, all you works of his,
  in all places of his dominion.
  Bless the LORD, O my soul.

Psalm 104

1   Bless the Lord, O my soul.
      O Lord my God, how excellent is your greatness!
      you are clothed with majesty and splendor.

2   You wrap yourself with light as with a cloak,
      and spread out the heavens like a curtain.

3   You lay the beams of your chambers in the waters above;
      you make the clouds your chariot;
      you ride on the wings of the wind.

4   You make the winds your messengers,
      and flames of fire your servants.

5   You have set the earth upon its foundations,
      so that it never shall move at any time.

6   You covered it with the Deep as with a mantle;
      the waters stood higher than the mountains.

7   At your rebuke they fled;
      at the voice of your thunder they hastened away.

8   They went up into the hills,
    and down to the valleys beneath,
      to the places you had appointed for them.

9   You set the limits that they should not pass;
      they shall not again cover the earth.

10   You send the springs into the valleys;
      they flow between the mountains.

11   All the beasts of the field drink their fill of them,
      and the wild asses quench their thirst.

12   Beside them the birds of the air make their nests,
      and sing among the branches.

13   You water the mountains from your dwelling on high;
         the earth is satisfied by the fruit of your works.

14   You make the grass grow for the cattle,
         and plants for the use of men;

15   That they may bring forth food from the earth,
         and wine to make glad the heart of man;

16   Oil to give man a cheerful countenance,
         and bread to strengthen his heart.

17   The trees of the LORD are full of sap,
         the cedars of Lebanon which he planted;

18   In which the birds build their nests,
         and in whose tops the stork makes his dwelling.

19   The high hills are a refuge for the mountain-goats,
         and the stony cliffs for the badgers.

20   You appointed the moon to mark the seasons,
         and the sun knows the time of its setting.

21   You make darkness that it may be night,
         in which all the beasts of the forest prowl about.

22   The lions roar after their prey;
         they seek their food from God.

23   The sun rises and they slip away,
         and lay themselves down in their dens.

24   Man goes forth to his work,
         and to his labor, until the evening.

25   O LORD, how manifold are your works!
         in wisdom you have made them all;
         the earth is full of your creatures.

26 Yonder is the great and wide sea,
    with its living things too many to number,
    creatures both small and great.

27 There move the ships,
    and there is that leviathan,
    which you have made for the sport of it.

28 All of them look to you,
    to give them their food in due season.

29 You give it to them, they gather it;
    you open your hand,
    and they are filled with good things.

30 You hide your face, and they are terrified;
    you take away their breath, and they die,
    and return to their dust.

31 You send forth your breath, and they are created;
    and so you renew the face of the earth.

32 May the glory of the LORD endure for ever;
    may the LORD rejoice in all his works.

33 He looks at the earth, and it trembles;
    he touches the mountains, and they smoke.

34 I will sing to the LORD as long as I live;
    I will praise my God while I have my being.

35 May these words of mine please him;
    I will rejoice in the LORD.

36 Let sinners be consumed out of the earth,
    and the wicked be no more.

37 Bless the LORD, O my soul;
    Hallelujah!

Psalm 108

1   My heart is fixed, O God;
    my heart is fixed;
        I will sing and make melody.

2   Wake up, my spirit;
    awake, lute and harp;
        I myself will waken the morning.

3   I will confess you among the peoples, O LORD;
        I will sing praises to you among the nations.

4   For your loving-kindness is greater than the heavens,
        and your faithfulness reaches to the clouds.

5   Exalt yourself above the heavens, O God,
        and your glory over all the earth.

6   Deliver those who are dear to you;
        save with your right hand, and answer me.

7   God spoke from his holy place, and said:
        I will exult, and parcel out Shechem;
        I will divide up the valley of Succoth.

8   Gilead is mine, and Manasseh is mine;
        Ephraim is my helmet, and Judah my scepter.

9   As for Moab, she is my wash-basin;
        on Edom I throw down my sandal,
        and over Philistia will I shout in triumph.

10 Who will lead me into the strong city?
        who will bring me to Edom?

11   Have you not cast us off, O God?
        you no longer go out with our armies.

12   Grant us your help against the enemy,
        for vain is the help of man.

13   With God we will do valiant deeds,
        and he shall tread our enemies under foot.

Psalm 110

1   The LORD said to my Lord:
        "Sit at my right hand,
        until I make your enemies your footstool."

2   The LORD will send the scepter of your power out of Zion,
        saying, "Rule over your enemies round about you."

3   In the day of battle, your people will offer themselves freely
                    upon the holy mountain;
        Your young men will come to you
                    like dew from the womb of the morning.

4   The LORD has sworn, and he will not retract:
        "You are a Priest for ever,
        after the order of Melchizedek."

5   The Lord who is at your right hand
        will smite kings in the day of his wrath.

6   So the king will judge among the nations;
        he will heap high the corpses;
            he will smash heads over the wide earth.

7   He will drink from the brook beside the road;
        therefore, he will lift high his head.

Psalm 111

1 Hallelujah!
  I will give thanks to the LORD with my whole heart,
    in the assembly of the upright, in the congregation.

2 Great are the works of the LORD!
    they are studied by all who delight in them.

3 His work is full of majesty and splendor,
    and his righteousness endures for ever.

4 He makes his marvelous works to be remembered;
    the LORD is gracious and compassionate.

5 He gives food to those who fear him;
    he is ever mindful of his covenant.

6 He has shown his people the power of his works,
    in giving them the lands of the nations.

7 The works of his hands are faithfulness and justice;
    all his commandments are sure.

8 They stand fast for ever and ever,
    because they are done in truth and equity.

9 He sent redemption to his people;
  he commanded his covenant for ever;
    holy and awesome is his Name.

10 The fear of the LORD is the beginning of wisdom;
    those who act accordingly have a good understanding;
    his praise endures for ever.

Psalm 112

1   Hallelujah!
How blest is the man who fears the LORD,
   and has great delight in his commandments!

2   His descendants will be mighty in the land;
   the generation of the upright shall be blest.

3   Wealth and riches shall be in his house,
   and his righteousness shall last for ever.

4   Light shines in the darkness for the upright;
   the righteous man is merciful and compassionate.

5   It is good for a man to be generous in lending,
   and to manage his affairs with justice.

6   For he will never be shaken;
   the righteous shall be kept in everlasting remembrance.

7   He shall not be afraid of any evil rumors;
   his heart is right;
   he puts his trust in the LORD.

8   His heart is established, and will not shrink,
   until he sees his desire upon his enemies.

9   He has given freely to the poor;
   his righteousness stands fast for ever;
   he will hold up his head with honor.

10   The wicked shall see it, and be angry;
   he shall gnash his teeth, and pine away;
   the desires of the wicked shall perish.

Psalm 113

1 Hallelujah!
Give praise, you servants of the LORD;
   praise the Name of the LORD.

2 Let the Name of the LORD be blest,
   from this time forth for evermore.

3 From the rising of the sun to its going down,
   let the Name of the LORD be praised.

4 The LORD is high above all nations,
   and his glory above the heavens.

5 Who is like the LORD our God,
who sits enthroned on high,
   but stoops to behold the heavens and the earth?

6 He takes up the weak out of the dust,
   and lifts up the poor out of the ashes.

7 He sets him with the princes,
   with the princes of his people.

8 He makes the woman of a childless house
   to be a joyful mother of children.
Hallelujah!

Psalm 114

1 When Israel came out of Egypt,
   the house of Jacob from among a people of strange speech,

2 Judah became the sanctuary of the LORD,
   and Israel his dominion.

3 The sea beheld it, and fled;
   and Jordan turned and went back.

4 The mountains skipped like rams,
   and the little hills like young sheep.

5 What ails you, O sea, that you fled?
   O Jordan, that you turned back?

6 You mountains, that you skipped like rams?
   You little hills, like young sheep?

7 Tremble, O earth, at the presence of the LORD;
   at the presence of the God of Jacob,

8 Who turned the hard rock into a pool of water,
   and the flint-stone into a flowing spring.

Psalm 116

1 I love the LORD, because he has heard
the voice of my entreaty;
because he has inclined his ear to me
whenever I called upon him.

2 The cords of death entangled me,
the grip of the grave took hold of me;
I came to grief and sorrow.

3 Then I called upon the Name of the LORD:
"O LORD, I pray you, save my life."

4 Gracious is the LORD, and righteous;
our God is full of compassion.

5 The LORD watches over the innocent:
I was brought very low, and he helped me.

6 Turn again to your rest, O my soul;
for the LORD has treated you well.

7 For you have rescued my life from death,
my eyes from tears, and my feet from stumbling.

8 I will walk in the presence of the LORD
in the land of the living.

9 I believed, even when I said,
"I have been brought very low."
In my distress I said, "All men are liars."

10 How shall I repay the LORD
for all the good things he has done for me?

11 I will lift up the cup of salvation,
and call upon the Name of the LORD,

12 I will fulfill my vows to the LORD
in the presence of all his people.

13 Precious in the sight of the LORD
       is the death of his servants.

14 O LORD, I am your servant;
       I am your servant, and the son of your handmaiden;
       you have freed me from my bonds.

15 I will offer you the sacrifice of thanksgiving,
       and call upon the Name of the LORD.

16 I will fulfill my vows to the LORD
    in the presence of all his people,
       in the courts of the LORD's house,
          in the midst of you, O Jerusalem. Hallelujah!

Psalm 117

1 Praise the LORD, all you nations;
       praise him, all you peoples.

2 For his loving-kindness toward us is great;
       and the faithfulness of the LORD endures for ever.
    Hallelujah!

Psalm 118

1   Give thanks to the LORD, for he is good;
    for his love endures for ever.

2   Let Israel now proclaim,
    "His love endures for ever."

3   Let the house of Aaron now proclaim,
    "His love endures for ever."

4   Let those who fear the LORD now proclaim,
    "His love endures for ever."

5   I called to the LORD in my distress;
    he answered by setting me free.

6   The LORD is on my side;
    therefore I will not fear;
      what can man do to me?

7   The LORD is on my side to help me;
    I will triumph over those who hate me.

8   It is better to rely on the LORD
    than to put any trust in man.

9   It is better to rely on the LORD
    than to put any trust in princes.

10 All nations compass me round about;
    in the Name of the LORD I will repel them.

11 They compass me, they compass me round about;
    in the Name of the LORD I will repel them.

12 They swarm about me like bees;
  they blaze like a fire of thorns;
    in the Name of the LORD I will repel them.

13 I was pressed so hard that I almost fell;
    but the LORD came to my help.

14 The LORD is my strength and my song,
  and he has become my salvation.

15 There is a sound of exultation and victory
    in the tents of the righteous:

16 "The right hand of the LORD has triumphed!
    the right hand of the LORD is exalted!
    the right hand of the LORD has triumphed!"

17 I shall not die, but live,
    and declare the works of the LORD.

18 The LORD has punished me sorely;
    but he did not hand me over to death.

19 Open for me the gates of righteousness;
    I will enter them;
    I will offer thanks to the LORD.

20 "This is the gate of the LORD,
    he who is righteous may enter."

21 I will give thanks to you, for you answered me,
   and have become my salvation.

22 The same stone which the builders rejected
   has become the chief corner-stone.

23 This is the LORD's doing,
   and it is marvelous in our eyes.

24 On this day the LORD has acted;
   we will rejoice and be glad in it.

25 Save us, LORD, we pray you;
   O LORD, grant us deliverance.

26 Blessed is he who comes in the Name of the LORD;
   we bless you from the house of the LORD.

27 God is the LORD; he has shined upon us;
   form a procession with branches
   up to the horns of the altar.

28 "You are my God, and I will thank you;
   you are my God, and I will exalt you."

29 Give thanks to the LORD, for he is good;
   for his love endures for ever,

Psalm 121

1 I will lift up my eyes to the hills.
    "Where is my help to come from?"

2 My help comes from the LORD,
    the Maker of heaven and earth.

3 He will not let your foot be moved,
    and he who watches over you will not fall asleep.

4 Behold, he who keeps watch over Israel
  shall neither slumber nor sleep:
    he who watches over you is the LORD.

5 The LORD is your shade at your right hand,
    so that the sun shall not strike you by day,
    nor the moon by night.

6 The LORD shall preserve you from all evil;
    it is he who shall keep you safe.

7 The LORD shall watch over your going out
                    and your coming in,
  from this time forth for evermore.

Psalm 122

1 I was glad when they said to me,
      "Let us go to the house of the LORD."

2 Now our feet are standing,
      Jerusalem, within your gates.

3 Jerusalem is built as a city
      that is at unity with itself;

4 To which the tribes go up, the tribes of the LORD,
            the assembly of Israel,
      to praise the Name of the LORD.

5 For there are the thrones of judgment,
      the thrones of the house of David.

6 Pray for the peace of Jerusalem:
      May they prosper who love you.

7 Peace be within your walls;
      and quietness within your towers.

8 For my brethren and companions' sake,
      I pray for your prosperity.

9 Because of the house of the LORD our God,
      I will seek to do you good.

Psalm 124

1 If the LORD had not been on our side,
   now may Israel say;

2 If the LORD had not been on our side,
   when men rose up against us;

3 Then would they have swallowed us up alive,
   in their fierce anger toward us;

4 Then would the waters have overwhelmed us,
   and the torrent gone over us;

5 Then would the raging waters
   have gone right over us.

6 Blessed be the LORD! he has not given us over
   to be a prey for their teeth.

7 We have escaped, like a bird from the snare of the fowler;
   the snare is broken, and we have escaped.

8 Our help is in the Name of the LORD,
   the maker of heaven and earth.

Psalm 126

1 When the LORD restored the fortunes of Zion,
   then were we like men who dream.

2 Then was our mouth filled with laughter,
   and our tongue with joy.

3 Then they said among the nations,
   "The LORD has done great things for them."

4 The LORD has done great things for us,
   and we are glad indeed.

5 Restore our fortunes, O LORD,
   like the water-courses of the Negev.

6 Those who sowed with tears,
   will reap with songs of joy.

7 He who goes out weeping, carrying the seed,
   will come again with joy, shouldering his sheaves.

Psalm 130

1 Out of the depths have I called to you, O Lord;
Lord, hear my voice;
   let your ears consider well the voice of my supplication.

2 If you, LORD, were to note what is done amiss,
O LORD, who could survive?
   but there is forgiveness with you;
   therefore you shall be feared.

3 I wait for the LORD; my soul waits for him;
   in his word is my hope.

4 My soul waits for the LORD,
more than watchmen for the morning,
   more than watchmen for the morning.

5 O Israel, wait for the LORD;
   for with the LORD there is mercy;

6 With him there is plenteous redemption;
   and he shall redeem Israel from all his sins.

Psalm 133

1 O, how good and pleasant it is,
   when brothers live together in unity!

2 It is like fine oil upon the head,
   that runs down upon the beard,

3 Upon the beard of Aaron,
   and runs down upon the collar of his robe.

4 It is like the dew of Hermon,
   that falls upon the hills of Zion.

5 For there the LORD has ordained the blessing,
   even life for evermore.

Psalm 134

1 Behold now, bless the LORD, all you servants of the LORD,
    you that stand by night in the house of the LORD.

2 Lift up your hands to the holy place, and bless the LORD.
    The LORD who made heaven and earth
        bless you out of Zion.

Psalm 139

1 LORD, you have searched me out, and known me;
    you know my sitting down, and my rising up again;
        you discern my thoughts from afar.

2 You trace my journeys, and my resting-places,
    and are acquainted with all my ways.

3 Indeed, there is not a word on my lips,
    but you, O LORD, know it altogether.

4 You press upon me behind and before,
    and lay your hand upon me.

5 Such knowledge is too wonderful for me;
    it is so high that I cannot attain to it.

6 Where can I go then from your Spirit?
    and where can I flee from your presence?

7 If I climb up to heaven, you are there;
    if I make the grave my bed, you are there also.

8 If I take the wings of the morning,
    and dwell in the uttermost parts of the sea,

9 Even there your hand will lead me,
    and your right hand hold me fast.

10 If I say, "Surely the darkness will cover me,
　　and the light around me turn to night",

11 Darkness is not dark to you;
　　the night is as bright as the day:
　　　darkness and light to you are both alike.

12 For you yourself created my inmost parts;
　　you knit me together in my mother's womb.

13 I will thank you because I am marvelously made;
　　your works are wonderful, and I know it well.

14 My body was not hidden from you,
　　while I was being made in secret,
　　　and woven in the depths of the earth.

15 Your eyes beheld my limbs, yet unfinished in the womb;
　　all of them were written in your book;
　　　they were fashioned day by day,
　　　when as yet there was none of them.

16 How deep I find your thoughts, O God!
　　how great is the sum of them!

17 If I were to count them, they would be more in number
　　　　　　than the sand;
　　to count them all, my life-span
　　would need to be like yours.

18 O that you would slay the wicked, O God!
　　You men of blood, depart from me.

19 They speak despitefully against you;
　　your enemies take your Name in vain.

20   Do I not hate them, O Lord, who hate you?
      and do I not loathe them who rise up against you?

21   I hate them with a perfect hatred;
      they have become my own enemies.

22   Search me out, O God, and know my heart;
      try me, and know my restless thoughts.

23   Look well whether there be any wickedness in me,
      and lead me in the way that is everlasting.

Psalm 142

1   I cry to the Lord with my voice;
      to the Lord I make loud supplication.

2   I pour out my complaint before him,
      and tell him all my trouble.

3   When my spirit languishes within me,
  you know my path;
      in the way wherein I walk they have hidden a trap for me.

4   I look to my right hand, and find no one who knows me;
      I have no place to flee to, and no one cares for me.

5   I cry out to you, O Lord;
  I say, "You are my refuge,
      my portion in the land of the living."

6   Listen to my cry for help, for I am very low;
      save me from those who pursue me,
      for they are too strong for me.

7   Bring me out of prison, that I may give thanks to your Name;
      when you have dealt bountifully with me,
      the righteous will gather around me.

Psalm 145

1 I will exalt you, O God my King,
   and bless your Name for ever and ever.

2 Every day will I bless you,
   and praise your Name for ever and ever.

3 Great is the LORD, and greatly to be praised;
   there is no end to his greatness.

4 One generation shall praise your works to another,
   and shall declare your power.

5 I will ponder the glorious splendor of your majesty,
   and all your marvelous works.

6 Men shall speak of the might of your wondrous acts;
   and I will tell of your greatness.

7 They shall publish the remembrance of your great goodness;
   they shall sing of your righteous deeds.

8 The LORD is gracious and compassionate,
   slow to anger, and of great kindness.

9 The LORD is loving to every man;
   and his compassion is over all his works.

10 All your works praise you, O LORD:
    and your faithful servants bless you.

11 They make known the glory of your kingdom,
    and speak of your power;

12 That men may know of your power,
    and the glorious splendor of your kingdom.

13 Your kingdom is an everlasting kingdom;
    your dominion endures throughout all ages.

14 The LORD is faithful in all his words,
and merciful in all his deeds.

15 The LORD upholds all those who fall;
he lifts up those who are bowed down.

16 The eyes of all wait upon you, O LORD:
and you give them their food in due season.

17 You open wide your hand,
and satisfy the needs of every living creature.

18 The LORD is righteous in all his ways,
and loving in all his works.

19 The LORD is near to all who call upon him,
to all who call upon him faithfully.

20 He fulfills the desire of those who fear him;
he hears their cry, and helps them.

21 The LORD preserves all those who love him;
but he destroys all the wicked.

22 My mouth shall speak the praise of the LORD;
let all flesh bless his holy Name,
for ever and ever.

Psalm 147

1 Hallelujah!
How good it is to sing praises to our God!
　　how pleasant it is to honor him with praise!

2 The LORD rebuilds Jerusalem;
　　he gathers the exiles of Israel.

3 He heals the broken-hearted,
　　and binds up their wounds.

4 He counts the number of the stars,
　　and calls them all by their names.

5 Great is our LORD, and mighty in power;
　　there is no limit to his wisdom.

6 The LORD gives relief to the lowly,
　　but casts the wicked to the ground.

7 Sing to the LORD with thanksgiving;
　　make music to our God upon the harp.

8 He covers the heavens with clouds,
and prepares rain for the earth;
　　he makes grass to grow upon the mountains,
　　and green plants for the use of men.

9 He provides food for the cattle,
　　and for the young ravens when they cry.

10 He is not impressed by the might of a horse;
　　he has no pleasure in the strength of a man.

11 But the LORD has pleasure in those who fear him,
    in those who await his gracious favor.

12 Worship the LORD, O Jerusalem;
    praise your God, O Zion.

13 For he has strengthened the bars of your gates;
    he has blessed your children within you.

14 He has established peace on your borders;
    he satisfies you with the finest wheat.

15 He sends out his command to the earth,
    and his word runs very swiftly.

16 He gives snow like wool;
    he scatters hoar-frost like ashes.

17 He scatters his ice like bread-crumbs;
    who can stand against his cold?

18 He sends forth his word, and melts them;
    he blows with his wind, and the waters flow.

19 He declares his word to Jacob,
    his statutes and his judgments to Israel.

20 He has not done so to any other nation;
    to them he has not revealed his judgments.
    Hallelujah!

Psalm 148

1 Hallelujah!
   Praise the LORD from the heavens;
      praise him in the heights.

2 Praise him, all you angels of his;
      praise him, all his host.

3 Praise him, sun and moon;
      praise him, all you shining stars.

4 Praise him, heavens of heavens,
      and you waters above the heavens.

5 Let them praise the Name of the LORD;
      for he commanded, and they were created.

6 He made them fast for ever and ever;
      he gave them a law which shall not pass away.

7 Praise the LORD from the earth,
      you sea-monsters and all deeps;

8 Fire and hail, snow and fog,
      tempestuous wind, doing his will;

9 Mountains and all hills,
      fruit-trees and all cedars;

10 Wild beasts and all cattle,
      creeping things and winged birds;

11 Kings of the earth and all peoples,
      princes and all rulers of the world;

12 Young men and maidens,
      old and young together;

13   Let them praise the Name of the LORD;
      for his Name only is exalted,
      his splendor is over earth and heaven.

14   He has raised up strength for his people,
    and praise for all his loyal servants,
      the children of Israel, a people that is near him.
    Hallelujah!

Psalm 150

1   Hallelujah!
    Praise God in his holy temple;
      praise him in the firmament of his power.

2   Praise him for his mighty acts;
      praise him for his excellent greatness.

3   Praise him with the blast of a horn;
      praise him with lyre and harp.

4   Praise him with timbrel and dance;
      praise him with strings and pipe.

5   Praise him with resounding cymbals;
      praise him with loud-clanging cymbals.

6   Let everything that breathes
      praise the LORD.
      Hallelujah!

THE DAILY OFFICE

SENTENCES FOR SEASONS
AND OTHER OCCASIONS

For use at any time at the discretion of the Minister

ADVENT SEASON

In the wilderness prepare the way of the LORD:
make straight in the desert a highway for our God.
The glory of the LORD shall be revealed,
and all flesh shall see it together.   [Isaiah 40:3, 5]
Rejoice: the Lord is at hand.   [Philippians 4:5]
Amen, Come, Lord Jesus.   [Revelation 22:20]

CHRISTMAS SEASON

Behold, I bring good news of great joy which will come to all
the people: for to you is born in the city of David a Savior,
who is Christ the Lord.   [Luke 2:10, 11]
Glory to God in the highest and on earth peace among men.
[Luke 2:14]
Behold the dwelling of God is with men. He will dwell with
them and they shall be his people:
God himself shall be with them, and be their God.
[Revelation 21:3]

EPIPHANY SEASON

I will give you as a light to the nations, that my salvation
may reach to the end of the earth.   [Isaiah 49:6]
Nations shall come to your light, and kings to the brightness
of your rising.   [Isaiah 60:3]
If we walk in the light, as he is in the light, we have fellowship with one another:
And the blood of Jesus his Son cleanses us from all sin.
[1 John 1:7]

LENT AND HOLY WEEK

Jesus said, If any man would come after me, let him deny himself and take up his cross and follow me.
For whoever would save his life will lose it; and whoever loses his life for my sake and the gospel's will save it.

[Mark 8:34, 35]

All we like sheep have gone astray; we have turned every one to his own way;
And the LORD has laid on him the iniquity of us all.

[Isaiah 53:6]

EASTER SEASON INCLUDING ASCENSION DAY AND THE DAY OF PENTECOST

Alleluia. He has risen. [Mark 16:6]
The Lord has risen indeed. Alleluia. [Luke 24:34]
Worthy is the Lamb who was slain, to receive power and wealth and wisdom and might and honor and glory and blessing.
To him who sits on the throne and to the Lamb be blessing and honor and glory and might for ever and ever.

[Revelation 5:12, 13]

God's love has been poured into our hearts,
Through the Holy Spirit who has been given to us.

[Romans 5:5]

ALL SAINTS AND OTHER FESTIVALS

Since we are surrounded by so great a cloud of witnesses, let us lay aside every weight, and sin which clings so closely,
And let us run with perseverance the race which is set before us, looking to Jesus, the pioneer and perfecter of our faith.

[Hebrews 12:1–2]

Let the nations be glad and sing for joy.
For God judges the peoples with equity,
and guides all the nations upon earth.   [Psalm 67:4]

The LORD is in his holy temple:
Let all the earth keep silence before him. [Habakkuk 2:20]
Worship the LORD in the beauty of holiness;
Let the whole earth tremble before him.   [Psalm 96:9]
God is spirit, and those who worship him
must worship in spirit and truth.   [John 4:24]
Let the words of my mouth and the meditation of my heart
be acceptable in your sight,
O LORD, my strength and my redeemer.   [Psalm 19:14]

THE INVITATORY ANTIPHONS

In the seasons and on the days named the following may be sung
or said with the Invitatory Psalms which begin the Psalter.

IN ADVENT

Our King and Savior now draws near: Come let us adore
him. Alleluia.

IN CHRISTMAS SEASON

Unto us a child is born: Come let us adore him. Alleluia.

IN THE EPIPHANY SEASON AND ON TRANSFIGURATION

The Lord has shown forth his glory: Come let us adore
him. Alleluia.

Alleluia. The Lord is risen indeed: Come let us adore him. Alleluia.

ON ASCENSION DAY

Alleluia. Christ the Lord is ascended to heaven: Come let us adore him. Alleluia.

ON THE DAY OF PENTECOST

Alleluia. The Spirit of the Lord renews the face of the earth: Come let us adore him. Alleluia.

ON TRINITY SUNDAY

Father, Son, and Holy Spirit, one God: holy is his Name: Come let us adore him. Alleluia.

In Lent, the Alleluias in the following antiphons are omitted:

ON FEASTS OF THE INCARNATION

The Word was made flesh and dwelt among us: Come let us adore him. (Alleluia.)

ON OTHER FESTIVALS

The Lord is glorious in his saints: Come let us adore him. (Alleluia.)

In Easter Season, the following forms are used instead:

ON FEASTS OF THE INCARNATION

Alleluia. The Word was made flesh and dwelt among us: Come let us adore him. Alleluia.

ON OTHER FESTIVALS

Alleluia. The Lord is glorious in his saints: Come let us adore him. Alleluia.

CONCERNING THE SERVICE

In the Offices of Morning and Evening Prayer, the term "Minister" is used to denote the person, whether a clergyman or a lay person, leading the service.

Proper Antiphons which may be used as refrains with the Invitatory Psalm will be found on pages 240–241.

Antiphons in the words of the opening Sentences given in the Offices, or other words of Scripture, may be used with the Psalms and with the Gospel Canticles.

The Apostles' Creed is normally recited at both Morning and Evening Prayer on Sundays and other major Feasts (except when the Eucharist with its own Creed is to follow). It is desirable that the Creed be recited in at least one of the Offices on other days.

At celebrations of the Holy Eucharist, the Order for Morning or Evening Prayer may be used in place of all that precedes the Offertory, provided that a Lesson from the Gospel is always included and that the Intercession conforms to the directions on page 307.

Additional Directions and Suggestions are on pages 306–307.

MORNING AND EVENING PRAYER

FIRST ORDER

The Minister begins the service with one or more of these Sentences of Scripture, or of those on pages 238–240.

The Sentences in italics may be used as responses by the people or as separate Sentences.

Grace to you and peace from God our Father and the Lord Jesus Christ. [Romans 1:7]

Thanks be to God who gives us the victory through our Lord Jesus Christ. [1 Corinthians 15:57]

Lord, I love the habitation of thy house, and the place where thy glory dwells. [Psalm 26:8]

Let my prayer be counted as incense before thee, and the lifting up of my hands as an evening sacrifice. [Psalm 141:2]

OCCASIONS OF THANKSGIVING

O give thanks to the Lord, call on his name, make known his deeds among the people.

Sing to him, sing praises to him, tell of all his wonderful works. [Psalm 105:1, 2]

PENITENTIAL

Seek the Lord while he may be found, call upon him while he is near; let the wicked forsake his way, and the unrighteous man his thoughts.

Let him return to the Lord that he may have mercy upon him, and to our God, for he will abundantly pardon.

[Isaiah 55:6, 7]

The following Confession of Sin, or the form on page 256, may then be said; or the office may continue at once with "O Lord, open thou our lips" all still standing.

CONFESSION OF SIN

Minister

Let us humbly confess our sins unto Almighty God.

SILENCE may be kept

Minister and People together, all kneeling

Almighty and most merciful Father, We have erred and strayed from thy ways like lost sheep. We have followed too much the devices and desires of our own hearts. We have offended against thy holy laws. We have left undone those things which we ought to have done; And we have done those things which we ought not to have done. But thou, O Lord, have mercy upon us; Spare thou those who confess their faults; Restore thou those who are penitent; According to thy promises declared unto mankind in Christ Jesus our Lord; And grant that hereafter we may live a godly, righteous and sober life, To the glory of thy holy Name.
                                                                Amen.

The Minister says this prayer.

Almighty God have mercy on us, forgive us all our sins, through our Lord Jesus Christ; strengthen us in all goodness, and by the power of the Holy Spirit, keep us in eternal life. *Amen.*

If a Bishop or Priest is present, he may substitute an absolution.

The Psalter

All stand

Minister O Lord, open thou our lips,

People And our mouth shall show forth thy praise.

Minister and People

Glory be to the Father, and to the Son, and to the Holy Spirit; as it was in the beginning, is now and ever shall be, world without end. Amen.

Except in Lent **Alleluia.**

In the morning shall be, and in the evening may be, sung or said

VENITE (Psalm 95: 1–7; 96: 9, 13)

O come let us sing unto the LORD;
    let us heartily rejoice in the strength of our salvation.
Let us come before his presence with thanksgiving;
    and show ourselves glad in him with psalms.

For the LORD is a great God;
    and a great King above all gods.
In his hand are all the corners of the earth;
    and the strength of the hills is his also.
The sea is his and he made it;
    and his hands prepared the dry land.

O come let us worship and fall down
    and kneel before the LORD our Maker.
For he is the Lord our God;
    and we are the people of his pasture,
    and the sheep of his hand.

O worship the LORD in the beauty of holiness;
    let the whole earth stand in awe of him.
For he cometh, for he cometh to judge the earth;
    and with righteousness to judge the world,
    and the peoples with his truth.

or this:

JUBILATE (Psalm 100)

O be joyful in the LORD all ye lands:
 serve the LORD with gladness,
  and come before his presence with a song.

Be ye sure that the LORD he is God;
it is he that hath made us and not we ourselves;
 we are his people and the sheep of his pasture.

O go your way into his gates with thanksgiving,
and into his courts with praise;
 be thankful unto him and speak good of his Name.

For the LORD is gracious, his mercy is everlasting;
 and his truth endureth from generation to generation.

In the evening, for the Invitatory, the Hymn "O Gracious Light"
may be used. And during Easter Season, the Easter Canticle may be
used for the Invitatory both in the morning and in the evening.

Then follows THE PSALM OR PSALMS APPOINTED

And at the end of the Psalter the Minister and People sing or say
together

Glory be to the Father, and to the Son, and to the Holy
Spirit; as it was in the beginning, is now and ever shall be,
world without end. Amen.

THE WORD OF GOD

Then is read a selection from the Old Testament and a selection from the New Testament.

And NOTE: 1. Silence may be kept after each reading;
2. One of the readings may be omitted;
3. A Canticle from those provided on pages 272–291 may be sung or said after each reading; but there shall be one at the conclusion of the Scripture.

Here, or in one of the other places appointed,
a SERMON or MEDITATION may follow.

THE APOSTLES' CREED

Minister and People together, all standing

I believe in God, the Father almighty,
    creator of heaven and earth.
I believe in Jesus Christ, his only Son, our Lord.
    He was conceived by the power of the Holy Spirit
        and born of the Virgin Mary.
    He suffered under Pontius Pilate,
        was crucified, died, and was buried.
    He descended to the dead.
    On the third day he rose again.
    He ascended into heaven,
        and is seated at the right hand of the Father.
    He will come again to judge the living and the dead.
I believe in the Holy Spirit,
    the holy catholic Church,
    the communion of saints,
    the forgiveness of sins,
    the resurrection of the body,
    and the life everlasting.

Instead of the above, the text of the Creed in the Book of Common Prayer may be used.

The Prayers

The prayers follow, the People standing or kneeling.

Minister The Lord be with you.
People   And also with you.
Minister Let us pray.

The text of the Lord's Prayer in the Second Order may be used in place of the following.

Minister and People

> Our Father, who art in heaven,
>   hallowed be thy Name,
>   thy Kingdom come,
>   thy will be done,
>   on earth as it is in heaven.
> Give us this day our daily bread.
> And forgive us our trespasses,
>   as we forgive those who trespass against us.
> And lead us not into temptation,
>   but deliver us from evil.
>
> For thine is the kingdom, and the power,
>   and the glory, for ever and ever. Amen.

Then follows

Minister Show us thy mercy, O Lord:
People   And grant us thy salvation.
Minister Clothe thy ministers with righteousness:
People   Let thy people sing with joy.
Minister Give peace, O Lord, in all the world:
People   For only in thee can we live in safety.
Minister Lord, keep this Nation under thy care:
People   And guide us in the way of justice and truth.

Minister Let thy way be known upon earth:

People Thy saving health among all nations.

Minister Let not the needy, O Lord, be forgotten:

People Nor the hope of the poor be taken away.

Minister Create in us clean hearts, O God:

People And sustain us with thy Holy Spirit.

or this:

Minister Save thy people, Lord, and bless thine inheritance:

People Govern and uphold them, now and always.

Minister Day by day we bless thee.

People We praise thy Name for ever.

Minister Lord, keep us from all sin today.

People Have mercy on us, Lord, have mercy.

Minister Lord, show us thy love and mercy;

People For we put our trust in thee.

Minister In thee, Lord, is our hope:

People May we never be confounded.

The Minister then says

THE COLLECT OF THE DAY

On Fridays and Saturdays, not Holy Days, the Collect for Good Friday and Holy Saturday may be substituted for the above.

In the morning there follows

O heavenly Father, in whom we live and move and have our being: We humbly pray thee so to guide and govern us by thy Holy Spirit, that in all the cares and occupations of life, we may never forget thee, but remember that we are ever walking in thy sight; through Jesus Christ our Lord. *Amen.*

or this:

O Lord, our heavenly Father, Almighty and Everlasting God, who hast safely brought us to the beginning of this day; Defend us in the same with thy mighty power; and grant that this day we fall into no sin, neither run into any kind of danger; but that we, being ordered by thy governance, may always do what is righteous in thy sight; through Jesus Christ our Lord. *Amen.*

In the evening is said

O God, from whom all holy desires, all good counsels, and all just works do proceed: Give unto thy servants that peace which the world cannot give; that our hearts may be set to obey thy commandments, and also that by thee, we, being defended from the fear of enemies, may pass our time in rest and quietness, through the merits of Jesus Christ our Savior.

Amen.

or this:

Lighten our darkness, we beseech thee, O Lord; and by thy great mercy defend us from all perils and dangers of this night; for the love of thy only Son, our Savior, Jesus Christ.

Amen.

The following Collect is always added:

Almighty and everlasting God, by whose Spirit the whole body of the Church is governed and sanctified: Receive our supplications and prayers, which we offer before thee for all members of thy holy Church, that every member of the same, in his vocation and ministry, may truly and godly serve thee; through our Lord and Savior Jesus Christ. *Amen.*

Here may follow a Hymn or Anthem.

Authorized Intercessions and Thanksgivings may follow.

Before the close of the Office one or both of the following
may be used:

A GENERAL THANKSGIVING

Minister and People

Almighty God, Father of all mercies,
we thine unworthy servants,
do give thee most humble and hearty thanks
for all thy goodness and loving-kindness to us,
and to all men.

We bless thee for our creation, preservation,
and all the blessings of this life;
but above all for thine inestimable love
in the redemption of the world by our Lord Jesus Christ;
for the means of grace, and for the hope of glory.

And, we beseech thee, give us that due sense
of all thy mercies,
that our hearts may be unfeignedly thankful;
And that we show forth thy praise,
not only with our lips, but in our lives,
by giving up our selves to thy service,
and by walking before thee
in holiness and righteousness
all our days;
through Jesus Christ our Lord,
to whom, with thee and the Holy Spirit,
be all honor and glory, world without end.
Amen.

A PRAYER OF ST. CHRYSOSTOM

Minister and People

Almighty God,
who hast given us grace at this time
with one accord to make our common supplications
 unto thee;
and dost promise, through thy well-beloved Son,
that when two or three shall agree in his Name
thou wilt grant their requests:
Fulfill now, O Lord, the desires and petitions of thy
 servants,
as may be best for them;
Granting us in this world knowledge of thy truth,
and in the world to come life everlasting;
Through the same thy Son, Jesus Christ our Lord.
Amen.

The Minister then concludes the Office with one of the following:

The grace of our Lord Jesus Christ, and the love of God,
and the fellowship of the Holy Spirit, be with us all evermore. *Amen.*   [2 Corinthians 13:4]

May the God of hope fill us with all joy and peace in believing through the power of the Holy Spirit. *Amen.*
        [Romans 15:13]

Glory to God whose power, working in us, can do infinitely
more than we can ask or imagine: Glory to him from generation to generation, in the Church, and in Christ Jesus, for
ever and ever. *Amen.*   [Ephesians 3:20, 21]

MORNING AND EVENING PRAYER

SECOND ORDER

CONCERNING THE SERVICE

In the Offices of Morning and Evening Prayer, the term "Minister" is used to denote the person, whether a clergyman or a lay person, leading the service.

Proper Antiphons which may be used as refrains with the Invitatory Psalm will be found on pages 240–241.

Antiphons in the words of the opening Sentences given in the Offices, or other words of Scripture, may be used with the Psalms and with the Gospel Canticles.

The Apostles' Creed is normally recited at both Morning and Evening Prayer on Sundays and other major Feasts (except when the Eucharist with its own Creed is to follow). It is desirable that the Creed be recited in at least one of the Offices on other days.

At celebrations of the Holy Eucharist, the Order for Morning or Evening Prayer may be used in place of all that precedes the Offertory, provided that a Lesson from the Gospel is always included and that the Intercession conforms to the directions on page 307.

Additional Directions and Suggestions are on pages 306–307.

MORNING AND EVENING PRAYER

SECOND ORDER

The Minister begins the service with one or more of these Sentences of Scripture, or of those on pages 238–240.

The Sentences in italics may be used as responses by the people or as separate Sentences.

Grace to you and peace from God our Father and the Lord Jesus Christ. [Romans 1:7]

Thanks be to God who gives us the victory through our Lord Jesus Christ. [1 Corinthians 15:57]

Lord, I love the splendor of your house, the place where your glory dwells. [Psalm 26:8]

Let my prayer rise up before you like incense, the lifting of my hands as an evening offering. [Psalm 141:2]

OCCASIONS OF THANKSGIVING

Give thanks to the Lord, call on his Name, make his deeds known among the peoples.

Sing to him, sing praises to him, tell of all his wonderful works. [Psalm 105:1, 2]

PENITENTIAL

Seek the Lord while he may be found, call upon him while he is near; let the wicked forsake his way, and the unrighteous man his thoughts.

Let him return to the Lord and he will have mercy on him, and to our God, for he will abundantly pardon.

[Isaiah 55:6, 7]

The following Confession of Sin, or the form on page 244, may then be said; or the office may continue at once with "Lord, open our lips," all still standing.

CONFESSION OF SIN

Minister

Dear friends in Christ, here in the presence of Almighty God, let us kneel in silence, and with humble and obedient hearts confess our sins, so that we may obtain forgiveness by his infinite goodness and mercy.

SILENCE *may be kept*

Minister and People together, all kneeling

Most merciful God,
we confess that we have sinned against you
in thought, word and deed:
we have not loved you with our whole heart;
we have not loved our neighbors as ourselves.
We pray you of your mercy
 forgive what we have been,
 amend what we are,
 direct what we shall be;
that we may delight in your will,
and walk in your ways,
through Jesus Christ our Lord. Amen.

The Minister says this prayer

Almighty God have mercy on us, forgive us all our sins, through our Lord Jesus Christ; strengthen us in all goodness, and by the power of the Holy Spirit, keep us in eternal life. *Amen.*

If a Bishop or Priest is present, he may substitute an absolution.

THE PSALTER

All stand

Minister Lord, open our lips.
People And our mouth shall proclaim your praise.

Minister and People
  Glory to the Father, and to the Son, and to the Holy
  Spirit: as in the beginning, so now, and for ever.
  Amen.

  Except in Lent Alleluia.

In the morning shall be, and in the evening may be, sung or said

VENITE (Psalm 95:1-7)

Come, let us sing to the LORD;
  let us shout for joy to the Rock of our salvation.
Let us come before his presence with thanksgiving;
  and raise a loud shout to him with psalms.

For the LORD is a great God;
  and a great King above all gods.
In his hand are the caverns of the earth;
  and the heights of the hills are his also.
The sea is his, for he made it;
  and his hands have molded the dry land.

Come, let us bow down, and bend the knee,
  and kneel before the LORD, our Maker.
For he is our God;
and we are the people of his pasture, and the sheep
                                        of his hand.
  O that today you would hearken to his voice!

or this:

JUBILATE (Psalm 100)

Be joyful in the LORD, all you lands;
> serve the LORD with gladness,
> and come before his presence with a song.

Know this: The LORD himself is God;
> he himself has made us, and we are his;
> we are his people and the sheep of his pasture.

Enter his gates with thanksgiving;
go into his courts with praise;
> give thanks to him, and call upon his Name.

For the LORD is good;
his mercy is everlasting;
> and his faithfulness endures from age to age.

In the evening, for the Invitatory, the Hymn "O Gracious Light"
may be used. And during Easter Season, the Easter Canticle may be
used for the Invitatory both in the morning and in the evening.

Then follows: THE PSALM OR PSALMS APPOINTED

And at the end of the Psalter the Minister and People sing or say
together

Glory to the Father, and to the Son, and to the Holy Spirit:
> as in the beginning, so now, and for ever. Amen.

The Word of God

Then is read a selection from the Old Testament and a selection from the New Testament.

And NOTE: 1. Silence may be kept after each reading;
2. One of the readings may be omitted;
3. A Canticle from those provided on pages 272–291 may be sung or said after each reading; but there shall be one at the conclusion of the Scripture.

Here, or in one of the other places appointed,
a SERMON or MEDITATION may follow.

THE APOSTLES' CREED

Minister and People together, all standing

I believe in God, the Father almighty,
creator of heaven and earth.
I believe in Jesus Christ, his only Son, our Lord.
He was conceived by the power of the Holy Spirit
and born of the Virgin Mary.
He suffered under Pontius Pilate,
was crucified, died, and was buried.
He descended to the dead.
On the third day he rose again.
He ascended into heaven,
and is seated at the right hand of the Father.
He will come again to judge the living and the dead.
I believe in the Holy Spirit,
the holy catholic Church,
the communion of saints,
the forgiveness of sins,
the resurrection of the body
and the life everlasting.

259

THE PRAYERS

The Prayers follow, the People standing or kneeling.

Minister The Lord be with you.
People And also with you.
Minister Let us pray.
Minister and People

> Our Father in heaven,
>> holy be your Name,
>> your kingdom come,
>> your will be done,
>>> on earth as in heaven.
> Give us today our daily bread.
> Forgive us our sins
>> as we forgive those who sin against us.
> Do not bring us to the test
>> but deliver us from evil.
>
> For the kingdom, the power, and the glory are yours
>> now and for ever. Amen.

Then follows

Minister Show us your mercy, O Lord:
People And grant us your salvation.
Minister Clothe your ministers with righteousness:
People Let your people sing with joy.
Minister Give peace, O Lord, in all the world:
People For only in you can we live in safety.
Minister Lord, keep this Nation under your care:
People And guide us in the way of justice and truth.
Minister Let your way be known upon earth:
People Your saving health among all nations.

Minister Let not the needy, O Lord, be forgotten:

People   Nor the hope of the poor be taken away.

Minister Create in us clean hearts, O God:

People   And sustain us with your Holy Spirit.

Or this:

Minister Save your people, Lord, and bless your inheritance:

People   Govern and uphold them, now and always.

Minister Day by day we bless you.

People   We praise your Name for ever.

Minister Lord, keep us from all sin today.

People   Have mercy on us, Lord, have mercy.

Minister Lord, show us your love and mercy:

People   For we put our trust in you.

Minister In you, Lord, is our hope:

People   May we never be confounded.

The Minister then says

THE COLLECT OF THE DAY

On Fridays and Saturdays, not Holy Days, the Collect for Good Friday and Holy Saturday may be substituted for the above.

In the morning there follows

Heavenly Father, in you we live and move and have our being: We humbly pray you so to guide and govern us by your Holy Spirit, that in all the cares and occupations of our life we may not forget you, but remember that we are ever walking in your sight; through Jesus Christ our Lord. *Amen.*

Or this:

Lord God, almighty and everlasting Father, you have brought us in safety to this new day: Preserve us with your mighty power, that we may not fall into sin, nor be overcome in adversity; and in all we do, direct us to the fulfilling of your purpose; through Jesus Christ our Lord. *Amen.*

In the evening is said

Most holy God, the source of all good desires, all right judgments, and all just works: Give to us, your servants, that peace which the world cannot give, so that our minds may be fixed on the doing of your will, and that we, being delivered from the fear of enemies, may live in peace and quietness; through the mercies of Christ Jesus our Savior. *Amen.*

The following Collect is always added:

Almighty and everlasting God, by whose Spirit the whole company of your faithful people is governed and sanctified: Receive our prayers which we now offer before you for all members of your holy Church, that in their vocation and ministry they may truly and devoutly serve you, to the glory of your Name; through our Lord and Savior Jesus Christ. *Amen.*

Here may follow a Hymn or Anthem.

Authorized Intercessions and Thanksgivings may follow.

Before the close of the Office one or both of the following
may be used:

A GENERAL THANKSGIVING

Minister and People

Almighty God, Father of all mercies,
we your unworthy servants give you humble thanks
for all your goodness and loving-kindness to us
and to all men.
We bless you for our creation, preservation,
and all the blessings of this life;
but above all for your incomparable love
in the redemption of the world by our Lord Jesus Christ;
for the means of grace, and for the hope of glory.

And, we pray, give us such an awareness of your mercies,
that with truly thankful hearts
we may make known your praise,
not only with our lips, but in our lives,
by giving up our selves to your service,
and by walking before you in holiness and righteousness
all our days;
through Jesus Christ our Lord,
to whom, with you and the Holy Spirit,
be all honor and glory throughout all ages.
Amen.

A PRAYER OF ST. CHRYSOSTOM

Minister and People

Almighty God,
by your grace we have come together at this time
to offer you our common petitions;
and you have promised by your Son Jesus Christ
that when two or three are gathered in his Name
he will be in the midst of them.
Fulfill now, O Lord, our desires and petitions,
as may be best for us;
Granting us in this world knowledge of your truth,
and in the world to come life everlasting;
Through your Son, Jesus Christ our Lord.
Amen.

The Minister then concludes the Office with one of the following:

The grace of our Lord Jesus Christ, and the love of God,
and the fellowship of the Holy Spirit, be with us all evermore. *Amen.*   [2 Corinthians 13:4]

May the God of hope fill us with all joy and peace in believing through the power of the Holy Spirit. *Amen.*

[Romans 15:13]

Glory to God whose power, working in us, can do infinitely
more than we can ask or imagine: Glory to him from generation to generation, in the Church, and in Christ Jesus,
for ever and ever. *Amen.*   [Ephesians 3:20, 21]

FIRST ORDER

OPENING PRECES

Minister   O Lord, open thou our lips,

People   And our mouth shall show forth thy praise.

All together   Glory be to the Father, and to the Son, and to

the Ho - ly Spir - it; as it was in the beginning, is

now and ever shall be, world without end. A - men.

Except in Lent   Al - le - lu - ia.

SECOND ORDER

OPENING PRECES

Minister   Lord, o - pen our lips.

People   And our mouth shall pro - claim your praise.

All together   Glory to the Father, and to the Son, and

to the Ho - ly Spir - it;   as in the beginning,

so now,   and for - ev - er. A - men.

Except in Lent   Al - le - lu - ia.

Both Orders of Service

The Suffrages

Minister   **The Lord be with you.**

Answer   **And al - so with you.**   Minister   **Let us pray.**

Minister and People together

Our Father who art in heaven . . .

OR   Our Father in heaven,
   holy be your Name,
   your kingdom come,
   your will be done,
      on earth as in heaven.
   Give us today our daily bread.
   Forgive us our sins
      as we forgive those who sin against us.
   Do not bring us to the test
      but deliver us from evil.

   For the kingdom, the power, and the glory are yours

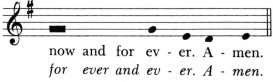

   now and for ev - er. A - men.
   for   ever and ev - er. A - men.

The Versicles may be sung by the Minister or a Cantor, the Choir and Congregation joining in the Responses.

V. Show us your mer - cy, O Lord:
thy

R. And grant us your sal - va - tion.
thy

V. Clothe your min - i - sters with right - eous - ness:
thy

R. Let your people sing with joy.
thy

V. Give peace, O Lord, in all the world:

R. For only in you can we live in safe - ty.
thee

V. Lord, keep this Nation un - der your care:
thy

R. And guide us in the way of jus - tice and truth.

V. Let your way be known up - on earth:
thy

R. Your saving health a - mong all na - tions.
Thy

V. Let not the needy, O Lord, be for - got - ten:

R. Nor the hope of the poor be ta - ken a - way.

V. Create in us clean hearts, O God:

R. And sustain us with your Ho - ly Spir - it.
thy

Or else these Versicles and Responses

V. Save your people, Lord,
        thy

and bless your in - her - i - tance.
        thine

R. Govern and uphold them, now and al - ways.

V. Day by day we bless you.
        thee

R. We praise your Name for ev - er.
        thy

V. Lord, keep us from all sin to - day.

R. Have mercy on us, Lord, have mer - cy.

V. Lord, show us your love and mer - cy;
thy

R. For we put our trust in you.
thee

V. In you, Lord, is our hope:
thee

R. May we never be con - foun - ded.

At the conclusion of the sung Collects, all respond

A - men.

CANTICLES FOR USE AFTER THE READING
OF THE SCRIPTURES

After any of the Canticles (except Benedictus es, Benedicite, Te Deum laudamus, Gloria in excelsis, and Phos hilaron) the following may be sung or said:

Glory to the Father, and to the Son, and to the Holy Spirit:
as in the beginning, so now, and for ever. Amen.

In musical settings, the following form may be used instead:

Glory to the Father, and the Son, and the Holy Spirit:
as in the beginning, so now, and for ever. Amen.

The designated places for the Canticles are suggestions only. They may be used after any reading at the discretion of the Minister.

A. After Readings from the Old Testament and Apocrypha

1. THE SONG OF ZECHARIAH *(Benedictus)*
(Luke 1:69–79)

Blessed be the Lord God of Israel;
  for he hath visited and redeemed his people;
And hath raised up a mighty salvation for us,
  in the house of his servant David;
As he spake by the mouth of his holy Prophets,
  which have been since the world began;
That we should be saved from our enemies,
  and from the hand of all that hate us.

To perform the mercy promised to our forefathers,
  and to remember his holy covenant;
To perform the oath which he sware to our
                    forefather Abraham,
  that he would give us;
That we being delivered out of the hand of our enemies
  might serve him without fear;
In holiness and righteousness before him,
  all the days of our life.

And thou, child, shalt be called the prophet of the Highest:
  for thou shalt go before the face of the Lord
                    to prepare his ways;
To give knowledge of salvation unto his people
  for the remission of their sins,
Through the tender mercy of our God;
  whereby the day-spring from on high hath visited us;
To give light to them that sit in darkness,
and in the shadow of death,
  and to guide our feet into the way of peace.

2. THE SONG OF ZECHARIAH *(Benedictus)*
(Luke 1:69–79)

Blessed be the Lord, the God of Israel;
  he has come to his people and set them free.
He has raised up for us a mighty savior,
  born of the house of his servant David.
Through his holy prophets he promised of old,
that he would save us from our enemies,
  from the hands of all who hate us.

He promised to show mercy to our fathers
and to remember his holy covenant.

This was the oath he swore to our father Abraham,
to set us free from our enemies' hand,

free to worship him without fear,
holy and righteous in his sight,
all the days of our life.

And you, my child, shall be called the prophet
of the Most High,
for you will go before the Lord to prepare his way,

to give his people knowledge of salvation
by forgiveness of their sins.

In the tender compassion of our God
the dawn from on high shall break upon us,

to shine on those who dwell in darkness
and the shadow of death,
and to guide our feet on the road to peace.

3. THE SONG OF THE THREE YOUNG MEN
(*Benedictus es, Domine*)
(*verses 29–34*)

Blessed art thou, O Lord God of our fathers:
praised and exalted above all for ever.

Blessed art thou for the Name of thy Majesty:
praised and exalted above all for ever.

Blessed art thou in the temple of thy holiness:
praised and exalted above all for ever.

Blessed art thou that beholdest the depths,
and dwellest between the Cherubim:
   praised and exalted above all for ever.

Blessed art thou on the glorious throne of thy kingdom:
   praised and exalted above all for ever.

Blessed art thou in the firmament of heaven:
   praised and exalted above all for ever.

Blessed art thou, O Father, Son, and Holy Spirit:
   praised and exalted above all for ever.

4. THE SONG OF THE THREE YOUNG MEN
(Benedictus es, Domine)
(verses 29–34)

Lord God of our fathers, you are blest and adored,
   praised and exalted above all for ever.

For the glory of your holy Name you are blest and adored,
   praised and exalted above all for ever.

In the splendor of your Temple you are blest and adored,
   praised and exalted above all for ever.

On the throne of your majesty you are blest and adored,
   praised and exalted above all for ever.

Throned upon Cherubim, plumbing the depths, you are
                        blest and adored,
   praised and exalted above all for ever.

In the high vault of heaven you are blest and adored,
   praised and exalted above all for ever.

Father, Son, and Holy Spirit, you are blest and adored,
   praised and exalted above all for ever.

275

5. A SONG OF CREATION
(*Benedicite, omnia opera Domini*)
(*Song of the Three Young Men: verses 35–65*)

O all ye works of the Lord, bless ye the Lord:
praise him and magnify him for ever.
O ye angels of the Lord, bless ye the Lord:
praise him and magnify him for ever.

O ye heavens, bless ye the Lord;
O ye waters that be above the firmament, bless ye the Lord;
O all ye powers of the Lord, bless ye the Lord:
praise him and magnify him for ever.

O ye sun and moon, bless ye the Lord;
O ye stars of heaven, bless ye the Lord;
O ye showers and dew, bless ye the Lord:
praise him and magnify him for ever.

O ye winds of God, bless ye the Lord;
O ye fire and heat, bless ye the Lord;
O ye winter and summer, bless ye the Lord:
praise him and magnify him for ever.

O ye dews and frosts, bless ye the Lord;
O ye frost and cold, bless ye the Lord;
O ye ice and snow, bless ye the Lord:
praise him and magnify him for ever.

O ye nights and days, bless ye the Lord;
O ye light and darkness, bless ye the Lord;
O ye lightnings and clouds, bless ye the Lord:
praise him and magnify him for ever.

O let the earth bless the Lord;
O ye mountains and hills, bless ye the Lord;
O all ye green things upon the earth, bless ye the Lord;
   praise him and magnify him for ever.

O ye wells, bless ye the Lord;
O ye seas and floods, bless ye the Lord;
O ye whales and all that move in the waters,
                            bless ye the Lord:
   praise him and magnify him for ever.

O all ye fowls of the air, bless ye the Lord;
O all ye beasts and cattle, bless ye the Lord;
O ye children of men, bless ye the Lord:
   praise him and magnify him for ever.

O ye people of God, bless ye the Lord;
O ye priests of the Lord, bless ye the Lord;
O ye servants of the Lord, bless ye the Lord:
   praise him and magnify him for ever.

O ye spirits and souls of the righteous, bless ye the Lord;
O ye holy and humble men of heart, bless ye the Lord;
Let us bless the Father, the Son, and the Holy Spirit:
   praise him and magnify him for ever.

6. A SONG OF CREATION
(*Benedicite, omnia opera Domini*)
(*Song of the Three Young Men: verses 35–65*)

Let all the works of the Lord celebrate the Lord,
   praise him and exalt him above all for ever.
You angels of the Lord, celebrate the Lord,
   praise him and exalt him above all for ever.

You heavens and all waters above the heavens,
                   celebrate the Lord;
All powers—sun and moon, stars of the sky—
               celebrate the Lord;
   praise him and exalt him above all for ever.

Each shower of rain and fall of dew, celebrate the Lord;
All winds, and fire and heat, celebrate the Lord;
   praise him and exalt him above all for ever.

Chill and cold, drops of dew and flakes of snow,
                 celebrate the Lord;
Frost and cold, ice and sleet, celebrate the Lord;
   praise him and exalt him above all for ever.

Nights and days, light and darkness, celebrate the Lord;
Storm clouds and thunderbolts, celebrate the Lord;
   praise him and exalt him above all for ever.

Let the earth celebrate the Lord;
Mountains and hills and all that grows upon the earth,
                 celebrate the Lord;
   praise him and exalt him above all for ever.

O springs of water, seas and streams, celebrate the Lord;
O whales, and all that move in the waters,
                        celebrate the Lord;
  praise him and exalt him above all for ever.

All birds of the air, celebrate the Lord;
Cattle and wild animals, and sons of men,
                        celebrate the Lord;
  praise him and exalt him above all for ever.

Let Israel celebrate the Lord;
O priests and servants of the Lord, celebrate the Lord;
  praise him and exalt him above all for ever.

O spirits and souls of the righteous, celebrate the Lord;
  praise him and exalt him above all for ever.
O holy and humble-hearted men, celebrate the Lord;
  praise him and exalt him above all for ever.

Let us celebrate the Father and the Son and the Holy Spirit;
  let us praise him and exalt him above all for ever.

> In musical settings of the Benedicite, the grouping of verses
> and the frequency of the refrain are at the discretion of the
> composer or musical editor.

7. THE FIRST SONG OF ISAIAH
(Ecce, Deus)
(Isaiah 12:2–6)

Surely, it is God who saves me;
  I will trust in him and not be afraid.
For the LORD is my stronghold and my sure defense,
  and he will be my Savior.
Therefore you shall draw water with rejoicing
  from the springs of salvation.
And on that day you shall say,
  Give thanks to the LORD, and call upon his Name;
Make his deeds known among the peoples;
  see that they remember that his Name is exalted.
Sing the praises of the LORD, for he has done great things,
  and this is known in all the world.
Cry aloud, ring out your joy, inhabitants of Zion,
  for the great one in the midst of you is the Holy One
                                        of Israel.

8. THE SECOND SONG OF ISAIAH
(*Quaerite Dominum*)
(*Isaiah 55:6–11*)

The Second Song of Isaiah is suggested for use on Fridays, and in the Season of Lent.

Seek the LORD while he wills to be found;
    call upon him when he draws near.
Let the wicked forsake his way,
    and the evil man his thoughts;
And let him turn to the LORD, and he will have compassion,
    and to our God, for he will richly pardon.
For my thoughts are not your thoughts,
    nor your ways my ways, says the LORD.
For as the heavens are higher than the earth,
    so are my ways higher than your ways,
    and my thoughts than your thoughts.
For as rain and snow fall from the heavens,
    and return not again, but water the earth,
Bringing forth life, and giving growth,
    seed for sowing and bread for eating,
So is my word that goes forth from my mouth:
    it will not return to me empty;
But it will accomplish that which I have purposed,
    and prosper in that for which I sent it.

B. After Readings from the New Testament

9. THE SONG OF MARY (*Magnificat*)
(*Luke 1:46–55*)

My soul doth magnify the Lord,
 and my spirit hath rejoiced in God my Savior.

For he hath regarded
 the lowliness of his handmaiden.

For behold from henceforth
 all generations shall call me blessed.

For he that is mighty hath magnified me;
 and holy is his Name.

And his mercy is on them that fear him
 throughout all generations.

He hath showed strength with his arm;
 he hath scattered the proud in the imagination
                              of their hearts.

He hath put down the mighty from their seat,
 and hath exalted the humble and meek.

He hath filled the hungry with good things;
 and the rich he hath sent empty away.

He remembering his mercy hath holpen his servant Israel;
 as he promised to our forefathers,
 Abraham and his seed for ever.

10. THE SONG OF MARY *(Magnificat)*
(Luke 1:46–55)

My soul proclaims the greatness of the Lord,
   my spirit rejoices in God my Savior;
   for he has looked with favor on his lowly servant,
   and from this day all generations will call me blessed.

The Almighty has done great things for me:
   holy is his Name.

He has mercy on those who fear him
   in every generation.

He has shown the strength of his arm,
   he has scattered the proud in their conceit.

He has cast down the mighty from their thrones,
   and has lifted up the lowly.

He has filled the hungry with good things,
   and sent the rich away empty-handed.

He has come to the help of his servant Israel,
   for he remembered his promise of mercy,
   the promise he made to our fathers,
   to Abraham and his children for ever.

11. THE SONG OF SIMEON
(Nunc Dimittis)
(Luke 2:29–32)

Lord, now lettest thou thy servant depart in peace,
   according to thy word.

For mine eyes have seen thy salvation,
   which thou hast prepared before the face of all people;

To be a light to lighten the Gentiles,
   and to be the glory of thy people Israel.

12. THE SONG OF SIMEON
(Nunc Dimittis)
(Luke 2:29–32)

Lord, you have fulfilled your word;
   now let your servant depart in peace.
With my own eyes I have seen the salvation,
   which you have prepared in the sight of every people:
A Light to reveal you to the nations,
   and the glory of your people Israel.

13. A SONG TO THE LAMB
(Dignus es)
(Revelation 4:11; 5:9–10, 13)

Splendor and honor and kingly power
are yours by right, O Lord our God,
   for you created everything that is,
   and by your will they were created and have their being;

And yours by right, O Lamb that was slain,
for with your Blood you have redeemed for God,
   from every family, language, people, and nation,
   a kingdom of priests to serve our God.

And so, to him who sits upon the throne,
and to Christ the Lamb,
   be worship and praise, dominion and splendor,
   for ever, and for evermore.

14. THE SONG OF THE LAMB
(*Magna et mirabilia*)
(*Revelation 15:3–4*)

O ruler of the universe, Lord God,
    great deeds are they that you have done,
    surpassing human understanding.
Your ways are ways of righteousness and truth,
    O King of all the ages.

Who can fail to do you homage, Lord,
    and sing the praises of your Name?
    for you only are the holy One.
All nations will draw near, and fall down before you,
    because your just and holy works have been revealed.

Canticles 13 and 14 may be sung as one Canticle.
A metrical version of Canticle 14 will be found in The Hymnal 1940, number 260.

15. WE PRAISE THEE
(*Te Deum laudamus*)

We praise thee O God; we acknowledge thee to be the Lord.
　All the earth doth worship thee, the Father everlasting.
To thee all Angels cry aloud:
the Heavens and all the Powers therein;
　To thee Cherubim and Seraphim continually do cry,
Holy, Holy, Holy, Lord God of Sabaoth;
　Heaven and earth are full of the Majesty of thy glory.
The glorious company of the Apostles praise thee.
　The goodly fellowship of the Prophets praise thee.
The noble army of Martyrs praise thee.
　The holy Church throughout all the world doth
　　　　　　　　　　　　　　acknowledge thee;
The Father of an infinite Majesty;
Thine adorable, true, and only Son;
　Also the Holy Ghost the Comforter.

Thou art the King of Glory, O Christ.
　Thou art the everlasting Son of the Father.
When thou tookest upon thee to deliver man,
　thou didst humble thyself to be born of a Virgin.
When thou hadst overcome the sharpness of death,
　thou didst open the Kingdom of Heaven to all believers.
Thou sittest at the right hand of God,
　in the glory of the Father.
We believe that thou shalt come to be our Judge.
　We therefore pray thee, help thy servants,
　whom thou hast redeemed with thy precious blood.
Make them to be numbered with thy Saints,
　in glory everlasting.

16. YOU ARE GOD
(*Te Deum laudamus*)

You are God: we praise you;
You are the Lord: we acclaim you;
You are the eternal Father:
All creation worships you.
To you all angels, all the powers of heaven,
Cherubim and Seraphim, sing in endless praise:
    Holy, holy, holy Lord, God of power and might,
    heaven and earth are full of your glory.
The glorious company of apostles praise you.
The noble fellowship of prophets praise you.
The white-robed army of martyrs praise you.
Throughout the world the holy Church acclaims you:
    Father, of majesty unbounded,
    your true and only Son, worthy of all worship,
    and the Holy Spirit, Advocate and Guide.
You, Christ, are the king of glory,
eternal Son of the Father.
When you became man to set us free
you did not disdain the Virgin's womb.
You overcame the sting of death
and opened the Kingdom of heaven to all believers.
You are seated at God's right hand in glory.
We believe that you will come and be our judge.
    Come then, Lord, sustain your people,
    bought with the price of your own blood,
    and bring us with your saints
    to everlasting glory.

17. GLORY BE TO GOD
(*Gloria in excelsis*)

Glory be to God on high,
    and on earth peace, good will towards men.
We praise thee, we bless thee, we worship thee,
    we glorify thee, we give thanks to thee
    for thy great glory,
O Lord God, heavenly King,
    God the Father Almighty.
O Lord, the only-begotten Son, Jesus Christ;
    O Lord God, Lamb of God, Son of the Father,
that takest away the sins of the world,
    have mercy upon us.
Thou that takest away the sins of the world,
    receive our prayer.
Thou that sittest at the right hand of God the Father,
    have mercy upon us.
For thou only art holy;
    thou only art the Lord;
thou only, O Christ, with the Holy Ghost,
    art most high in the glory of God the Father. Amen.

18. GLORY TO GOD
(Gloria in excelsis)

Glory to God in the highest,
   and peace to his people on earth.
Lord God, heavenly King,
almighty God and Father,
   we worship you, we give you thanks,
   we praise you for your glory.
Lord Jesus Christ, only Son of the Father,
Lord God, Lamb of God,
you take away the sin of the world:
   have mercy on us;
you are seated at the right hand of the Father:
   receive our prayer.
For you alone are the Holy One,
you alone are the Lord,
you alone are the Most High,
   Jesus Christ,
   with the Holy Spirit,
   in the glory of God the Father. Amen.

C. CANTICLES FOR USE IN PLACE OF THE INVITATORY PSALM

19. O GRACIOUS LIGHT
(Phos hilaron)

O gracious light,
pure brightness of the everliving Father in heaven,
O Jesus Christ, holy and blessed!

Now as we come to the setting of the sun,
and our eyes behold the vesper light,
we sing your praises, O God: Father, Son,
and Holy Spirit.

You are worthy at all times to be praised by happy voices,
O Son of God, O Giver of life,
and to be glorified through all the worlds.

Metrical versions of this Canticle will be found in The Hymnal 1940, numbers 173 and 176. Other versions may also be used.

20. CHRIST OUR PASSOVER
(1 Corinthians 5:7–8; Romans 6:9–11;
1 Corinthians 15:20–22)

Christ our Passover is sacrificed for us:
    therefore let us keep the feast,
Not with old leaven,
neither with the leaven of malice and wickedness;
    but with the unleavened bread of sincerity and truth.

Christ being raised from the dead dieth no more;
    death hath no more dominion over him.
For in that he died, he died unto sin once:
    but in that he liveth, he liveth unto God.

Likewise reckon ye also yourselves to be
dead indeed unto sin,
but alive unto God through Jesus Christ our Lord.

Christ is risen from the dead,
and became the first fruits of them that slept.
For since by man came death,
by man came also the resurrection of the dead.
For as in Adam all die,
even so in Christ shall all be made alive.

21. CHRIST OUR PASSOVER
(1 Corinthians 5:7–8; Romans 6:9–11;
1 Corinthians 15:20–22)

Alleluia. Alleluia.
Christ our Passover has been sacrificed for us;
therefore let us celebrate the feast,
Not with the old leaven, the leaven of malice and evil,
but with the unleavened bread of sincerity and truth.
Alleluia.

Christ being raised from the dead will never die again;
death no longer has dominion over him.
The death that he died, he died to sin, once for all;
but the life he lives, he lives to God.
So also consider yourselves dead to sin,
and alive to God in Jesus Christ our Lord. Alleluia.

Christ has been raised from the dead,
the first fruits of those who have fallen asleep.
For since by a man came death,
by a man has come also the resurrection of the dead.
For as in Adam all die,
so also in Christ shall all be made alive. Alleluia.

291

AN ORDER OF SERVICE FOR NOONDAY
OR OTHER TIMES

Leader Our help is in the Name of the Lord.

People The maker of heaven and earth.

Leader and People

> Glory to the Father and to the Son, and to the Holy Spirit: as in the beginning, so now, and for ever. Amen.

> Except in Lent **Alleluia.**

Then follows a Hymn or a Psalm, or both.
(Psalm 67 or a section of Psalm 119 is suggested.)

One of the following, or some other passage of Scripture, is then read:

To the king of ages, immortal, invisible, the only God, be honor and glory for ever and ever.   [1 Timothy 1:17]

If anyone is in Christ he is a new creation; the old has passed away, behold, the new has come. All this is from God, who through Christ reconciled us to himself and gave us the ministry of reconciliation.   [2 Corinthians 5:17–18]

From the rising of the sun to its going down, let the Name of the Lord be praised! The Lord is high above all nations, and his glory above the heavens.   [Psalm 113:3–4]

People Thanks be to God.

A Meditation, silent or spoken, may follow.

The Leader then says to the People

The Lord be with you.
People **And also with you.**
Leader **Let us pray.**

Lord, have mercy.
Christ, have mercy.
Lord, have mercy.

The Lord's Prayer

The Collect of the Day may then be said, and one or more of the following:

Blessed Savior, at this hour you hung upon the cross, stretching out your loving arms: Grant that all the peoples of the earth may look to you and be saved; for your mercies' sake. *Amen.*

Almighty Savior, who at noonday called your servant Saint Paul to be an apostle to the Gentiles: We pray you to illumine the world with the radiance of your glory, that all nations may come and worship you, who with the Father and the Holy Spirit live and reign, one God, for ever and ever. *Amen.*

Lord Jesus Christ, you said to your Apostles, "Peace I give to you; my own peace I leave with you": Regard not our sins, but the faith of your Church, and give to us the peace and unity of that heavenly city, where with the Father and the Holy Spirit you live and reign, now and for ever. *Amen.*

Free intercessions may be offered.

The Service concludes as follows:

Leader **Let us praise the Lord.**
Answer **Thanks be to God.**

AN ORDER OF SERVICE
FOR THE CLOSE OF DAY
(COMPLINE)

When the people are assembled the Leader says

The Lord Almighty grant us a peaceful night and a perfect
end.

People Amen.

Leader Lord, you are in the midst of us, and we are called
by your Name:
People Do not forsake us, O Lord our God.
Leader Be pleased, O Lord, to deliver us:
People O Lord, make haste to help us.
Leader Our help is in the Name of the Lord:
People The maker of heaven and earth.

The Leader may then say

Let us ask God's pardon for our failures
and shortcomings this day.

SILENCE may be kept for a time.

Leader and People

Almighty God, our heavenly Father:
We have sinned against you,
through our own fault,
in thought, and word, and deed,
and in what we have left undone.

294

For your Son our Lord Jesus Christ's sake,
forgive us all our offenses;
and grant that we may serve you
in newness of life,
to the glory of your Name. Amen.

Leader **May the Almighty God grant us forgiveness of all our sins, and the grace and comfort of the Holy Spirit.** *Amen.*

The Leader and People then say together

Glory to the Father, and to the Son, and to the Holy Spirit: as in the beginning, so now, and for ever. Amen.

Except in Lent **Alleluia.**

One or more of the following Psalms is then sung or said (or other suitable selections from the Psalter):

[Psalm 4]

Answer me when I call, O God, defender of my right;
    you set me at liberty when I am hard-pressed;
    have pity on me and hear my petition.
O man, how long will you dishonor my Glory?
    how long will you worship dumb idols and resort
                    to false gods?
Know this, that the LORD looks with favor on him
                  who serves him.
The LORD will listen when I call to him.

Tremble, then, and do not sin;
  ponder these things in your heart,
  upon your bed, and be silent.
Offer the rightful sacrifices,
  and put your trust in the LORD.
While many are saying, "Who will show us any favor?",
  Lift up upon us the light of your countenance, LORD.
You have put joy in my heart,
  more than when one sees his grain and wine
                    and oil increase.
Let me lie down and sleep in peace,
  for only you, Lord, make me dwell in safety.

                         [Psalm 33:1–5, 12–14, 18–22]
Rejoice in the LORD, O you righteous;
  to sing praises is becoming to the upright.
Praise the LORD with the harp;
  play to him upon the psaltery and lyre.
Sing for him a new song;
  sound a fanfare with all your skill upon the trumpet.
For the word of the LORD is right,
  and all his works are sure.
He loves righteousness and justice;
  the loving-kindness of the LORD fills the whole earth.

Happy is the nation whose God is the LORD!
  happy the people he has chosen to be his own!
The LORD looks down from heaven,
  and beholds all the children of men.
From where he sits enthroned he turns his gaze
  on all who dwell on the earth.

Behold, the eye of the LORD is upon those who fear him,
  on those who wait upon his love.
To pluck their lives from death,
  and to keep them in the time of famine.
Our soul waits for the LORD;
  he is our help and our shield.
Indeed, our heart rejoices in him,
  for in his holy Name we put our trust.
Let your loving-kindness, O LORD, be upon us,
  as we have put our trust in you.

[Psalm 134]

Behold now, bless the LORD, all you servants of the LORD,
  you that stand by night in the house of the LORD.
Lift up your hands to the holy place, and bless the LORD.
  The LORD who made heaven and earth
        bless you out of Zion.

The following Psalms are also suggested:
Psalms 31:1–6, 34, 77, 91

After the Psalter all say together

Glory to the Father, and to the Son, and to the Holy Spirit:
  as in the beginning, so now, and for ever. Amen.

One of the following, or some other short passage of Scripture, is
then read.

Come to me, all who labor and are heavy-laden, and I will
give you rest. Take my yoke upon you, and learn from me;
for I am gentle and lowly in heart, and you will find rest for
your souls. For my yoke is easy, and my burden is light.

[Matthew 11:28–30]

May the God of peace who brought again from the dead our Lord Jesus, the great shepherd of the sheep, by the blood of the eternal covenant, equip you with everything good that you may do his will, working in you that which is pleasing in his sight, through Jesus Christ; to whom be glory for ever and ever.   [Hebrews 13:20-21]

People **Thanks be to God.**

A Hymn suitable for the evening may then be sung or said.

Then follows

Leader Into your hands, O Lord, I commend my spirit:
People For you have redeemed me, O Lord, O God of truth.
Leader Keep us, O Lord, as the apple of an eye:
People Hide us under the shadow of your wings.
Leader Lord, hear our prayer:
People And let our cry come to you.
Leader Let us pray.

> Lord, have mercy.
> *Christ, have mercy.*
> Lord, have mercy.

Leader and People

Our Father in heaven,
   holy be your Name,
   your Kingdom come,
   your will be done,
      on earth as in heaven.
Give us today our daily bread.
Forgive us our sins
   as we forgive those who sin against us.
Do not bring us to the test
   but deliver us from evil.

Intercession may be offered in the following form:

Eternal God, to you, our heavenly Father, the darkness and the light are both alike, and the night is as clear as the day. We therefore pray you to be with those who watch and work throughout the night on behalf of others:

> Here the Leader or members of the congregation may mention specific persons and occupations.

Grant them courage in danger, diligence in emergencies, and the presence of your Holy Spirit in the long and lonely hours. When we awake may we be thankful for their labors and take thought in turn for their needs: through Jesus Christ our ever-reigning Lord. *Amen.*

> Silence may be kept; and free intercessions and thanksgivings may be offered.

> One of the following Collects is then said:

Lighten our darkness, Lord, we pray; and in your mercy defend us from all the dangers of the night; for the love of your only Son, Jesus Christ. *Amen.*

Be present, O merciful God, and protect us through the hours of this night, so that we who are wearied by the changes and chances of this life may rest in your eternal changelessness; through Jesus Christ our Lord. *Amen.*

Look down, O Lord, from your heavenly throne, and illumine the darkness of this night with your celestial brightness; and from the children of light banish the deeds of darkness; through Jesus Christ our Lord. *Amen.*

The Service concludes with the Song of Simeon with this Antiphon, which is sung or said by all.

Guide us waking, O Lord, and guard us sleeping; that awake we may watch with Christ, and asleep we may rest in peace.

In Easter Season add **Alleluia, Alleluia, Alleluia.**

Lord, you have fulfilled your word;
  now let your servant depart in peace.
With my own eyes I have seen the salvation,
  which you have prepared in the sight of every people;
A Light to reveal you to the nations,
  and the glory of your people Israel.

All repeat the Antiphon

Guide us waking, O Lord, and guard us sleeping; that awake we may watch with Christ, and asleep we may rest in peace.

In Easter Season add **Alleluia, Alleluia, Alleluia.**

Leader Let us praise the Lord.
People Thanks be to God.
Leader The almighty and merciful Lord, Father, Son, and Holy Spirit, bless us and keep us. *Amen.*

DAILY DEVOTIONS
FOR INDIVIDUALS AND FAMILIES

When more than one person is present, the devotions, except for the Reading, may be said in unison. Individuals may find it helpful, when possible, to say the devotions aloud.

The Readings may be taken from:

The Psalms or Lessons for the day listed in the Prayer Book Lectionary (pages x to xli)

The Lessons or Gospels for Sundays and Holy days in the Prayer Book (pages 90 to 269)

Some other manual of devotion which provides daily selections for the Church Year.

IN THE MORNING

AN ACT OF PRAISE [Psalm 103:1–4, 22]

Bless the Lord, O my soul;
and all that I am, bless his holy Name.
Bless the Lord, O my soul,
and never forget his goodness.
He forgives all my sins,
and heals all my infirmities.
He saves my life from death,
and crowns me with mercy and love.
Bless the Lord, all his creation,
in every place where he rules;
Bless the Lord, O my soul.

A READING

followed, when possible, by silent meditation.
A Hymn or Canticle may follow.
The Apostles' Creed may be recited.

THE PRAYERS

Heavenly Father, in you we live and move and have our being: We humbly pray you so to guide and govern us by your Holy Spirit, that in all the cares and occupations of our life we may not forget you, but remember that we are ever walking in your sight; through Jesus Christ our Lord. *Amen.*

Remember today, O Lord, especially . . . .

(Here may be mentioned names and particular concerns)

We ask this in the Name of Jesus Christ.
Amen.

THE LORD'S PRAYER

At Noon

AN ACT OF RECOLLECTION

O God, you will keep him in perfect peace,
  whose mind is steadfast in you;
For in returning and rest we shall be saved;
  in quietness and trust shall be our strength.

[Isaiah 26:3, 30:15]

THE READING

From the rising of the sun to its going down, let the Name of the Lord be praised! The Lord is high above all nations, and his glory above the heavens.   [Psalm 113:3–4]

THE PRAYERS

Either or both of the following:

Blessed Savior, at this hour you hung upon the cross, stretching out your loving arms: Grant that all the peoples of the earth may look to you and be saved; for your mercies' sake. *Amen.*

Lord Jesus Christ, you said to your Apostles, "Peace I give to you; my own peace I leave with you": Regard not our sins, but the faith of your Church, and give to us the peace and unity of that heavenly city, where with the Father and the Holy Spirit you live and reign, now and for ever. *Amen.*

Other prayers may be added.

THE LORD'S PRAYER

At the Close of Day

[Psalm 67]

God be merciful to us, and bless us;
  show us the light of his countenance, and come to us.
Let your ways be known upon earth,
  your saving health among all nations.
Let the peoples praise you, O God;
  let all the peoples praise you.

A READING

  followed, when possible, by silent meditation.
  The Song of Simeon may be said:

Lord, you have fulfilled your word;
  now let your servant depart in peace.
With my own eyes I have seen the salvation,
  which you have prepared in the sight of every people.
A Light to reveal you to the nations,
  and the glory of your people Israel.

THE PRAYERS

THE LORD'S PRAYER

Most holy God, the source of all good desires, all right judgments, and all just works: Give to us your servants that peace which the world cannot give, so that our minds may be fixed on the doing of your will; and that we, being delivered from the fear of enemies, may live in peace and quietness; through the mercies of Christ Jesus our Savior. *Amen.*

  Other prayers may be added. Those from the Service for the Close of Day are suggested (page 299).

CONCLUSION

Let me lie down and sleep in peace, O Lord;
  for only you, Lord, make me dwell in safety.

ADDITIONAL DIRECTIONS AND SUGGESTIONS
FOR FIRST ORDER AND SECOND ORDER

ADDITIONAL DIRECTIONS AND SUGGESTIONS

The Psalm or Psalms to be used in the Office are those appointed in the Lectionary or the daily course in the Psalter of the Book of Common Prayer; or chosen from some other approved scheme, or from a Selection of Psalms for Special Occasions.

The Readings from Scripture are to be taken from an authorized Lectionary, and if the Office is read only once in the day may be taken from either the morning or evening course. On Sundays and Holy Days, the Readings may be taken from the Proper for the Eucharist; and, when desired, there may be three Readings.

Any of the Readings may be lengthened at the discretion of the Minister. Note that the Old Testament Reading may be from the Apocrypha.

Readings are announced in one of the following forms (the titles are given by way of illustration) :

Old Testament: The [First] Reading is from . . .

    . . . the Book of Genesis

    . . . the first Book of Kings

    . . . the Book of the prophet Amos

New Testament: The [Second] Reading is from . . .

    . . . The Gospel according to Matthew

    . . . The Acts of the Apostles

    . . . The Epistle of Paul to the Romans

    . . . The Epistle to the Hebrews

    . . . The first Epistle of Peter

    . . . The Revelation of John

Or, Hear the Word of God from . . .

At the end of each Reading may be said: Here ends the Reading.

In special circumstances, in place of a Canticle, a Hymn may be sung.

One or two versions of each of the Canticles are printed with the Orders of Service. Other translations may be used when they are associated with particular musical settings.

The Sermon or Meditation is optional. One place for it is indicated in the text. Other appropriate places are

After the Hymn or Anthem after The Prayers (the Lord's Prayer and Collects)

After the Intercessions and Thanksgivings (see pages 250 and 262)

After the Office

The Meditation may, on occasion, take the form of readings from non-Biblical Christian literature.

When Morning or Evening Prayer is used as the Ministry of the Word at the Eucharist, the Nicene Creed may take the place of the Apostles' Creed; and the Intercessions shall include prayer for

The Universal Church and all its members

The Nation and all in authority

The welfare of the world

The concerns of the local community

Those who suffer and those in any trouble

The departed (with commemoration of a saint when appropriate).

The forms of the Intercession given on pages 93–112 are recommended.

When Communion is not to follow, an Offering may be received and presented at the time of the Hymn or Anthem which precedes the Intercessions and Thanksgivings; or immediately before the devotions which conclude the Office (see pages 251 and 263).

In the Intercessions and Thanksgivings, opportunity may be given for the members of the congregation to express intentions or objects of prayer and thanksgiving, either at the bidding, or in the course of the prayer; and opportunity may be given for silent prayer.

PASTORAL OFFICES

Concerning the Service

Christian Marriage is a solemn and public covenant between a man and a woman. In the Episcopal Church it is required that one, at least, of the parties must be a baptized Christian; that the ceremony be attested by at least two witnesses; and that the marriage conform to the laws of the State and the Canons of this Church.

A priest or a bishop normally presides at the Celebration and Blessing of a Marriage, because such Ministers alone have the function of pronouncing the nuptial Blessing, and of celebrating the Holy Eucharist.

When both a bishop and a priest are present and officiating, the bishop should pronounce the Blessing and preside at the Eucharist.

A deacon, or an assisting priest, may deliver the charge and ask for the declaration of intention, read the Gospel, and perform other assisting functions at the Eucharist.

Where it is permitted by civil law that deacons may perform marriages, and no priest or bishop is available, the deacon may use the service which follows, omitting only the priestly Blessing, beginning, "God the Father, God the Son . . ."

It is desirable that Lessons from the Old Testament and the Epistles be read by lay persons and that the newly married couple present the offerings of Bread and wine at the Offertory.

In the opening exhortation (at the symbol of *N.N.*), the full names of the persons to be married are to be declared. Subsequently, only their Christian names are used.

Additional Directions and Suggestions may be found on pages 321–322

THE CELEBRATION AND BLESSING OF A MARRIAGE

At the time appointed, the persons to be married, with their witnesses, assemble with the Minister in the church or some other appropriate place.

During their entrance, a Psalm, Hymn, or Anthem may be sung; or instrumental music may be used.

Then the presiding Minister, facing the People and the persons to be married, with the woman on his right and the man on his left, addresses the congregation and says

Good people, we have come together in the presence of God to witness and proclaim the joining together of this man and this woman in marriage. The bond of marriage was established by God at creation, and our Lord Jesus Christ himself adorned this manner of life by his presence and first miracle at a wedding in Cana of Galilee. It signifies to us the union between Christ and his Church, and Holy Scripture commends it to be honored among all men.

The union of man and woman in heart, body, and mind is intended by God for their mutual joy; for the help and comfort given one another in prosperity and adversity; and, when it is God's will, for the procreation of children and their nurture in the knowledge and love of the Lord. Therefore marriage is not to be entered into unadvisedly or lightly, but reverently, deliberately, and in accord with the purposes for which it was instituted by God.

Into this holy union *N.N.* and *N.N.* come now to be joined. If any of you can show just cause why they may not lawfully be married, speak now, or for ever hold your peace.

Then the Minister says to the persons to be married

I require and charge you both in the Name of God, that if either of you know any reason why you may not be united in marriage lawfully and in accordance with God's Word, you confess it now.

The Minister then says to the man

N., Will you have this woman to be your wife, to live together in a holy marriage? Will you love her, comfort her, honor and keep her, in sickness and in health, and forsaking all others, be faithful to her as long as you both shall live?

The man answers

I will by God's help.

The Minister then says to the woman

N., Will you have this man to be your husband to live together in a holy marriage? Will you love him, comfort him, honor and keep him in sickness and in health, and forsaking all others, be faithful to him as long as you both shall live?

The woman answers

I will by God's help.

Will you who witness these vows do all in your power to support and uphold this marriage in the years ahead?

We will.

Who gives this woman to be married to this man?

I do.

The Lord be with you.
Answer   And also with you.
Minister   Let us pray.

THE COLLECT   The People standing

Eternal God, creator and sustainer of all men, giver of all grace, author of salvation: Look with favor upon this man and this woman, that they may grow in love and peace together; through Jesus Christ your Son our Lord, who lives and reigns with you in the unity of the Holy Spirit, one God, now and for ever. *Amen.*

Then one or more of the following passages from Holy Scripture is read. If there is to be a Communion, a passage from the Gospels is always included.

THE LESSON

Genesis 2:4-9, 15-24
Colossians 3:12-17
Ephesians 5:20-33
1 Corinthians 13
1 John 4:7-16

THE GOSPEL

Mark 10:6-9
Matthew 7:21, 24-29
Matthew 5:13-16
John 15:11-17

Between the Readings, Psalm 128, 113, or 100, or some other Psalm, Hymn, or Anthem may be sung or said.

After the Readings (or after the homily if there is one), the Service continues with

THE MARRIAGE

All stand, and the man facing the woman, and taking her right hand in his, says

I, N., take you, N., to be my wife, to have and to hold from this day forward, for better for worse, for richer for poorer, in sickness and in health, to love and to cherish, until we are parted by death. This is my solemn vow.

Then they loose their hands and the woman, still facing the man, takes his right hand in hers and says

I, N., take you, N., to be my husband, to have and to hold from this day forward, for better for worse, for richer for poorer, in sickness and in health, to love and to cherish, until we are parted by death. This is my solemn vow.

They loose their hands.

The Minister may ask God's blessing on the ring (or rings) as follows:

Bless, O Lord, this ring that *he* who gives it and *she* who wears it may live in your peace, and continue in your favor, all the days of their life; through Jesus Christ our Lord. *Amen.*

The giver places the ring on the ring-finger of the other's hand, and says,

N., I give you this ring as a symbol of my vow, and with all that I am, and all that I have, I honor you, in the Name of God.

Then the Minister joins the right hands of the husband and wife and says

Now that N. and N. have given themselves to each other by solemn vows, with the joining of hands and the giving and receiving of *a ring* (rings), I pronounce that they are husband and wife, in the Name of the Father, and of the Son, and of the Holy Spirit.

Those whom God has joined together let not man put asunder.

The Congregation responds *Amen.*

When Communion is to follow, the Service continues on page 319.

When there is no Communion, the Service continues on the following page.

THE BLESSING OF THE MARRIAGE

The Minister sàys

Let us pray together in the words our Savior taught us:

Standing, all say

Our Father in heaven,
  holy be your Name,
  your kingdom come,
  your will be done,
        on earth as in heaven.
Give us today our daily bread.
Forgive us our sins
  as we forgive those who sin against us.
Do not bring us to the test
  but deliver us from evil.

For the kingdom, the power, and the glory are yours
  now and for ever. Amen.

The Minister says this prayer over the couple:

Almighty God, look graciously, we pray, on this man
and this woman, and on all whom you make to be one
flesh in holy marriage. Make their lives together a
sacrament of your love to this broken world, so that
unity may overcome estrangement, forgiveness heal
guilt, and joy triumph over despair; in the Name of our
Lord Jesus Christ, to whom be all honor and glory, now
and forever. *Amen.*

He may then add one or more of the following three prayers:

Almighty God, Creator of mankind, the source of all life, grant to N. and N., if it be your will, the gift and heritage of children, and the grace to nurture them in the knowledge and love of your Name; through Jesus Christ our Lord. *Amen.*

Almighty God, giver of life and love, bless N. and N. whom you have now joined in holy matrimony. Grant them wisdom and devotion in the ordering of their common life that each may be to the other a strength in need, a counsellor in perplexity, a comfort in sorrow, and a companion in joy. And so knit their wills together in your will, and their spirits in your spirit, that they may live together in love and in peace all the days of their life, through Jesus Christ our Lord. *Amen.*

Almighty God, by whose love the whole world is created, sustained and redeemed, so fill N. and N. with the overflowing abundance of your grace that their lives may reflect your compassion for all men. May their love for each other not blind them to the brokenness in the world. As you teach them to bind up each other's wounds, teach them also to heal the hurts of others. As their mutual respect orders their common life within the family, direct them to their share also in the shaping of a society in which human dignity may flourish and abound. At all times and in all seasons may they rejoice to serve you and to give you thanks, through Jesus Christ our Lord. *Amen.*

The following prayer is always added, the couple kneeling:

O God, who consecrated the state of Marriage to be a sign of the spiritual unity between Christ and his Church; Bless these your servants, that they may love, honor, and cherish each other in faithfulness and patience, in wisdom and true godliness, and that their home may be a haven of blessing and of peace; through Jesus Christ our Lord, who lives and reigns with you and the Holy Spirit, one God, now and for ever. *Amen.*

The husband and wife still kneeling, the Priest pronounces this nuptial Blessing:

God the Father, God the Son, God the Holy Spirit, bless, preserve and keep you; the Lord mercifully with his favor look upon you and fill you with all spiritual benediction and grace, that you may faithfully live together in this life, and in the world to come have life everlasting. *Amen.*

The Peace may now be exchanged.

As the wedding party leaves the Church, a Psalm, Hymn, or Anthem may be sung; or instrumental music may be used.

One of the Ministers may dismiss the Congregation.

AT THE EUCHARIST:
THE BLESSING OF THE MARRIAGE

For the Intercession, the Deacon or person appointed says

Almighty God, in whom we live and move and have our being: Look graciously upon the world which you have made, and on the Church for which your Son gave his life; and especially on all whom you make to be one flesh in holy marriage:

Grant that their lives together may be a sacrament of your love to this broken world, so that unity may overcome estrangement, forgiveness heal guilt, and joy overcome despair. *Amen.*

Grant that *N.* and *N.* may so live together, that the strength of their love may enrich our common life and become an example of your faithfulness. *Amen.*

The following suffrage may be omitted:

Grant that they may have children, if it be your will, and may bring them up by your help to know and love you. *Amen.*

Grant them such fulfillment of their mutual affection that they may reach out in concern for others, to the praise of your Name. *Amen.*

Grant that all married persons who have witnessed this exchange of vows may find their union strengthened and their loyalty confirmed. *Amen.*

Grant that the bonds of our common humanity which unite every man to his neighbor, and the living to the dead, may be transformed by your grace, that justice and peace may prevail and your will be done on earth as it is in heaven. *Amen.*

Then, while the congregation remains standing, the husband and wife kneel, and the Priest says the following prayer:

O God, who consecrated the state of Marriage to be a sign of the spiritual unity between Christ and his Church; Bless these your servants, that they may love, honor, and cherish each other in faithfulness and patience, in wisdom and true godliness, and that their home may be a haven of blessing and of peace; through Jesus Christ our Lord, who lives and reigns with you and the Holy Spirit, one God, now and for ever. *Amen.*

The husband and wife still kneeling, the Priest pronounces this nuptial Blessing:

God the Father, God the Son, God the Holy Spirit, bless, preserve and keep you; the Lord mercifully with his favor look upon you and fill you with all spiritual benediction and grace, that you may faithfully live together in this life, and in the world to come have life everlasting. *Amen.*

The Peace is now exchanged.

The Liturgy continues with the Offertory.

The following Proper Preface may be used at the Eucharist:

TRADITIONAL	CONTEMPORARY
Because thou hast ordained the solemn covenant of love between husband and wife as a witness of the union of thy son Jesus Christ with the holy fellowship of all faithful people:	Because you have ordained the solemn covenant of love between husband and wife as a witness of the union of your son Jesus Christ with the holy fellowship of all faithful people:

Additional Directions and Suggestions

The Celebration and Blessing of a Marriage may be used with any authorized liturgy for the Holy Eucharist. This Order of Service will then replace the Ministry of the Word, and the Eucharist will begin with the Offertory. When this Service is used with the Order for the Holy Communion in the Book of Common Prayer, the Prayer for the Church and the Confession of Sin may be omitted.

After the declaration of intention (betrothal), it is fitting that the man and woman to be married remain where they may conveniently hear the reading of Scripture. They may then approach the altar either for the marriage vows or for the prayers and nuptial Blessing.

It is appropriate that all remain standing until the conclusion of the Collect. Seating may be provided for the wedding party, so that all may be seated for the Lessons and the Homily.

The Apostles' Creed may be recited after the Lessons (or after the Homily, if there is one).

At the Offertory, it is desirable that the bread and wine be offered to the Ministers by the newly married persons. They may then remain before the Lord's Table and receive Holy Communion before other members of the congregation.

At the Peace, the newly married couple shall first greet each other, after which greetings may be exchanged throughout the congregation.

A THANKSGIVING FOR THE BIRTH OF A CHILD

As soon as convenient after the birth of a child, the parents, with other members of the family, should give thanks to Almighty God in his Church.

If this service is used at the hospital or the home, and not in the church, the Minister may omit the Psalm.

At a Sunday Service, after the Announcements, the Minister invites the parents and other members of the family to present themselves before the altar.

The Minister begins with these or similar words:

Since it has pleased our heavenly Father to bestow upon N. and N. the gift of a child, let us, together with them, give thanks to God, and say

[From Psalm 116]

I love the LORD, because he has heard
the voice of my entreaty;
    because he has inclined his ear to me
    whenever I called upon him.

Gracious is the LORD, and righteous;
    our God is full of compassion.

How shall I repay the LORD
    for all the good things he has done for me?

I will lift up the cup of salvation,
    and call upon the Name of the LORD,

323

I will fulfill my vows to the LORD
in the presence of all his people,
   in the courts of the LORD's house,
   in the midst of you, O Jerusalem. [Hallelujah!]

Glory to the Father, and to the Son, and to the Holy
   Spirit: as in the beginning, so now, and for ever.
   Amen.

Or this Psalm may be said: [*Psalm* 121]

I will lift up my eyes to the hills.
   "Where is my help to come from?"
My help comes from the LORD,
   the Maker of heaven and earth.
He will not let your foot be moved,
   and he who watches over you will not fall asleep.
Behold, he who keeps watch over Israel
shall neither slumber nor sleep:
   he who watches over you is the LORD.
The LORD is your shade at your right hand,
   so that the sun shall not strike you by day,
   nor the moon by night.
The LORD shall preserve you from all evil;
   it is he who shall keep you safe.
The LORD shall watch over your going out and
your coming in,
   from this time forth for evermore.

Glory to the Father, and to the Son, and to the Holy
   Spirit: as in the beginning, so now, and for ever.
   Amen.

When this office is used separately, the Lord's Prayer is said here.

The Minister then says one or more of the following prayers:

O God, our heavenly Father, we thank you and praise your glorious Name for your blessing upon your servant(s) in your gift to her (*them*) of a child: Grant most merciful Father, that *N*. (*and her husband*) may diligently lead this child in the way of righteousness, to her (*their*) own great joy, and to the glory of your Name; through Jesus Christ our Lord. *Amen.*

Almighty God, heavenly Father: you have blessed us with the joy and care of children: Give us wisdom and strength to bring them up to love what is true and pure, and honorable, and good, following the example of their Savior Jesus Christ. *Amen.*

Almighty God, our heavenly Father, we commend to your continual care the homes in which your people dwell. Put far from them all bitterness, selfishness, and pride of life. Fill them with faith, courage, knowledge, temperance, patience, godliness. Knit together in constant affection those who in holy marriage have been made one flesh. Turn the hearts of parents to their children, and the hearts of children to their parents; and so enkindle charity among us all, that we may evermore be bound together in your love; through Jesus Christ our Lord. *Amen.*

The Minister may add this or some other Blessing:

Unto God's gracious mercy and protection we commit you. The Lord bless you, and keep you. The Lord make his face to shine upon you, and be gracious unto you. The Lord lift up his countenance upon you, and give you peace, both now and evermore. *Amen.*

325

Concerning the Service

This form may be used when a person wishes to re-affirm his commitment to the service of Christ in the world, either in general terms, or because he is called to some special responsibility.

The questions and answers in the baptismal service may be used at any time for the renewal of one's baptismal promises. It is preferable, however, that this be done in the context of a public service of Baptism. The renewal of baptismal vows by this means is most appropriate at the Service of Easter Eve.

It is desirable that the statement of purpose, or the questions and answers to be used, be determined in advance during a private consultation between the Minister and the person concerned.

A FORM OF COMMITMENT TO CHRISTIAN SERVICE

Before the Offertory at the Eucharist, the person, standing before the congregation, states his purpose, either in his own words, or in response to a question or questions.

After this, the Minister says these or similar words:

May the Holy Spirit guide and strengthen you, that in this and all things you may do God's will in the service of the kingdom of his Christ. *Amen.*

In the name of this congregation I commend you to this work, and pledge you our prayerful encouragement and support.

The Minister then says this or some similar prayer, first saying to the Congregation

Let us pray.

Almighty God, look with favor upon this person who has now reaffirmed *his* commitment to follow Christ and to serve in his name. Give *him* courage, patience, and vision; and strengthen us all in our Christian vocation of witness to the world, and of service to our fellow men; through Jesus Christ our Lord. *Amen.*

A prayer for the special work in which the person will be engaged may be added.

The Service then continues with the exchange of the Peace and the Offertory.

Concerning the Service

One or more of the four parts of this Service may be used upon a single occasion; but when two or more are used together, they should be used in the order set forth in the Service: Part I being The Ministry of the Word; Part II, Confession and Absolution; Part III, Anointing of the Sick or Laying on of hands; Part IV, Communion of the Sick.

The Ministration should always include the Lord's Prayer and a blessing.

Unless otherwise indicated, any part of this Service may be used by a deacon or by a lay person.

In Part I, the Readings (Epistle-Psalm-Gospel) are intended for use as units, but the Minister may, at his discretion, combine Readings from different groups, or use only one or two from any group.

THE MINISTRATION TO
THE SICK AND SUFFERING

PART I. THE MINISTRY OF THE WORD

If a group of people are present, the Minister may begin:

Grace be to you, and peace, from God our Father and from the Lord Jesus Christ.

> The Lord be with you.
> Answer And also with you.

Then he says the Collect below. In the absence of a group, he begins the Collect without introduction.

O God of peace, who taught us that in returning and rest we shall be saved, in quietness and confidence shall be our strength; by the might of your Spirit lift us, we pray, to your presence, where we may be still and know that you are God; through Jesus Christ our Lord. *Amen.*

Then one or more of the following portions of Scriptures are read. In the Psalms, the bracketed verses may be omitted.

The Epistle. 2 Corinthians 1:3–5

Blessed be the God and Father of our Lord Jesus Christ, the Father of mercies and God of all comfort, who comforts us in all our affliction, so that we may be able to comfort those who are in any affliction, with the comfort with which we ourselves are comforted by God. For as we share abundantly in Christ's sufferings, so through Christ we share abundantly in comfort too.

Psalm 103

Bless the LORD, O my soul;
   and all that is within me, bless his holy Name.
Bless the LORD, O my soul;
   and forget not all his benefits.
He forgives all my sins,
   and heals all my infirmities;
He redeems my life from the grave,
   and crowns me with mercy and loving-kindness;
He satisfies me with good things,
   and my youth is renewed like an eagle's.

[The LORD executes righteousness,
  and judgment for all who are oppressed.
He made his ways known to Moses;
  and his works to the children of Israel.
The LORD is full of compassion and mercy,
  slow to anger and of great kindness.
He will not always accuse us,
  nor will he keep his anger forever.
He has not dealt with us according to our sins,
  nor rewarded us according to our wickedness.
For as the heavens are high over the earth,
  so is his mercy great over those who fear him.
Far as the east is from the west,
  so far has he removed our sins from us.]

As a father cares for his children,
  so does the LORD care for those who fear him.
For he himself knows whereof we are made;
  he remembers that we are but dust.

[The days of man are like the grass:
  he flourishes like a flower of the field;
When the wind goes over it, it is gone;
  and its place shall know it no more.

But the merciful goodness of the LORD
endures for ever and ever on those who fear him,
   and his righteousness on children's children;
On those who keep his covenant;
   and remember his commandments and do them.
The LORD has set his throne in heaven;
   and his kingship has dominion over all.]

Bless the LORD, you angels of his;
   you mighty ones who do his bidding,
   and hearken to the voice of his word.
Bless the LORD, all you his hosts,
   you ministers of his who do his will.
Bless the LORD, all you works of his,
in all places of his dominion.
   Bless the LORD, O my soul.

The Gospel. St. Matthew 9:2–8

They brought to *Jesus* a paralytic, lying on his bed;
and when Jesus saw their faith he said to the paralytic,

"Take heart, my son; your sins are forgiven." And behold, some of the scribes said to themselves, "This man is blaspheming." But Jesus, knowing their thoughts, said, "Why do you think evil in your hearts? For which is easier, to say, 'Your sins are forgiven,' or to say, 'Rise and walk'? But that you may know that the Son of man has authority on earth to forgive sins"—he then said to the paralytic—"Rise, take up your bed and go home." And he rose and went home. When the crowds saw it, they were afraid, and they glorified God, who had given such authority to men.

*   *   *   *   *

The Epistle. Galatians 2:20

I have been crucified with Christ; it is no longer I who live, but Christ who lives in me; and the life I now live in the flesh I live by faith in the Son of God, who loved me and gave himself for me.

Psalm 91

He who dwells in the shelter of the Most High,
   abides under the shadow of the Almighty.
He shall say to the LORD,
"You are my refuge and my stronghold,
   my God in whom I put my trust."
He shall deliver you from the snare of the hunter,
   and from the deadly pestilence.
He shall cover you with his pinions,
and you shall find refuge under his wings;
   his faithfulness shall be a shield and buckler.
You shall not be afraid of any terror by night,
   nor of the arrow that flies by day;
Of the plague that stalks in the darkness,
   nor of the sickness that lays waste at mid-day.

[A thousand shall fall at your side,
and ten thousand at your right hand;
   but it shall not come near you.
Your eyes have only to behold,
   to see the reward of the wicked.]

Because you have made the LORD your refuge,
and the Most High your habitation,
there shall no evil happen to you,
neither shall any plague come near your dwelling.
For he shall give his angels charge over you,
to keep you in all your ways.

[They shall bear you in their hands,
lest you dash your foot against a stone,
You shall tread upon the lion and adder;
you shall trample the young lion and the serpent
under your feet.]

Because he is bound to me in love, therefore
will I deliver him;
I will protect him, because he knows my Name.
He shall call upon me, and I will answer him;
I am with him in trouble;
I will rescue him and bring him to honor.
With long life will I satisfy him,
and show him my salvation."

The Gospel. St. Luke 6:6–10

On another sabbath, when *Jesus* entered the synagogue and taught, a man was there whose right hand was withered. And the scribes and the Pharisees watched him, to see whether he would heal on the sabbath, so that they might find an accusation against him. But he knew their thoughts, and he said to the man who had the withered hand, "Come and stand here." And he rose and stood there. And Jesus said to them, "I ask you, is it lawful on the sabbath to do good or to do harm, to save life or to destroy it?" And he looked around on them all, and said to him, "Stretch out your hand." And he did so, and his hand was restored.

*   *   *   *   *

The Epistle. Romans 8:15b–18

When we cry, "Abba! Father!" it is the Spirit himself bearing witness with our spirit that we are children of God, and if children, then heirs, heirs of God and fellow heirs with Christ, provided we suffer with him in order that we may also be glorified with him. I consider that the sufferings of this present time are not worth comparing with the glory that is to be revealed to us.

Psalm 27:1–8

The LORD is my light and my salvation;
whom then shall I fear?
    the LORD is the strength of my life;
    of whom then shall I be afraid?
When evildoers came upon me to eat up my flesh,
    it was they, my foes and my adversaries, who
                         stumbled and fell.
Though an army should encamp against me,
yet shall not my heart be afraid;
    and though war should rise up against me,
    yet will I put my trust in him.
For one thing have I asked of the Lord;
for one think I seek:
    that I may dwell in the house of the LORD
                all the days of my life;
To behold the fair beauty of the LORD,
    and to seek him in his temple.

For in the day of trouble he shall keep me safe
in his shelter;
  he shall hide me in the secrecy of his dwelling,
  and set me up upon a rock of stone.
Even now he lifts up my head
  above my enemies round about me.
Therefore I will offer in his dwelling an oblation,
with sounds of great gladness;
  I will sing and make music to the LORD.

The Gospel. St. John 6:47–51

Jesus said, "Truly, truly, I say to you, he who believes has eternal life. Your fathers ate the manna in the wilderness, and they died. This is the bread which comes down from heaven, that a man may eat of it and not die. I am the living bread which came down from heaven; if any one eats of this bread, he will live for ever; and the bread which I shall give for the life of the world is my flesh."

* * * * *

The Epistle. St. James 5:14–16

Is any sick among you? Let him call for the presbyters of the Church; and let them pray over him, anointing him with oil in the Name of the Lord: and the prayer of faith shall save the sick, and the Lord shall raise him up. And if he have committed sins, absolution shall be given him. Confess therefore your sins to one another, and pray for one another, that you may be healed. The prayer of a righteous man has great power.

Psalm 23

The Lord is my shepherd;
  nothing, therefore, shall I lack.
He makes me lie down in green pastures;
  and leads me beside still waters.
He revives my soul,
  and guides me along safe pathways for his
                  Name's sake.
Though I walk through the valley of the shadow
                     of death,
I shall fear no evil;
  for you are with me;
  your rod and your staff, they comfort me.

You spread a table before me,
in the presence of those who trouble me;
    you have anointed my head with oil,
    and my cup is full.
Surely your goodness and mercy shall follow me
                      all the days of my life;
    and I will dwell in the house of the Lord for ever.

The Gospel. St. Mark 6:7, 12–13

Jesus called to him the twelve, and began to send them
out two by two, and gave them authority over the un-
clean spirits. So they went out and preached that men
should repent. And they cast out many demons, and
anointed with oil many that were sick and healed them.

> After any lesson the Minister may comment upon it briefly.
> Prayers and Thanksgivings may be offered.

PART II. CONFESSION AND ABSOLUTION

Here may be used the Confession of Sin given below, or any of the forms provided for the Eucharist, or the Form for the Reconciliation of a Penitent (page 345).

Minister and People

Most merciful God,
we confess that we have sinned against you
in thought, word and deed:
we have not loved you with our whole heart;
we have not loved our neighbors as ourselves.
We pray you of your mercy
    forgive what we have been,
    amend what we are,
    direct what we shall be;
that we may delight in your will,
and walk in your ways,
through Jesus Christ our Lord. Amen.

The Minister says this prayer

Almighty God have mercy on us, forgive us all our sins, through our Lord Jesus Christ; strengthen us in all goodness, and by the power of the Holy Spirit, keep us in eternal life. *Amen.*

If a Bishop or Priest is present, he may substitute an absolution.

PART III. ANOINTING OR LAYING ON OF HANDS

The Form on pages 347–348 of this Book is used.

PART IV. THE COMMUNION OF THE SICK

The Order for Private Communions on pages 351–359 is used, beginning with the Offertory; or, if Communion is to be administered from the Sacrament already consecrated, beginning with the Lord's Prayer.

When necessary, or when desired, it is fitting that the Sacrament be administered by intinction.

Additional Prayers

FOR THE RECOVERY OF A SICK PERSON

O merciful God, giver of life and health; bless we pray you your servant, *N.*, and those who minister to *him* of your healing gifts; that *he* may be restored to health of body and mind; through Jesus Christ our Lord. *Amen.*

FOR ONE ABOUT TO UNDERGO SURGERY

Almighty God our Heavenly Father, we beseech you graciously to comfort your servant in *his* suffering, and to bless the persons and means made use of for *his* cure. Fill *his* heart with confidence, that though *he* be sometime afraid *he* may yet put *his* trust in you; through Jesus Christ our Lord. *Amen.*

FOR THOSE IN MENTAL STRESS

Heavenly Father, you know all our needs before we ask: Make this your servant know that you are nearer to *him* than the breath *he* breathes; grant that in struggles of mind, *he* may turn to your light, and in the midst of turmoil may find that peace which passes all understanding; through Jesus Christ our Lord. *Amen.*

FOR THOSE WHO SUFFER FROM ADDICTION

Mercifully regard, O Lord, this your servant who is bound with the chains of harmful addiction. Give *him* strength that *he* may be freed from fear and guilt and be restored in you to the liberty of the sons of God; now and forever. *Amen.*

A THANKSGIVING FOR RECOVERY

Glory be to you, O Lord God, for the deliverance which you have granted this your servant from illness of body and mind. Grant, O Gracious God, that *he* may employ the powers restored to *him* to your glory and to the salvation of *his* soul, for the sake of Jesus Christ. *Amen.*

Concerning the Rite

This form may be used at any private occasion of reconciliation.

The secrecy of a confession is absolute, and must under no circumstances be broken. Under extraordinary circumstances, in the absence of a priest, a deacon or a lay person may hear the confession of another Christian, if he is asked to do so. The deacon or lay confessor must make it clear to the penitent that he is not a priest.

The obligation to maintain the secrecy of a confession is no less absolute for a deacon or a lay person than it is for a priest.

THE RECONCILIATION
OF A PENITENT

The person who comes to confess may begin as follows:

Answer me when I call, O God my protector: you have set me at liberty when I was hard pressed; have mercy on me and hear my prayer.

or Bless me, a sinner.

Priest May the love of God who gave his only Son that none should perish but have eternal life, be in your heart and on your lips to bring you to true repentance; through Jesus Christ our Lord. *Amen.*

Penitent I confess to Almighty God and before his Church that I have sinned in thought, word, and deed, and in what I have left undone, by my own fault, especially . . .. Therefore, I humbly beg forgiveness of God and his Church.

Here the priest may offer counsel, direction, and comfort.

THE ABSOLUTION

Our Lord Jesus Christ who has left power to his Church to absolve all sinners who truly repent and believe in him, of his great mercy forgive you all your offences; and by his authority committed to me, I absolve you from all your sins: In the Name of the Father, and of the Son, and of the Holy Spirit. *Amen.*

Or

Our Lord Jesus Christ, who offered himself to be sacrificed for us to the Father, and who conferred power on his Church to forgive sins, absolve you through my ministry by the grace of the Holy Spirit, and restore you in the perfect peace of the Church. *Amen.*

The Priest may add the Lord's Prayer, or other suitable prayers, and a Blessing.

The Priest concludes by saying

Go (*or* abide) in peace. The Lord has put away all your sins; and of your charity pray for me who am also a sinner.

FORM OF ABSOLUTION BY A DEACON OR LAY PERSON

Our Lord Jesus Christ who offered himself to be sacrificed for us to the Father, forgive your sins by the grace of the Holy Spirit. *Amen.*

In conclusion, the Lord's Prayer may be said together.

THE ANOINTING
OF THE SICK

The Anointing of the Sick may take place in the course of the Ministration to the Sick and Suffering, or at a public celebration of the Eucharist, or separately.

When the Anointing takes place at the Eucharist, it is desirable that it precede the distribution of Holy Communion; and it is recommended that it take place immediately after the Intercession.

In cases of necessity, a Deacon or lay person may perform the Anointing, using oil blessed by a Bishop or Priest.

The Minister says

The Almighty Lord, who is a most strong tower to all who trust in him, be now and evermore your defense, and make you know that the only Name given for health and salvation is the Name of our Lord Jesus Christ.

THE ANOINTING

The Priest anoints the sick person with blessed oil on the forehead, or elsewhere when necessary, saying

N., I anoint you in the name of the Father, and of the Son, and of the Holy Spirit:

As you are outwardly anointed with this holy oil, so may our heavenly Father grant you the inward anointing of the Holy Spirit. Of his great mercy, may he forgive you your sins, release you from suffering, and restore you to wholeness and strength. May he deliver you from all evil, preserve you in all goodness, and bring you to everlasting life; through Jesus Christ our Lord. *Amen.*

THE LAYING ON OF HANDS

If the laying on of hands is used in connection with, or instead of, the Anointing, the following may be said:

(N.) I lay my hand upon you in the name of the Father, and of the Son, and of the Holy Spirit: Beseeching the mercy of our Lord Jesus Christ, that, putting to flight all sickness of body and spirit, he may give you that victory of life and peace which will help you to serve him both now and evermore. *Amen.*

A FORM FOR THE BLESSING OF OIL

The oil for the Anointing of the Sick is blessed by a Bishop or Priest, using the form below. The oil may be blessed immediately before the Anointing; or if it is intended for use on subsequent occasions it may be blessed at the Eucharist, immediately before the Lord's Prayer.

Priest **The Lord be with you.**

Answer **And also with you.**

Priest **Let us pray.**

O Lord, Holy Father, giver of health and salvation: Send your Holy Spirit, we beseech you, to sanctify this oil; that as your holy Apostles anointed many that were sick, and healed them; so those who in faith and repentance receive this holy unction may be made whole; through Jesus Christ our Lord, who lives and reigns with you and the Holy Spirit, one God, for ever and ever. *Amen.*

Concerning the Service

This form is intended for use with those who for reasonable cause cannot be present at a regular public celebration of the Eucharist.

Especially when persons are unable to be present for extended periods of time, it is desirable that the Priest arrange to celebrate with them privately, on a regular basis.

It is desirable that fellow-parishioners, relatives, and friends be present, when possible, to communicate with them.

At other times, or when desired, it is fitting that they be communicated from the Reserved Sacrament.

The Collect and Lessons may be taken from the Proper of the Day, or from those appointed for Special Occasions.

If it is necessary to shorten the service, the Priest may begin the celebration at the Offertory.

THE ORDER FOR PRIVATE COMMUNIONS

The Minister may begin the Service with the salutation
The Lord be with you, and with this or some other Collect:

Almighty God, to you all hearts are open, all desires known, and from you no secrets are hid: Cleanse the thoughts of our hearts by the inspiration of your Holy Spirit, that we may perfectly love you, and worthily magnify your holy Name; through Christ our Lord. *Amen.*

One or more passages from Scripture may be read: a brief commentary may follow.

The Apostles' Creed may be said.

A Confession and Absolution may be used.

Minister

Let us confess our sins against God and our neighbor.

A period of silence may be observed.

Minister and People

Most merciful God,
we confess that we have sinned against you
in thought, word and deed:
we have not loved you with our whole heart;
we have not loved our neighbors as ourselves.
We pray you of your mercy
   forgive what we have been,
   amend what we are,
   direct what we shall be;
that we may delight in your will,
and walk in your ways,
through Jesus Christ our Lord. Amen.

THE ABSOLUTION

Almighty God have mercy on you, forgive you all your sins, through our Lord Jesus Christ; strengthen you in all goodness, and by the power of the Holy Spirit, keep you in eternal life. *Amen.*

Appropriate Intercessions and Thanksgivings may be offered.

[If Communion is to be administered from the Reserved Sacrament, the Lord's Prayer is now said, the Minister first saying, Let us pray in the words our Savior Christ hath *(has)* taught us. The Ministration of the Sacrament follows immediately. See page 359]

AT THE OFFERTORY AND CONSECRATION

The bread and cup of wine to be consecrated are placed on a suitable table. The Priest says one of the following Eucharistic Prayers:

I

Priest The Lord be with you.

People And with thy spirit.

Priest Lift up your hearts.

People We lift them up unto the Lord.

Priest Let us give thanks unto our Lord God.

People It is meet and right so to do.

Priest

It is very meet, right, and our bounden duty, that we should at all times, and in all places, give thanks unto thee, O Lord, Holy Father, Almighty, Everlasting God.

A proper Preface may be said.

Therefore with Angels and Archangels, and with all the company of heaven, we laud and magnify thy glorious Name; evermore praising thee, and saying,

Priest and People

HOLY, HOLY, HOLY, Lord God of Hosts:
Heaven and earth are full of thy glory.
Glory be to thee, O Lord Most High.

Here may be added

Blessed is He that cometh in the Name of the Lord:
Hosanna in the highest!

Then the Priest continues

All glory be to thee, Almighty God, our heavenly Father,
for that thou, of thy tender mercy, didst give thine only
Son Jesus Christ to suffer death upon the Cross for our
redemption; who made there, by his one oblation of
himself once offered, a full, perfect, and sufficient sacrifice for the sins of the whole world; and did institute,
and in his holy Gospel command us to continue, a
perpetual memory of that his precious death and sacrifice, until his coming again:

At the following words concerning the Bread, the Priest is to hold it,
or lay his hand upon it. And at the words concerning the Cup, he
is to hold, or lay his hand upon, the Cup and any other vessel containing wine to be consecrated.

For in the night in which he was betrayed, he took bread;
and when he had given thanks, he brake it, and gave it
to his disciples, saying, "Take, eat: This is my Body which
is given for you. Do this in remembrance of me."

Likewise, after supper, he took the cup; and when he
had given thanks, he gave it to them, saying, "Drink this,
all of you: For this is my Blood of the New Covenant,
which is shed for you, and for many, for the remission of
sins. Do this, as oft as ye shall drink it, in remembrance
of me."

Wherefore, O Lord and heavenly Father, we, thy humble servants, do celebrate and make here before thy Divine Majesty, with these thy holy Gifts, which we now offer unto thee, the memorial thy Son hath commanded us to make; having in remembrance his blessed passion and precious death, his mighty resurrection and glorious ascension; rendering unto thee most hearty thanks for the innumerable benefits procured unto us by the same.

And we most humbly beseech thee, O merciful Father, to hear us; and, of thy almighty goodness, vouchsafe to bless and sanctify, with thy Word and Holy Spirit, these Gifts of bread and wine; that we, receiving them according to thy Son our Savior Jesus Christ's holy institution, may be partakers of his most blessed Body and Blood.

And we earnestly desire thy fatherly goodness, mercifully to accept this our sacrifice of praise and thanksgiving; through Jesus Christ our Lord; by whom, and with whom, in the unity of the Holy Ghost, all honor and glory be unto thee, O Father Almighty, world without end.
Amen.

And now, as our Savior Christ hath taught us, we are bold to say,

People and Priest

Our Father, who art in heaven,
  hallowed be thy Name,
  thy kingdom come,
  thy will be done,
    on earth as it is in heaven.
Give us this day our daily bread.
And forgive us our trespasses,
  as we forgive those who trespass against us.
And lead us not into temptation,
  but deliver us from evil.
For thine is the kingdom, and the power, and the glory,
  for ever and ever. *Amen.*

The Priest then breaks the consecrated Bread, and communicates himself and the other persons present.

The Service continues on page 359.

II

Priest The Lord be with you.
People And also with you.
Priest Lift up your hearts.
People We lift them up to the Lord.
Priest Let us give thanks to the Lord our God.
People It is right to give him thanks and praise.

Priest

It is right, and a good and joyful thing, always and everywhere to give thanks to you, Father Almighty, Creator of heaven and earth:

A Proper Preface may be said.

Therefore we praise you,
joining our voices with angels and archangels
and with all the company of heaven,
who for ever sing this hymn
to proclaim the glory of your Name:

Priest and People

Holy, holy, holy Lord, God of power and might,
heaven and earth are full of your glory.
   Hosanna in the highest.
Blessed is he who comes in the name of the Lord.
   Hosanna in the highest.

Then the Priest continues

All glory is yours, Almighty God, Holy Father:
You made us in your own image;
and when we had fallen into sin,
you gave your only-begotten Son Jesus Christ,
to take our nature upon him,
and to suffer death upon the Cross for our redemption.
He made there, by his one oblation of himself,
a full and perfect sacrifice for the whole world;
And instituted and commanded us to continue
this memorial of his precious death and sacrifice,
until his coming again.

At the following words concerning the Bread, the Priest is to hold it, or lay his hand upon it. And at the words concerning the Cup, he is to hold, or lay his hand upon, the Cup and any other vessel containing wine to be consecrated.

For in the night in which he was betrayed, he took bread;
and when he had given thanks to you,
he broke it, and gave it to his disciples, and said,
"Take, eat: This is my Body which is given for you.
Do this in remembrance of me."

After supper, he took the cup;
and when he had given thanks, he gave it to them
   and said,
"Drink this, all of you: For this is my Blood of the New
   Covenant
which is poured out for you and for many
for the forgiveness of sins.
Do this, as often as you drink it, in remembrance of me."

Therefore, O Lord and Holy Father, we your people
celebrate here before your Divine Majesty,
with these holy Gifts which we offer to you,
the memorial of the blessed Passion
and precious Death of your dear Son,
his mighty Resurrection and glorious Ascension,
looking for his Coming again in power and great glory.
And with these Gifts, O Lord, we offer to you ourselves,
for this is our duty and service.
And we pray you, in your goodness and mercy, to accept,
through the eternal mediation of our Savior Jesus Christ,
this our sacrifice of praise and thanksgiving.

Gracious Father, in your almighty power,
bless and sanctify us and these holy Mysteries
with your Life-giving Word and Holy Spirit;
fill with your grace all who partake
of the Body and Blood of our Lord Jesus Christ;
makes us one Body that he may dwell in us
   and we in him.
And grant that with boldness
we may confess your Name in constancy of faith,
and at the last Day enter with all your Saints
into the joy of your eternal kingdom:

Through Jesus Christ our Lord,
by whom, and with whom, and in whom,
in the unity of the Holy Spirit
all honor and glory is yours,
O Father Almighty,
now and for ever.
Amen.

As our Savior Christ has taught us, we now pray,

People and Priest

Our Father in heaven,
   holy be your Name,
   your kingdom come,
   your will be done,
      on earth as in heaven.

Give us today our daily bread.
Forgive us our sins
  as we forgive those who sin against us.
Do not bring us to the test
  but deliver us from evil.
For the kingdom, the power, and the glory are yours
  now and for ever. *Amen.*

The Priest then breaks the consecrated Bread, and communicates himself and the other persons present.

THE MINISTRATION OF THE SACRAMENT

The Sacrament is ministered with these or other words:

The Body [*and Blood*] of our Lord Jesus Christ keep you unto everlasting life.

or

The Body of Christ, the Bread of heaven.
The Blood of Christ, the Cup of salvation.

After Communion, a suitable prayer may be said.

The Service concludes with this or some other Blessing:

The Peace of God, which passeth all understanding, keep your hearts and minds in the knowledge and love of God, and of his Son Jesus Christ our Lord: And the Blessing of God Almighty, the Father, the Son, and the Holy Ghost, be amongst you, and remain with you always. *Amen.*

PRAYERS FOR THE DYING

A Prayer for a Person near Death

Almighty God, look on this your servant, lying in great weakness, and comfort *him* with the promise of life everlasting given in the resurrection of your Son, Jesus Christ our Lord. *Amen.*

LITANY FOR THE DYING

God the Father,
Have mercy upon your servant.

God the Son,
Have mercy upon your servant.

God the Holy Spirit,
Have mercy upon your servant.

Holy Trinity, one God,
Have mercy upon your servant.

From all evil, from all sin, from all tribulation,
Good Lord, deliver him.

By your holy Incarnation, by your Cross and Passion, by your precious Death and Burial,
Good Lord, deliver him.

By your glorious Resurrection and Ascension, and by the coming of the Holy Spirit,
Good Lord, deliver him.

We sinners beseech you to hear us, Lord Christ: That it may please you to deliver your servant from fear and loneliness, from the power of evil, and from eternal death,
We beseech you to hear us, good Lord.

That it may please you mercifully to pardon all *his* sins.
We beseech you to hear us, good Lord.

That it may please you to grant *him* a place of refreshment and everlasting blessedness;
We beseech you to hear us, good Lord.

That it may please you to give *him* joy and gladness in your kingdom, with your saints in light;
We beseech you to hear us, good Lord.

Lamb of God, you take away the sins of the world:
Have mercy on him.

Lamb of God, you take away the sins of the world:
Have mercy on him.

Lamb of God, you take away the sins of the world:
Grant him *your peace.*

Lord, have mercy.
Christ, have mercy.
Lord, have mercy.

Our Father, who art in heaven . . .

       or

Our Father in heaven,
  holy be your Name,
  your kingdom come,
  your will be done,
    on earth as in heaven.

Give us today our daily bread.
Forgive us our sins
  as we forgive those who sin against us.
Do not bring us to the test
  but deliver us from evil.

Let us pray.

Deliver your servant, O Sovereign Lord, from all evil, and set *him* free from every bond; that *he* may rest with all your saints in the eternal habitations; where with the Father and the Holy Spirit you live and reign, one God, for ever and ever. *Amen.*

A COMMENDATION AT THE TIME OF DEATH

Depart, O Christian soul, out of this world,
In the name of God the Father Almighty
                  who created you.
In the name of Jesus Christ who redeemed you.
In the name of the Holy Spirit who sanctifies you.
May your rest be this day in peace, and your dwelling
               place in the Paradise of God.

A COMMENDATORY PRAYER

Into your hands, O merciful Saviour, we commend your servant *N.* Acknowledge, we humbly beseech you, a sheep of your own fold, a lamb of your own flock, a sinner of your own redeeming. Receive *him* into the arms of your mercy, into the blessed rest of everlasting peace, and into the glorious company of the saints in light. *Amen.*

May *his* soul and the souls of all the faithful, through the mercy of God, rest in peace. *Amen.*

363

Concerning the Service

The death of a member of the Church should be reported to the Minister as soon as possible, and arrangements for the funeral should be made in consultation with him.

Baptized Christians are properly buried from the church, except for weighty reasons; and the service in the church should be held at a time when the congregation has opportunity to be present.

The word "Body" is used to denote the mortal remains of the departed, whether in a coffin, or prepared for burial at sea, or in an urn after cremation. The coffin is to be closed before the service begins, and shall remain closed throughout the service. It should be covered with a pall or a national flag.

If necessary, or if desired, the whole or a part of the service at the grave may be said in the church.

At the Burial of a Child, the passages from Lamentations, First John, and St. John 6, together with Psalm 23, are recommended.

It is customary that the Minister meet the Body, and go before it into the church or towards the grave.

The Anthems at the beginning of the service are said or sung:

    1. As the Body is borne into the church

  or 2. During the entrance of the Ministers

  or 3. By the Minister, standing in his accustomed place.

The text of the Burial Anthems given in the Book of Common Prayer may be substituted for those in this Service when a musical setting composed for the Prayer Book text is used.

THE ORDER FOR THE BURIAL OF THE DEAD

FIRST SERVICE

All stand while the following Anthems are sung or said:

I am the Resurrection and the Life, says the Lord.
  He who believes in me shall live,
  even though he die.
Those who live and believe in me
  shall not die for ever.

I know that my Redeemer lives,
  and that he will rise up and stand
  here on the earth, at the Last Day;
and though my flesh shall have turned to dust,
  yet shall I see God.
I shall see him for myself;
  ·these eyes shall behold him;
  he will not be a stranger.

For none of us has life in himself,
  and none becomes his own master when he dies.
For if we have life, we are alive in the Lord,
  and if we die, we die in the Lord.
So, then, whether we live or die,
  we are the Lord's possession.

Blessed are the dead who die in the Lord!
So it is, says the Spirit,
  they may now rest from their labors,
  for they take with them the record of their deeds.

The Minister then says

Blessed be God: Father, Son, and Holy Spirit.

People   And blessed be his Kingdom, now and for ever. Amen.

Minister   The Lord be with you.

Answer   And with your spirit.

Minister   Let us pray.

THE COLLECT

O God, whose mercies cannot be numbered: Accept our prayers on behalf of thy servant, *N.*, and grant *him* an entrance into the land of light and joy, in the fellowship of thy saints; through Jesus Christ thy Son our Lord, who liveth and reigneth with thee and the Holy Spirit, one God, now and for ever. *Amen.*

THE COLLECT AT THE BURIAL OF A CHILD

O God, whose most dear Son took little children into his arms and blessed them: Give us grace to entrust the soul of this child to thy never-failing care and love, and bring us all to thy heavenly kingdom; through Jesus Christ our Lord, who liveth and reigneth with thee and the Holy Spirit, one God, now and for ever. *Amen.*

The People sit.
The Reader or Readers appointed announce and read one or two of the following Lessons:

FROM THE OLD TESTAMENT

Wisdom 3:1-5, 9

The souls of the righteous are in the hand of God, and no torment will ever touch them. In the eyes of the foolish they seemed to have died, and their departure was thought to be an affliction, and their going from us to be their destruction; but they are at peace. For though in the sight of men they were punished, their hope is full of immortality. Having been disciplined a little, they will receive great good, because God tested them and found them worthy of himself. Those who trust in him will understand truth, and the faithful will abide with him in love, because grace and mercy are upon his elect, and he watches over his holy ones.

Isaiah 61:1-3

The Spirit of the Lord God is upon me, because the Lord has anointed me to bring good tidings to the afflicted; he has sent me to bind up the brokenhearted, to proclaim liberty to the captives, and the opening of the prison to those who are bound; to proclaim the year of the Lord's favor, and the day of vengeance of our God; to comfort all who mourn; to grant to those who mourn in Zion—to give them a garland instead of ashes, the oil of gladness instead of mourning, the mantle of praise instead of a faint spirit; that they may be called oaks of righteousness, the planting of the Lord, that he may be glorified.

Lamentations 3:22–26, 31–33

The steadfast love of the Lord never ceases,
 his mercies never come to an end;
they are new every morning;
 great is thy faithfulness.
"The Lord is my portion," says my soul,
 "therefore I will hope in him."

The Lord is good to those who wait for him,
 to the soul that seeks him.
It is good that one should wait quietly
 for the salvation of the Lord.

For the Lord will not cast off for ever,
but, though he cause grief, he will have compassion
 according to the abundance of his steadfast love;
for he does not willingly afflict
 or grieve the sons of men.

FROM THE EPISTLES

1 Corinthians 15:20–26, 35–38, 42–44, 53–58

Christ has been raised from the dead, the first fruits of those who have fallen asleep. For as by a man came death, by a man has come also the resurrection of the dead. For as in Adam all die, so also in Christ shall all be made alive.

But each in his own order: Christ the first fruits, then at his coming those who belong to Christ. Then comes the end, when he delivers the kingdom to God the Father after destroying every rule and every authority and power. For he must reign until he has put all his enemies under his feet. The last enemy to be destroyed is death.

But some one will ask, "How are the dead raised? With what kind of body do they come?" You foolish man! What you sow does not come to life unless it dies. And what you sow is not the body which is to be, but a bare kernel, perhaps of wheat or of some other grain. But God gives it a body as he has chosen, and to each kind of seed its own body.

So is it with the resurrection of the dead. What is sown is perishable, what is raised is imperishable. It is sown in dishonor, it is raised in glory. It is sown in weakness, it is raised in power. It is sown a physical body, it is raised a spiritual body.

For this perishable nature must put on the imperishable, and this mortal nature must put on immortality. When the perishable puts on the imperishable, and the mortal puts on immortality, then shall come to pass the saying that is written: "Death is swallowed up in victory." "O death, where is thy victory? O death, where is thy sting?"

The sting of death is sin, and the power of sin is the law. But thanks be to God, who gives us the victory through our Lord Jesus Christ.

Therefore, my beloved brethren, be steadfast, immovable, always abounding in the work of the Lord, knowing that in the Lord your labor is not in vain.

Romans 8:14–19, 34–35, 37–39

All who are led by the Spirit of God are sons of God. For you did not receive the spirit of slavery to fall back into fear, but you have received the spirit of sonship. When we cry, "Abba! Father!" it is the Spirit himself bearing witness with our spirit that we are children of God, and if children, then heirs, heirs of God and fellow heirs with Christ, provided we suffer with him in order that we may also be glorified with him.

I consider that the sufferings of this present time are not worth comparing with the glory that is to be revealed to us. For the creation waits with eager longing for the revealing of the sons of God.

It is Christ Jesus, who died, yes, who was raised from the dead, who is at the right hand of God, who indeed intercedes for us. Who shall separate us from the love of Christ? Shall tribulation, or distress, or persecution, or famine, or nakedness, or peril, or sword?

No, in all these things we are more than conquerors through him who loved us. For I am sure that neither death, nor life, nor angels, nor principalities, nor things present, nor things to come, nor powers, nor height, nor depth, nor anything else in all creation, will be able to separate us from the love of God in Christ Jesus our Lord.

1 John 3:1–2

See what love the Father has given us, that we should be called children of God; and so we are. The reason why the world does not know us is that it did not know him. Beloved, we are God's children now; it does not yet appear what we shall be, but we know that when he appears we shall be like him, for we shall see him as he is.

One of the following Psalms, or a suitable Hymn or Canticle, may be said or sung after each of the preceding Readings.

PSALM 23

The LORD is my shepherd;
   therefore can I lack nothing.

He shall feed me in a green pasture,
   and lead me forth beside the waters of comfort.

He shall convert my soul,
   and bring me forth in the paths of righteousness
   for his Name's sake.

Yea though I walk through the valley
of the shadow of death,
I will fear no evil;
   for thou art with me;
   thy rod and thy staff comfort me.

Thou shalt prepare a table before me
in the presence of them that trouble me;
   thou hast anointed my head with oil,
   and my cup shall be full.

Surely thy loving-kindness and mercy
shall follow me all the days of my life;
   and I will dwell in the house of the LORD for ever.

PSALM 23 (King James Version)

The LORD is my shepherd;
   I shall not want.

He maketh me to lie down in green pastures:
   he leadeth me beside the still waters.

He restoreth my soul:
   he leadeth me in the paths of righteousness
   for his Name's sake.

Yea, though I walk through the valley of
               the shadow of death,
I will fear no evil:
  for thou art with me;
  thy rod and thy staff they comfort me.

Thou preparest a table before me
in the presence of mine enemies:
  thou anointest my head with oil;
  my cup runneth over.

Surely goodness and mercy
shall follow me all the days of my life:
  and I will dwell in the house of the LORD for ever.

PSALM 121

I will lift up mine eyes unto the hills;
  from whence cometh my help?

My help cometh even from the LORD,
  who hath made heaven and earth.

He will not suffer thy foot to be moved;
  and he that keepeth thee will not sleep.

Behold, he that keepeth Israel
  shall neither slumber nor sleep.

The LORD himself is thy keeper;
  the LORD is thy defence upon thy right hand;

So that the sun shall not burn thee by day,
  neither the moon by night.

The LORD shall preserve thee from all evil;
  yea, it is even he that shall keep thy soul.

The LORD shall preserve thy going out, and thy
                  coming in,
  from this time forth for evermore.

PSALM 130

Out of the deep have I called unto thee, O LORD;
  Lord, hear my voice.

O let thine ears consider well
  the voice of my complaint.

If thou, LORD, wilt be extreme to mark what is
                              done amiss,
  O LORD who may abide it?

For there is mercy with thee;
  therefore shalt thou be feared.

I look for the LORD; my soul doth wait for him;
  in his word is my trust.

My soul fleeth unto the LORD before the morning watch;
  I say, before the morning watch.

O Israel, trust in the LORD;
for with the LORD there is mercy,
  and with him is plenteous redemption.

And he shall redeem Israel
  from all his sins.

The following Psalms * are also appropriate

65:1–8
139:1–11
116:1–9
116:9–16

* The verse references are to *The Book of Common Prayer.*

THE GOSPEL

Then, all standing, the Minister appointed reads the Gospel, first saying

The Holy Gospel of our Lord Jesus Christ, according to ———.

The People respond **Glory be to thee, O Lord.**

At the end of the Gospel, the Minister says

The Gospel of the Lord.

The People respond **Praise be to thee, O Christ.**

St. John 6:37–40

Jesus said, "All that the Father gives me will come to me; and him who comes to me I will not cast out. For I have come down from heaven, not to do my own will, but the will of him who sent me; and this is the will of him who sent me, that I should lose nothing of all that he has given me, but raise it up at the last day. For this is the will of my Father, that every one who sees the Son and believes in him should have eternal life; and I will raise him up at the last day."

or

St. John 11:21–27

Martha said to Jesus, "Lord, if you had been here, my brother would not have died. And even now I know that whatever you ask from God, God will give you."

Jesus said to her, "Your brother will rise again." Martha said to him, "I know that he will rise again in the resurrection at the last day." Jesus said to her, "I am the resurrection and the life; he who believes in me, though he die, yet shall he live, and whoever lives and believes in me shall never die. Do you believe this?" She said to him, "Yes, Lord; I believe that you are the Christ, the Son of God, he who is coming into the world."

or

St. John 14:1-6

Jesus said, "Let not your hearts be troubled; believe in God, believe also in me. In my Father's house are many rooms; if it were not so, would I have told you that I go to prepare a place for you? And when I go and prepare a place for you, I will come again and will take you to myself, that where I am you may be also. And you know the way where I am going." Thomas said to him, "Lord, we do not know where you are going; how can we know the way?" Jesus said to him, "I am the way, and the truth, and the life; no one comes to the Father, but by me."

Here a Sermon or Homily may be preached, the People being seated.

THE APOSTLES' CREED may be said here, the People standing:

I believe in God the Father Almighty, Maker of heaven and earth:

And in Jesus Christ his only Son our Lord: Who was conceived by the Holy Ghost, Born of the Virgin Mary:

376

Suffered under Pontius Pilate, Was crucified, dead, and buried: He descended into hell; The third day he rose again from the dead: He ascended into heaven, And sitteth on the right hand of God the Father Almighty: From thence he shall come to judge the quick and the dead.

I believe in the Holy Ghost: The holy Catholic Church; The Communion of Saints: The Forgiveness of sins: The Resurrection of the body: And the Life everlasting. Amen.

When there is to be a Communion, the Service continues on page 379.

When there is no Communion, the Service is concluded as follows:

Minister In the words our Savior taught us, let us say together,

Our Father, who art in heaven, Hallowed be thy Name. Thy kingdom come. Thy will be done, On earth as it is in heaven. Give us this day our daily bread. And forgive us our trespasses, As we forgive those who trespass against us. And lead us not into temptation; But deliver us from evil. For thine is the kingdom, and the power, and the glory, for ever and ever. Amen.

Almighty God, with whom do live the spirits of those who depart hence in the Lord, and with whom the souls of the faithful, after they are delivered from the burden of the flesh, are in joy and felicity: We give thee hearty thanks for the good examples of all those thy servants, who, having finished their course in faith, do now rest from their labors. And we beseech thee, that we, with all those who are departed in the true faith of thy holy Name, may have our perfect consummation and bliss, both in body and soul, in thy eternal and everlasting glory; through Jesus Christ our Lord. *Amen.*

Almighty God, Father of mercies and giver of comfort; Deal graciously, we pray, with all who mourn, that, casting all their care on thee, they may know the consolation of thy love; through Jesus Christ our Lord. *Amen.*

Other authorized prayers may follow.

Then the Minister, standing and facing the Body, says

Unto God's gracious mercy and protection we commit *him.* The Lord bless *him* and keep *him.* The Lord make his face to shine upon *him,* and be gracious unto *him.* The Lord lift up his countenance upon *him,* and give *him* peace, both now and evermore. *Amen.*

Or else, the Service of Committal takes place at this point.

A Priest (or the Bishop) may then bless the People.

A Canticle or Hymn may be sung or said as the Body is borne from the Church (see pages 387–388 for Canticles).

If the Body is not then to be taken to the grave, the Deacon, or other Minister, dismisses the People:

Let us go forth in the Name of Christ.
Thanks be to God.

AT THE EUCHARIST

When Communion follows, this Prayer of Intercession may be used:

THE PRAYER OF INTERCESSION
(People Standing)

In Peace, let us pray to the Lord.

For the peace from above, for the salvation of mankind: that righteousness, mercy, and truth may prevail among all peoples and nations.

Hear us, good Lord.

For the well-being of thy holy Catholic Church in every place: that thou wilt confirm it in the truth of thy holy Word, and grant to all Christians to live in unity, love, and concord.

Hear us, good Lord.

Deal graciously, Lord, with all those who mourn, that, casting every care on thee they may know the consolation of thy love.

Hear us, good Lord.

Have mercy upon us, most merciful Lord; and in thy compassion forgive us all our sins and failures, known and unknown, things done and left undone; and so uphold us by thy Spirit, that we may end our days in peace, trusting in thy mercy at the day of judgment.

Have mercy upon us.

We commend to thy keeping all thy servants departed this life in thy faith and fear, and especially thy servant, *N.:* that thou wilt grant them continual growth in thy love and service. May we with them and with all thy saints be partakers of thine everlasting kingdom; through Jesus Christ, our only Mediator and Advocate.

To thee be honor, glory, and dominion, now and forever. Amen.

The Service then continues with the Offertory.

After the postcommunion Prayer, the Minister, standing before the Body, says

Unto God's gracious mercy and protection we commit *him.* The Lord bless *him* and keep *him.* The Lord make his face to shine upon *him,* and be gracious unto *him.* The Lord lift up his countenance upon *him,* and give *him* peace, both now and evermore. *Amen.*

Or else, the Service of Committal takes place at this point.

A Priest (or the Bishop) may then bless the People.

A Canticle or Hymn may be sung or said as the Body is borne from the Church (see pages 387–388 for Canticles).

If the Body is not then to be taken to the grave, the Deacon, or other Minister, dismisses the People:

Let us go forth in the Name of Christ.
Thanks be to God.

AT THE GRAVE

The following Anthems are sung or said:

In the midst of life we are in death;
  of whom may we seek for succor,
  but of thee, O Lord,
  who for our sins art justly displeased?
Yet, O Lord God most holy, O Lord most mighty,
O holy and most merciful Savior:
  Deliver us not into the bitter pains of eternal death.
Thou knowest, Lord, the secrets of our hearts;
  shut not thy merciful ears to our prayer;
But spare us, Lord most holy, O God most mighty,
O holy and merciful Savior,
thou most worthy Judge eternal:
  Suffer us not, at our last hour,
  for any pains of death, to fall from thee.

or these Anthems

Jesus said:
"All whom the Father gives me
    shall come to me;
and him who comes to me
    I will not cast out."

He who raised Christ Jesus from the dead
will give new life to our mortal bodies also,
    through his Spirit which dwells in us.

Therefore my heart is glad
    and my soul rejoices;
    my body shall rest in hope.

Thou shalt show me the path of life;
    in thy presence there is fulness of joy,
        and at thy right hand there is pleasure for evermore.

THE WORDS OF COMMITTAL

The Minister then says these words, during which earth may be
cast upon the coffin.

Unto Almighty God we commend our *brother N.*, as we
commit *his* Body to the ground*; earth to earth, ashes
to ashes, dust to dust; in sure and certain hope of the
resurrection to eternal life; through our Lord Jesus
Christ.

* or *the deep,* or *the elements,* or *this resting place*

Lord have mercy.
Christ have mercy.
Lord have mercy.

The LORD'S PRAYER may be said.

Then the Minister says one or more of the Prayers on pages 384–386, after which he may say

Rest eternal grant to *him,* O Lord:
And let light perpetual shine upon him.

May *his* soul and the souls of all the faithful,
through the mercy of God, rest in peace. *Amen.*

He concludes the Service as follows:

The God of peace, who brought again from the dead our Lord Jesus Christ, the great Shepherd of the sheep, through the blood of the everlasting covenant: Make you perfect in every good work to do his will, working in you that which is well pleasing in his sight; through Jesus Christ, to whom be glory for ever and ever. *Amen.*

ADDITIONAL PRAYERS, AND CANTICLES

Almighty God, with whom do live the spirits of those who depart hence in the Lord, and with whom the souls of the faithful, after they are delivered from the burden of the flesh, are in joy and felicity: We give thee hearty thanks for the good examples of all those thy servants, who, having finished their course in faith, do now rest from their labors. And we beseech thee, that we, with all those who are departed in the true faith of thy holy Name, may have our perfect consummation and bliss, both in body and soul, in thy eternal and everlasting glory; through Jesus Christ our Lord. *Amen.*

O Lord Jesus Christ, who by thy death didst take away the sting of death: Grant unto us thy servants so to follow in faith where thou hast led the way, that we may at length fall asleep peacefully in thee, and awake up after thy likeness; through thy mercy, who livest with the Father and the Holy Spirit, one God, now and for ever. *Amen.*

O God, whose days are without end, and whose mercies cannot be numbered: Make us, we beseech thee, deeply sensible of the shortness and uncertainty of human life; and let thy Holy Spirit lead us in holiness and righteousness all our days; that, when we shall have served thee in our generation, we may be gathered unto our fathers:

having the testimony of a good conscience; in the communion of the Catholic Church; in the confidence of a certain faith; in the comfort of a reasonable, religious and holy hope; in favor with thee our God, and in perfect charity with the world. All which we ask through Jesus Christ our Lord. *Amen.*

O Heavenly Father, who hast given us a true faith and a sure hope: Help us, we pray, in the midst of things we cannot understand, to believe and trust in thy fatherly care—in the communion of saints, the forgiveness of sins, and the resurrection to life everlasting; and strengthen, we beseech thee, this faith and hope in us all the days of our life; through the love of thy Son, our Savior Jesus Christ. *Amen.*

O Merciful God, the Father of our Lord Jesus Christ who is the Resurrection and the Life; in whom whosoever believeth shall live, though he die; and whosoever liveth and believeth in him shall not die eternally; who also hath taught us by his holy Apostle Saint Paul not to be sorry, as men without hope, for those who sleep in him: We humbly beseech thee, O Father, to raise us from the death of sin unto the life of righteousness; that when we shall depart this life we may rest in him; and that at the general Resurrection, we may be found acceptable in thy sight; and receive that blessing which thy well-beloved Son shall then pronounce to all who love and fear thee, saying, "Come, ye blessed of my Father, receive the kingdom prepared for you from the beginning of the world." Grant this, we beseech thee, O merciful Father, through Jesus Christ, our Mediator and Redeemer. *Amen.*

Grant, O Lord, to all who are bereaved the spirit of faith and courage, that they may have strength to meet the days to come with steadfastness and patience; not sorrowing as those without hope, but in thankful remembrance of all the manifestations of thy great goodness, and in the joyful expectation of eternal life with those they love. And this we ask in the name of Jesus Christ our Savior. *Amen.*

Almighty God, Father of mercies and giver of comfort; Deal graciously, we pray, with all who mourn, that, casting all their care on thee, they may know the consolation of thy love; through Jesus Christ our Lord. *Amen.*

The Song of Zechariah (Benedictus)
(Luke 1:69-79)

Blessed be the Lord God of Israel;
  for he hath visited and redeemed his people;
And hath raised up a mighty salvation for us,
  in the house of his servant David;
As he spake by the mouth of his holy Prophets,
  which have been since the world began;
That we should be saved from our enemies,
  and from the hand of all that hate us.

To perform the mercy promised to our forefathers,
  and to remember his holy covenant;
To perform the oath which he sware to our
                forefather Abraham,
  that he would give us;
That we being delivered out of the hand
             of our enemies
  might serve him without fear;
In holiness and righteousness before him,
  all the days of our life.

And thou, child, shalt be called the prophet
of the Highest:
for thou shalt go before the face of the Lord
to prepare his ways;
To give knowledge of salvation unto his people
for the remission of their sins,
Through the tender mercy of our God;
whereby the day-spring from on high hath visited us;
To give light to them that sit in darkness,
and in the shadow of death,
and to guide our feet into the way of peace.

The Song of Simeon (Nunc dimittis)
(Luke 2:29–32)

Lord, now lettest thou thy servant depart in peace,
according to thy word.
For mine eyes have seen thy salvation,
which thou hast prepared before the face of all people;
To be a light to lighten the Gentiles,
and to be the glory of thy people Israel.

THE CONSECRATION OF A GRAVE

FROM THE BOOK OF OFFICES, 1960

If the Grave is in a place that has not previously been set apart for Christian burial, the Priest may use the following form, either before the service at the grave or at some other convenient time:

In the place where Jesus was crucified there was a garden, and in the garden a new sepulcher wherein was never man yet laid.

The eternal God is thy refuge.
And underneath are the everlasting arms.

Let us pray.

O God, whose blessed Son was laid in a sepulcher in the garden: Bless, we beseech thee, this grave, that *he* whose Body is [is to be] buried here may dwell with Christ in paradise, and may come to thy heavenly Kingdom; through the same Jesus Christ, our Lord. *Amen.*

Concerning the Service

The death of a member of the Church should be reported to the Minister as soon as possible, and arrangements for the funeral should be made in consultation with him.

Baptized Christians are properly buried from the church, except for weighty reasons; and the service in the church should be held at a time when the congregation has opportunity to be present.

The word "Body" is used to denote the mortal remains of the departed, whether in a coffin, or prepared for burial at sea, or in an urn after cremation. The coffin is to be closed before the service begins, and shall remain closed throughout the service. It should be covered with a pall or a national flag.

If necessary, or if desired, the whole or a part of the service at the grave may be said in the church.

At the Burial of a Child, the passages from Lamentations, First John, and St. John 6, together with Psalm 23, are recommended.

It is customary that the Minister meet the Body, and go before it into the church or towards the grave.

The Anthems at the beginning of the service are said or sung:

    1. As the Body is borne into the church

  or 2. During the entrance of the Ministers

  or 3. By the Minister, standing in his accustomed place.

The text of the Burial Anthems given in the Book of Common Prayer may be substituted for those in this Service when a musical setting composed for the Prayer Book text is used.

THE ORDER FOR THE BURIAL OF THE DEAD

SECOND SERVICE

All stand while the following Anthems are sung or said:

I am Resurrection and I am Life, says the Lord.
  Whoever has faith in me shall have life,
  even though he die.
And everyone who has life,
and has committed himself to me in faith,
  shall not die for ever.

I know for sure that my Redeemer lives
  and that at the Last he will stand upon the earth.
After my awaking, he will raise me up;
  and in my body I shall see God.
I myself shall see, and my eyes behold him
  who is my Friend and not a Stranger.

For none of us has life in himself,
  and none becomes his own master when he dies.
For if we have life, we are alive in the Lord,
  and if we die, we die in the Lord.
So, then, whether we live or die,
  we are the Lord's possession.

How blest, from now on,
  are those who die in the Lord!
So it is, says the Spirit,
for the record of their deeds goes with them,
  that they may have rest from their weary toil.

The Minister then says

Blessed be God: Father, Son, and Holy Spirit.

People   And blessed be his Kingdom, now and for ever. Amen.

Minister   The Lord be with you.

People   And also with you.

Minister   Let us pray.

THE COLLECT

O God, whose mercies cannot be numbered: Accept our prayers on behalf of your servant, *N.,* and grant *him* an entrance into the land of light and joy, in the fellowship of your saints; through Jesus Christ our Lord, who lives and reigns with you and the Holy Spirit, one God, now and for ever. *Amen.*

THE COLLECT AT THE BURIAL OF A CHILD

O God, whose most dear Son took little children into his arms and blessed them: Give us grace to entrust the soul of this child to your never-failing care and love, and bring us all to your heavenly kingdom; through Jesus Christ our Lord, who lives and reigns with you and the Holy Spirit, one God, now and for ever. *Amen.*

The People sit.

The Reader or Readers appointed announce and read one or two of the following Lessons:

FROM THE OLD TESTAMENT

Wisdom 3:1-5, 9

The souls of the just are in God's hand, and torment shall not touch them. In the eyes of foolish men they seemed to be dead; their departure was reckoned as defeat, and their going from us as disaster. But they are at peace, for though in the sight of men they may be punished, they have a sure hope of immortality; and after a little chastisement they will receive great blessings, because God has tested them and found them worthy to be his. Those who have put their trust in him shall understand that he is true, and the faithful shall attend upon him in love; they are his chosen, and grace and mercy shall be theirs.

Isaiah 61:1-3

The spirit of the Lord God is upon me
because the Lord has anointed me;
he has sent me to bring good news to the humble,
   to bind up the broken-hearted,
to proclaim liberty to captives
   and release to those in prison;
to proclaim a year of the Lord's favor
   and a day of the vengeance of our God;
   to comfort all who mourn,
to give them garlands instead of ashes,
   oil of gladness instead of mourners' tears,
   a garment of splendor for the heavy heart.
They shall be called Trees of Righteousness,
   planted by the Lord for his glory.

Lamentations 3:22–26, 31–33

The Lord's true love is surely not spent,
  nor has his compassion failed;
  they are new every morning,
  so great is his constancy.
The Lord, I say, is all that I have;
  therefore I will wait for him patiently.
The Lord is good to those who look for him,
  to all who seek him;
it is good to wait in patience and sigh
  for deliverance by the Lord.
For the Lord will not cast off.
  his servants for ever.
He may punish cruelly, yet he will have compassion
  in the fullness of his love;
he does not willingly afflict
  or punish any mortal man.

FROM THE EPISTLES

1 Corinthians 15:20–26, 35–38, 42–44, 53–58

Christ was raised to life—the firstfruits of the harvest of the dead. For since it was a man who brought death into the world, a man also brought resurrection of the dead. As in Adam all men die, so in Christ all will be brought to life; but each in his own proper place: Christ the firstfruits, and afterwards, at his coming, those who belong to Christ. Then comes the end, when he delivers up the kingdom to God the Father, after abolishing every kind of domination, authority, and power. For he is destined to reign until God has put all enemies under his feet; and the last enemy to be abolished is death.

But you may ask, how are the dead raised? In what kind of body? How foolish! The seed you sow does not come to life unless it has first died; and what you sow is not the body that shall be, but a naked grain, perhaps of wheat, or of some other kind; and God clothes it with the body of his choice, each seed with its own particular body.

So it is with the resurrection of the dead. What is sown in the earth as a perishable thing is raised imperishable. Sown in humiliation, it is raised in glory; sown in weakness, it is raised in power; sown as an animal body, it is raised as a spiritual body.

This perishable being must be clothed with the imperishable, and what is mortal must be clothed with immortality. And when our mortality has been clothed with immortality, then the saying of Scripture will come true: "Death is swallowed up; victory is won!" "O Death, where is your victory? O Death, where is your sting?" The sting of death is sin, and sin gains its power from the law; but God be praised, he gives us the victory through our Lord Jesus Christ.

Therefore, my beloved brothers, stand firm and immovable, and work for the Lord always, work without limit, since you know that in the Lord your labor cannot be lost.

Romans: 8:14–19, 34–35, 37–39

All who are moved by the Spirit of God are sons of God. The Spirit you have received is not a spirit of slavery leading you back into a life of fear, but a Spirit that makes us sons, enabling us to cry "Abba! Father!" In that cry the Spirit of God joins with our spirit in testifying that we are God's children; and if children, then heirs. We are God's heirs and Christ's fellow-heirs, if we share his sufferings now in order to share his splendor hereafter.

For I reckon that the sufferings we now endure bear no comparison with the splendor, as yet unrevealed, which is in store for us. For the created universe waits with eager expectation for God's sons to be revealed.

It is Christ—Christ who died, and, more than that, was raised from the dead—who is at God's right hand, and indeed pleads our cause. Then what can separate us from the love of Christ? Can affliction or hardship? Can persecution, hunger, nakedness, peril, or the sword? In spite of all, overwhelming victory is ours through him who loved us. For I am convinced that there is nothing in death or life, in the realm of spirits or superhuman powers, in the world as it is or the world as it shall be, in the forces of the universe, in heights or depths— nothing in all creation that can separate us from the love of God in Christ Jesus our Lord.

1 John 3:1–2

How great is the love that the Father has shown to us! We were called God's children, and such we are; and the reason why the godless world does not recognize us is that it has not known him. Here and now, dear friends, we are God's children; what we shall be has not yet been disclosed, but we know that when it is disclosed, we shall be like him, because we shall see him as he is.

One of the following Psalms, or a suitable Hymn or Canticle, may be said or sung after each of the preceding Readings.

PSALM 23

The LORD is my shepherd;
  nothing, therefore, shall I lack.
He makes me lie down in green pastures;
  and leads me beside still waters.
He revives my soul,
  and guides me along safe pathways
  for his Name's sake.
Though I walk through the valley of the shadow
                        of death,
I shall fear no evil;
  for you are with me;
  your rod and your staff, they comfort me.
You spread a table before me,
in the presence of those who trouble me;
  you have anointed my head with oil,
  and my cup is full.
Surely your goodness and mercy
shall follow me all the days of my life;
  and I will dwell in the house of the LORD
                     for ever.

PSALM 121

I will lift up my eyes to the hills.
   "Where is my help to come from?"
My help comes from the LORD,
   the Maker of heaven and earth.
He will not let your foot be moved,
   and he who watches over you will not fall asleep.
Behold, he who keeps watch over Israel
shall neither slumber nor sleep:
   he who watches over you is the LORD.
The LORD is your shade at your right hand,
   so that the sun shall not strike you by day,
   nor the moon by night.
The LORD shall preserve you from all evil;
   it is he who shall keep you safe.
The LORD shall watch over your going out
and your coming in,
   from this time forth for evermore.

PSALM 130

Out of the depths have I called to you, O LORD;
Lord, hear my voice;
    let your ears consider well the voice
                    of my supplication.
If you, LORD, were to note what is done amiss,
O LORD, who could survive?
    but there is forgiveness with you;
    therefore you shall be feared.
I wait for the LORD; my soul waits for him;
    in his word is my hope.
My soul waits for the LORD,
more than watchmen for the morning,
    more than watchmen for the morning,
O Israel, wait for the LORD;
    for with the LORD there is mercy;
With him there is plenteous redemption;
    and he shall redeem Israel from all his sins.

The following Psalms are also appropriate   65:1–8
                                        139:1–11
                                        116:1–8
                                        116:8–16

THE GOSPEL

The Holy Gospel of our Lord Jesus Christ, according to ———.

The People respond **Glory to you, Lord Christ.**

At the end of the Gospel, the Minister says

The Gospel of the Lord.

The People respond **Praise to you, Lord Christ.**

St. John 6:37–40

Jesus said, "All that the Father gives me will come to me, and the man who comes to me I will never turn away. I have come down from heaven, not to do my own will, but the will of him who sent me. It is his will that I should not lose even one of all that he has given me, but raise them all up on the last day. For it is my Father's will that everyone who looks upon the Son and puts his faith in him shall possess eternal life; and I will raise him up on the last day."

or

St. John 11:21–27

Martha said to Jesus, "If you had been here, sir, my brother would not have died. Even now I know that whatever you ask of God, God will grant you." Jesus said, "Your brother will rise again." "I know that he will rise again", said Martha, "at the resurrection on the

401

last day." Jesus said, "I am the resurrection and I am life. If a man has faith in me, even though he die, he shall come to life; and no one who is alive and has faith shall ever die. Do you believe this?" "Lord, I do," she answered; "I now believe that you are the Messiah, the Son of God who was to come into the world."

or

St. John 14:1–6

Jesus said, "Set your troubled hearts at rest. Trust in God always; trust also in me. There are many dwelling-places in my Father's house; if it were not so I should have told you; for I am going there on purpose to prepare a place for you. And if I go and prepare a place for you, I shall come again and receive you to myself, so that where I am you may be also; and my way there is known to you." Thomas said, "Lord, we do not know where you are going, so how can we know the way?" Jesus replied, "I am the way; I am the truth and I am life; no one comes to the Father except by me."

Here a Sermon or Homily may be preached, the People being seated.

THE APOSTLES CREED may be said here, the People standing:

I believe in God, the Father almighty,
 creator of heaven and earth.
I believe in Jesus Christ, his only Son, our Lord.
 He was conceived by the power of the Holy Spirit
  and born of the Virgin Mary.
 He suffered under Pontius Pilate,
  was crucified, died, and was buried.
 He descended to the dead.
 On the third day he rose again.
 He ascended into heaven.
  and is seated at the right hand of the Father.
 He will come again to judge the living and the dead.

I believe in the Holy Spirit,
 the holy catholic Church,
 the communion of saints,
 the forgiveness of sins,
 the resurrection of the body,
 and the life everlasting.

The version of the Creed in the Book of Common Prayer may be
used instead.

When there is to be a Communion, the Service continues on
page 406.

When there is no Communion, the Service is concluded as follows:

Minister In the words our Savior taught us, let us
say together,

Our Father in heaven,
holy be your Name,
your kingdom come,
your will be done,
on earth as in heaven.
Give us today our daily bread.
Forgive us our sins
as we forgive those who sin against us.
Do not bring us to the test
but deliver us from evil.
For the kingdom, the power, and the glory are yours
now and for ever. Amen.

The version of the Lord's Prayer in the Book of Common Prayer
may be used instead.

Minister

Almighty God, with whom still live the spirits of those
who die in the Lord, and with whom the souls of the
faithful, after they are delivered from the burden of
the flesh, are in joy and felicity: We give you heartfelt
thanks for the good examples of all your servants, who,
having finished their course in faith, now rest from
their labors. May we, with all those who have died in
the true faith of your holy Name, find perfect fulfillment and bliss, both in body and soul, in your eternal
and everlasting glory; through Jesus Christ our Lord.
Amen.

Almighty God, Father of mercies and giver of comfort: Deal graciously, we pray, with all who mourn, that, casting all their care on you, they may know the consolation of your love; through Jesus Christ our Lord. *Amen.*

Other authorized prayers may follow.

Then the Minister, standing and facing the Body, says

To God's loving care and protection we entrust *him.* The Lord bless *him*, and keep *him* safe; the Lord show *him* his glory, and be gracious to *him;* the Lord look upon *him* with favor, and give *him* peace; now, and for ever. *Amen.*

Or else, the Service of Committal takes place at this point.

A Priest (or the Bishop) may then bless the People.

A Canticle or Hymn may be sung or said as the Body is borne from the Church (see pages 415–416 for Canticles).

If the Body is not then to be taken to the grave, the Deacon, or other Minister, dismisses the People:

Let us go forth in the Name of Christ.
Thanks be to God.

AT THE EUCHARIST

When Communion follows, this Prayer of Intercession may be used:

THE PRAYER OF INTERCESSION
(People Standing)

In Peace, let us pray to the Lord.

For the peace from above, for the salvation of mankind: that righteousness, mercy, and truth may prevail among all peoples and nations.

Hear us, good Lord.

For the well-being of your holy Catholic Church in every place: that you will confirm it in the truth of your holy Word, and grant to all Christians to live in unity, love, and concord.

Hear us, good Lord.

Deal graciously, Lord, with all who mourn, that, casting every care on you, they may know the consolation of your love.

Hear us, good Lord.

Have mercy upon us, most merciful Lord; and in your compassion forgive us all our sins and failures, known and unknown, things done and left undone; and so uphold us by your Spirit, that we may end our days in peace, trusting in your mercy at the day of judgment.

Have mercy upon us.

We commend to your keeping all who have departed this life in your faith and fear, and especially your servant, N.: that you will grant them continual growth in your love and service. May we with them and with all your saints be partakers of your everlasting kingdom; through your Son Jesus Christ, our only Mediator and Advocate.

To you be honor, glory, and dominion, now and for ever. Amen.

The Service then continues with the Offertory.

After the postcommunion Prayer, the Minister, standing before the Body, says

To God's loving care and protection we entrust *him*. The Lord bless *him*, and keep *him* safe; the Lord show *him* his glory, and be gracious to *him;* the Lord look upon *him* with favor, and give *him* peace; now, and for ever. *Amen.*

Or else, the Service of Committal takes place at this point.

A Priest (or the Bishop) may then bless the People.

A Canticle or Hymn may be sung or said as the Body is borne from the Church (see pages 415–416 for Canticles).

If the Body is not then to be taken to the grave, the Deacon, or other Minister, dismisses the People:

Let us go forth in the Name of Christ.
Thanks be to God.

AT THE GRAVE

The following Anthems are sung or said:

In the midst of life, we are in death.
  To whom can we turn for help,
  but to you, only, Lord,
  who by our sins are justly angered.
Holy God, Holy and mighty, Holy and merciful
                                        Savior:
  Deliver us not into the bitter pain
              of eternal death.
You, Lord, know the secrets of our hearts.
  Close not your ears to our prayers;
  but spare us, worthy and eternal Judge.
Holy Lord, Holy and mighty, Holy and
                          merciful Savior:
  Let not the pains of death at our last hour
  turn us away from you.

or these Anthems

Jesus said:
"Everyone whom the Father gives me
  will come to me;
I will never turn away anyone
  who believes in me."

He who raised Christ Jesus from the dead
will also give new life to our mortal bodies,
  through his indwelling Spirit.

Because of this, my heart is glad,
  and my spirit sings for joy;
  my body shall rest in hope.

You will show me the path of life;
  you will fill me with joy in your presence,
  and with pleasures at your right hand, for ever.

THE WORDS OF COMMITTAL

The Minister then says these words, during which the earth may
be cast upon the coffin.

To Almighty God we commend our *brother, N.,* as we
commit *his* Body to *the ground**; earth to earth, ashes
to ashes, dust to dust; in sure and certain hope of the
resurrection to eternal life, through our Lord Jesus
Christ.

* or, *the deep,* or *the elements,* or *this resting place.*

Lord have mercy.
Christ have mercy.
Lord have mercy.

The LORD'S PRAYER may be said.

Then the Minister says one or more of the Prayers on pages 411–414; after which he may say

Give *him* eternal rest, O Lord:
Let your light shine upon him *for ever.*

May his soul and the souls of all the faithful, through the mercy of God, rest in peace. *Amen.*

He concludes the Service as follows:

The God of peace, who brought again from the dead our Lord Jesus Christ, the great Shepherd of the sheep, through the blood of the everlasting covenant: Make you perfect in every good work to do his will, working in you that which is well pleasing in his sight; through Jesus Christ, to whom be glory for ever and ever. *Amen.*

ADDITIONAL PRAYERS AND CANTICLES

Almighty God, with whom still live the spirits of those who die in the Lord, and with whom the souls of the faithful, after they are delivered from the burden of the flesh, are in joy and felicity: We give you heartfelt thanks for the good examples of all your servants, who, having finished their course in faith, now rest from their labors. May we, with all those who have died in the true faith of your holy Name, find perfect fulfillment and bliss, both in body and soul, in your eternal and everlasting glory; through Jesus Christ our Lord. *Amen.*

Lord Jesus Christ, who by your death have taken away the sting of death: Grant us so to follow in faith where you have led the way, that we may at length fall asleep peacefully in you, and wake up after your likeness; through your mercy, O Christ, who with the Father and the Holy Spirit live and reign, one God, for ever and ever. *Amen.*

O God, whose days are without end, and whose mercies cannot be numbered: Make us, we pray, deeply sensible of the shortness and uncertainty of human life; and let your Holy Spirit lead us in holiness and righteousness all our days; so that, when we shall have served you in our generation, we may be gathered to our fathers: having the testimony of a good conscience; in the communion of the Catholic Church; in the confidence of a

411

certain faith; in the comfort of a rational, religious and holy hope; in favor with you our God, and in perfect charity with the world. All which we ask through Jesus Christ our Lord. *Amen.*

Heavenly Father, giver of a true faith and a sure hope: Help us, we pray, in the midst of things we cannot understand, to believe and trust in your fatherly care— in the communion of saints, the forgiveness of sins, and the resurrection to life everlasting; and strengthen, we pray, this faith and hope in us all the days of our life; through Jesus Christ our Lord. *Amen.*

Father of all, we pray to you for those we love, but see no longer. Grant them your peace; let light perpetual shine upon them; and in your loving wisdom and almighty power, work in them the good purpose of your perfect will; through Jesus Christ our Lord. *Amen.*

Merciful God, Father of our Lord Jesus Christ who is the Resurrection and the Life, in whom whosoever believes shall live, even though he die, and whosoever lives and believes in him shall not die eternally; who also has taught us by his holy Apostle Saint Paul not to be sorry, as men without hope, for those who sleep in him: We humbly beseech you, O Father, to raise us from the death of sin to the life of righteousness; that when we shall depart this life we may rest in him, and that at the general Resurrection we may be found acceptable in your sight; and receive that blessing which your well-beloved Son shall then pronounce to all who love and fear you, saying, "Come you blessed of my Father, receive the kingdom prepared for you from the beginning of the world." Grant this, we beseech you, merciful Father, through Jesus Christ, our Mediator and Redeemer. *Amen.*

Grant, O Lord, to all who are bereaved the spirit of faith and courage, that they have strength to meet the days to come with steadfastness and patience; not sorrowing as those without hope, but in thankful remembrance of all the manifestations of your great goodness, and in the joyful expectation of eternal life with those they love. And this we ask in the Name of Jesus Christ our Savior. *Amen.*

Almighty God, Father of mercies and giver of comfort: Deal graciously, we pray, with all who mourn, that, casting all their care on you, they may know the consolation of your love; through Jesus Christ our Lord. *Amen.*

* Lord God, you were happy to give us
  the light of our eyes
  and let us be born.
  You did not make us
  for darkness and death,
  but so that we should, with all our hearts,
  live and come closer to you.
  Be merciful to us then
  and take us by the hand
  and lead us to life
  today and for ever.

For a dead person

* We thank you, God,
for this *man* who was so near and dear to us
and who has now been taken from us.
We thank you
for the friendship that went out from *him*
and the peace *he* brought.
We thank you
that through suffering *he* learned obedience
and that *he* became a person others could love
while *he* was with us here on earth.

For ourselves, who are still living

* Let us pray for ourselves,
who are severely tested by this death,
that we do not try to minimize this loss
or seek refuge from it in words
and also that we do not brood over it
so that it overwhelms us
and isolates us from others.
May God grant us new courage
and confidence to face life.

* From "Your Word is Near" by Huub Oosterhuis, Newman
Press, New York, N.Y. Reprinted by permission.

The Song of Zechariah (Benedictus)
(Luke 1:69-79)

Blessed be the Lord, the God of Israel;
   he has come to his people and set them free.
He has raised up for us a mighty savior,
   born of the house of his servant David.
Through his holy prophets he promised of old,
that he would save us from our enemies,
   from the hands of all who hate us.

He promised to show mercy to our fathers
   and to remember his holy covenant.
This was the oath he swore to our father Abraham,
   to set us free from our enemies' hand,
free to worship him without fear,
   holy and righteous in his sight,
   all the days of our life.

And you, my child, shall be called the prophet of the
                              Most High,
   for you will go before the Lord to prepare his way,
to give his people knowledge of salvation
   by forgiveness of their sins.
In the tender compassion of our God
   the dawn from on high shall break upon us,
to shine on those who dwell in darkness and the
                              shadow of death,
   and to guide our feet on the road to peace.

The Song of Simeon (Nunc dimittis)
(Luke 2:29–32)

Lord, you have fulfilled your word;
  now let your servant depart in peace.
With my own eyes I have seen the salvation,
  which you have prepared in the sight
                    of every people:
A Light to reveal you to the nations,
  and the glory of your people Israel.

THE CONSECRATION OF A GRAVE

ADAPTED FROM THE BOOK OF OFFICES, 1960

If the Grave is in a place that has not previously been set apart for Christian burial, the Priest may use the following form, either before the Service at the Grave, or at some other convenient time:

In the place where Jesus was crucified there was a garden, and in the garden a new sepulcher in which no man had been buried before.

The eternal God is your dwelling-place;
And underneath are the everlasting arms.

Let us pray.

O God, whose blessed Son was laid in a sepulcher in the garden: Bless, we pray, this grave, that *he* whose body is [is to be] buried here may dwell with Christ in paradise, and may come to your heavenly Kingdom; through the same Jesus Christ, our LORD. *Amen.*

THE ORDINATION
OF BISHOPS,
PRIESTS,
AND DEACONS

At the Ordination of a Bishop

When a Bishop is to be ordained, the Presiding Bishop of the Church, or a Bishop appointed by him, shall preside and serve as Chief Consecrator. At least two other Bishops shall serve as Co-consecrators. Representatives of the Presbyterate, Diaconate, and Laity of the Diocese for which the new Bishop is to be consecrated, are to be assigned appropriate duties in the service.

From the beginning of the service until the Offertory, it is desirable that the Presiding Bishop's chair be placed close to the People, so that all may see and hear what is done. The other Bishops, or a convenient number of them, should sit to his right and left.

The Bishop-elect is to be vested in a rochet or alb, without stole, tippet, or other vesture distinctive of ecclesiastical or academic rank or order.

When the Bishop-elect is presented, his full name (designated by the symbol *N.N.*) shall be used. Thereafter, it is appropriate to refer to him only by the Christian name by which he wishes to be known.

Additional Directions and Suggestions are on pages 432–433.

THE ORDINATION OF A BISHOP

A Psalm, or Hymn, or Anthem may be sung during the entrance of the Bishops and other Ministers.

The People being assembled, and all standing, a Bishop appointed says

Blessed be God: Father, Son, and Holy Spirit.

People

And blessed be his Kingdom, now and for ever. Amen.

From Easter Day through the Day of Pentecost, he says instead

Alleluia! Christ is risen.

People

The Lord is risen indeed. Alleluia!

Bishop

Almighty God, to you all hearts are open, all desires known, and from you no secrets are hid; cleanse the thoughts of our hearts by the inspiration of your Holy Spirit, that we may perfectly love you, and worthily magnify your holy Name; through Christ our Lord. *Amen.*

The Bishops and the People sit.

The Presentation

A Priest and a Lay Person, as representatives of the Diocese, present the man for whom they seek Consecration to the Presiding Bishop, saying

Reverend Father in God, the Clergy and People of the Diocese of *N.*, trusting in the guidance of the Holy Spirit, have chosen *N.N.* to be a Bishop and Chief Pastor. We therefore ask you to lay your hands upon him and in the power of the Holy Spirit to consecrate him a Bishop in the One, Holy, Catholic, and Apostolic Church.

The Presiding Bishop then directs that testimonials of the election be read.

When the reading of the testimonials is ended, the Presiding Bishop requires the following promise from the Bishop-elect:

In the Name of the Father, and of the Son, and of the Holy Spirit, I, *N.N.*, chosen Bishop of the Church in *N.*, do promise conformity and obedience to the Doctrine, Discipline, and Worship of The Episcopal Church.

All stand.

The Presiding Bishop then says the following, or similar words, and asks the response of the People.

Dear friends in Christ, you have heard testimony given that *N.N.* has been duly and lawfully elected to be a Bishop of the Church of God to serve in the Diocese of *N.* You have been assured of his suitability for this office, and that the Church has, through its authorized representatives, approved him for this sacred responsibility. We therefore present him to you as Bishop-elect. We ask you to voice your assent, and to express the loyalty which you will give to him as Bishop. Is he worthy?

The People respond with a loud voice saying these or other words, several times:

He is worthy.

The Presiding Bishop then says

The Scriptures tell us that our Savior Christ spent the whole night in prayer before he chose and sent forth his twelve Apostles. Likewise, the Apostles prayed before they appointed Matthias to be one of their number. Let us, therefore, follow their examples, and offer our prayers to Almighty God before we ordain this person for the work to which we trust the Holy Spirit has called him.

All kneel, and the Person appointed leads the Litany for the Ministry of the Church, or some other approved Litany. At the end of the Litany, after the Kyries, the Presiding Bishop stands and reads the Collect for the Day, or the following Collect, or both, first saying

	The Lord be with you.
Answer	**And also with you.**
Presiding Bishop	**Let us pray.**

The Collect

Almighty God, by whose Holy Spirit your people are provided with true and faithful pastors: By the same Spirit kindle in this your servant such love toward you, that he may witness to you in holiness of life, zealously proclaim the Gospel, and gather a people reconciled in your Son, Jesus Christ our Lord; who lives and reigns with you and the Holy Spirit, one God, now and ever. *Amen.*

At the Ministry of the Word

Three Lessons are to be read. Lay persons read the Old Testament Lesson and the Epistle. A Deacon reads the Gospel. The readings are ordinarily selected from the following list, except that on a major Feast, or on a Sunday, the Presiding Bishop may select readings from the Proper of the Day if they are appropriate.

Old Testament	Isaiah 61:1–8, or Isaiah 42:1–9
Suggested Psalms	99, or 40:1–14, or 100
Epistle	Hebrews 5:1–10, or 1 Timothy 3:1–7, or 2 Corinthians 3:4–9
Gospel	John 20:19–23, or John 17:1–9, 18–21, or Luke 24:44–49a

The Sermon

After the Sermon, the Congregation sings a Hymn.

The Examination

All now sit, except the Bishop-elect, who stands facing the Bishops. The Bishop-elect is questioned by one or more of the participating Bishops.

Bishop   My brother, the People have affirmed their trust in you by acclaiming your election. Will you fulfill this trust, in obedience to Christ?

Answer   I will obey Christ, and will serve in his Name.

Bishop   Will you be faithful in prayer, and in the study of Holy Scripture, that you may have the mind of Christ?

Answer   I will, for he is my help.

Bishop   Will you boldly proclaim and interpret the Gospel of Christ, enlightening the minds and stirring up the consciences of men?

Answer   I will, in the power of the Spirit.

Bishop   As a Chief Priest and Pastor, will you nourish your people from the riches of God's grace, pray for them without ceasing, and celebrate with them the Sacraments of our redemption?

Answer   I will, in the Name of Christ, the Shepherd and Bishop of our souls.

Bishop Will you guard the faith, unity, and discipline of the Church?

Answer I will, for the love of God.

Bishop Will you join with your brother Bishops in the government of the whole Church? Will you sustain your fellow Presbyters and take counsel with them? Will you guide and strengthen the Deacons and all others who minister in the Church?

Answer I will, by the grace given me.

Bishop Will you defend, and show compassion to, the poor and strangers and those who have no helper? And will you be merciful to all men?

Answer I will, for the sake of Christ Jesus.

All stand.

The Presiding Bishop then says

N., through these promises you have committed yourself to God, to serve his Church in the Office of Bishop. We therefore call upon you, chosen to be a guardian of the Church's faith, to lead us in confessing that faith.

[The version of the Creed which follows is recommended by the International Consultation on English Texts.]

Bishop-elect

We believe in one God.

Then all say together

We believe in one God,
 the Father, the Almighty,
 maker of heaven and earth,
 of all that is seen and unseen.

We believe in one Lord, Jesus Christ,
 the only Son of God,
 eternally begotten of the Father,
 God from God, Light from Light,
 true God from true God,
 begotten, not made, one in Being with the Father.
 Through him all things were made.
 For us men and for our salvation
  he came down from heaven:
 by the power of the Holy Spirit
  he was born of the Virgin Mary, and became man.
 For our sake he was crucified under Pontius Pilate;
  he suffered, died, and was buried.
  On the third day he rose again
   in fulfillment of the Scriptures;
  he ascended into heaven
   and is seated at the right hand of the Father.
 He will come again in glory to judge the living
  and the dead,
  and his kingdom will have no end.

We believe in the Holy Spirit, the Lord,
    the giver of life,
who proceeds from the Father.
With the Father and the Son he is worshiped
    and glorified.
He has spoken through the Prophets.
We believe in one holy catholic and apostolic Church.
We acknowledge one baptism
    for the forgiveness of sins.
We look for the resurrection of the dead,
    and the life of the world to come. Amen.

The Consecration of the Bishop

All continue to stand, except the Bishop-elect, who kneels before the Presiding Bishop. The other Bishops stand to the right and left of the Presiding Bishop.

The Hymn *Veni Creator Spiritus,* or the Hymn *Veni Sancte Spiritus,* is sung.

A period of silent prayer follows, the People still standing.

The Presiding Bishop then begins this Prayer of Consecration:

God and Father of our Lord Jesus Christ, Father of mercies and God of all comfort, dwelling on high but having regard for the lowly, knowing all things before they come to pass: We give you thanks that from the beginning you have gathered and prepared a people to be heirs of the covenant of Abraham, and have raised up prophets, kings, and priests, never leaving your temple untended. We praise you also that from the creation you have graciously accepted the ministry of those whom you have chosen.

The Presiding Bishop and other Bishops now lay their hands upon the head of the Bishop-elect, and say together

Pour out now upon *N*. the power of that princely Spirit whom you bestowed upon your beloved Son Jesus Christ, with whom he endowed the Apostles, and by whom your Church is built up in every place, to the glory and unceasing praise of your Name.

The Presiding Bishop continues

To you, O Father, all hearts are open; fill, we pray, the heart of this your servant whom you have chosen to be a Bishop in your Church, with such love of you and of all the people, that he may feed and tend the flock of Christ, and exercise without reproach the high priesthood to which you have called him: serving before you day and night in the ministry of reconciliation, offering the holy gifts, and wisely overseeing the life and work of the Church. In all things may he present before you the acceptable offering of a pure, and gentle, and holy life; through Jesus Christ your Son, to whom with you and the Holy Spirit be honor and power and glory in the Church, now and for ever.

The People in a loud voice respond AMEN.

The new Bishop now stands, and the rest of the vestments of his office are put upon him.

The Bible is then presented; after which he may be given other symbols of office.

The Peace

The Presiding Bishop turns the new Bishop toward the Congregation and presents him to his People.

The Clergy and People offer their applause.

The new Bishop then says

The Peace of the Lord be always with you.

Answer   **And also with you.**

The Presiding Bishop, and other Bishops, now greet the new Bishop. He may then greet other members of the Clergy, and his family, as convenient. Meanwhile, the People may greet one another.

At the Celebration of the Eucharist

The new Bishop says the Offertory Sentence.

Then, standing at the Lord's Table as chief celebrant, and joined by Bishops and other ministers, he proceeds with the celebration of the Eucharist.

After Communion

In place of the usual post-communion Prayer, one of the Bishops leads the People in the following Prayer:

430

Almighty Father, we thank you for feeding us with the holy food of the Body and Blood of your Son, and for uniting us through him in the fellowship of your Holy Spirit. We thank you for raising up among us faithful servants for the ministry of your Word and Sacraments. We pray that *N.* may be to us an effective example in word and action, in love and patience, and in holiness of life. Grant that we, with him, may serve you now, and always rejoice in your glory; through Jesus Christ your Son our Lord, who lives and reigns with you and the Holy Spirit, one God, now and for ever. Amen.

The new Bishop dismisses the People with this Blessing, first saying

	Our help is in the Name of the Lord:
Answer	The Maker of heaven and earth.
New Bishop	Blessed be the Name of the Lord.
Answer	From this time forth for evermore.

New Bishop The blessing, mercy, and grace of God Almighty, the Father, the Son, and the Holy Spirit, be upon you, and remain with you for ever. *Amen.*

The Hymn *Te Deum laudamus* is then sung as an act of thanksgiving.

Additional Directions and Suggestions

The celebration of the Holy Eucharist at an Ordination may be according to the 1928 Liturgy, or any other Liturgy of this Church authorized for public worship. In the former case, the Prayer for the Whole State of Christ's Church and the General Confession are to be omitted, the service proceeding at once from the Offertory to "Lift up your hearts," and what follows. If another Liturgy is used, the Penitential Order and the Prayer of Intercession are omitted. In all cases, the Summary of the Law, the Gloria in excelsis, and the usual post-communion Prayer are not to be used with this service of Ordination.

After the Old Testament Lesson, and after the Epistle, a Psalm, Hymn, or Canticle is sung or said.

The Hymn to the Holy Spirit before the Prayer of Consecration of the Bishop may be sung responsively between a Bishop and the Congregation, or in some other convenient manner.

Immediately after the People's *Amen* to the Consecration Prayer, and while the new Bishop is being clothed with the vesture and insignia of the Episcopate, organ or other instrumental music may be used.

In addition to the Bible, he may be presented with a Pectoral Cross, Pastoral Staff, or other suitable symbols. It is appropriate that Church bells be rung when he is presented to the People.

At the Offertory, the Deacons and other assisting ministers prepare the Lord's Table, placing the Bread and Wine upon it. For the Eucharistic Prayer, it is appropriate that some of the consecrating Bishops, and representative Presbyters of the Diocese, stand with the new Bishop at the altar as fellow-ministers of the Sacrament.

The newly-ordained Bishop, assisted by other Ministers, shall distribute Holy Communion to the People, who shall always be allowed opportunity to communicate. Since there are normally many communicants at such a service, advantage should be taken of the presence of a large number of Bishops, Priests, and Deacons to arrange for the orderly and expeditious administration of Communion; and, when necessary, at several different places in the Church.

When two or more Bishops are to be ordained at the same time, each shall have his own Presenters; and the Presentation, including the Promise of Conformity and the Acclamation of the People, shall take place separately for each Bishop-elect. Thereafter, in the Litany and subsequent parts of the service, references to the Bishop-elect in the singular shall be changed to the plural where necessary. All the Bishops-elect are to be examined together and shall lead the Creed in unison. During the Prayer of Consecration, the sentence, "Pour out now, etc.," is to be repeated in full over each Candidate while the Presiding Bishop and other Bishops lay their hands on his head. The new Bishops shall all join in the Peace and in the celebration of the Eucharist, one of them being designated to preside as chief celebrant.

The Bishops who are present shall not depart without signing the Letters of Consecration.

At the Ordination of a Priest

When the Bishop is to confer Holy Orders, at least two Presbyters shall be present.

From the beginning of the service until the Offertory, it is desirable that a seat for the Bishop be placed close to the People, and facing them, so that all may see and hear what is done in the Ordination.

The Ordinand is to be vested in a surplice or alb, without stole, tippet, or other vesture distinctive of ecclesiastical or academic rank or order.

When the Candidate is presented, his full name (designated by the symbol *N.N.*) shall be used. Thereafter, it is appropriate to refer to him only by the Christian name by which he wishes to be known.

The family of the newly Ordained may receive Communion before other members of the Congregation. And opportunity shall be given to the People to communicate.

Additional Directions and Suggestions are on pages 444–445.

THE ORDINATION
OF A PRIEST

A Psalm, or Hymn, or Anthem may be sung during the entrance of the Ministers.

The People being assembled, and all standing, the Bishop says

Blessed be God: Father, Son, and Holy Spirit.

People

And blessed be his Kingdom, now and for ever. Amen.

From Easter Day through the Day of Pentecost, he says instead

Alleluia! Christ is risen.

People

The Lord is risen indeed. Alleluia!

Bishop

Almighty God, to you all hearts are open, all desires known, and from you no secrets are hid; cleanse the thoughts of our hearts by the inspiration of your Holy Spirit, that we may perfectly love you, and worthily magnify your holy Name; through Christ our Lord. *Amen.*

The Presentation

The Bishop sits. A Priest and a Lay Person, standing before the Bishop, present to him the one proposed for ordination, saying

Reverend Father in God, on behalf of the Clergy and People of the Diocese of *N.*, we present to you *N.N.* to be ordained a Priest in Christ's Holy Catholic Church.

Bishop

Has he been selected in accordance with the Canons of this Church? And do you believe his manner of life to be suitable to the exercise of this Ministry?

Presenters

We certify to you that he has satisfied the requirements of the Canons, and we believe him qualified for this Order.

The Bishop says to the Person presented

Will you be loyal to the Doctrine, Discipline, and Worship of Christ as this Church has received them? And will you, in accordance with the Canons of this Church, obey your Bishop and other Ministers who may have authority over you and your work?

Answer I am willing and ready to do so.

The Bishop stands and says to the People

Dear friends in Christ, you know the importance of this Ministry, and the weight of your responsibility in presenting *N.N.* for ordination to the sacred Priesthood. Therefore, if any of you knows any impediment or crime because of which we should not proceed, let him come forward and make it known.

If no objection is made, the Bishop continues

I ask you then to declare your will that this Ministry be conferred on him. Is he worthy?

The People respond with a loud voice saying these or other words, several times:

He is worthy.

The Bishop then calls the People to prayer with these or similar words:

Let us pray to Almighty God for his blessing upon us and all men, and for the gift of his grace to those who are called to the ordained Ministry of his Church.

All kneel, and the Person appointed leads the Litany for the Ministry of the Church, or some other approved Litany. At the end of the Litany, after the Kyries, the Bishop stands and reads the Collect for the Day, or the following Collect, or both, first saying

<blockquote>

The Lord be with you.

Answer   **And also with you.**

Bishop   **Let us pray.**

</blockquote>

The Collect

Almighty God, the giver of all good gifts, who of your divine providence appointed various Orders in your Church: Give your grace, we humbly pray, to this person now called to the Order of Priests: and so replenish him with the truth of your doctrine, and endue him with holiness of life, that he may faithfully serve before you to the glory of your great Name, and to the benefit of your holy Church; through Jesus Christ our Lord, who lives and reigns with you in the unity of the Holy Spirit, one God, now and ever. *Amen.*

At the Ministry of the Word

Three Lessons are to be read. Lay persons read the Old Testament Lesson and the Epistle. A Deacon or Priest reads the Gospel. The readings are ordinarily selected from the following list, except that on a major Feast, or on a Sunday, the Bishop may select readings from the Proper of the Day if they are appropriate.

Old Testament	Isaiah 6:1–8, or Numbers 11:16–17, 24–25 (omitting the final clause)
Suggested Psalm	43, or 132:8–19
Epistle	1 Peter 5:1–4*, or Ephesians 4:7, 11–16, or Philippians 4:4–9

* It is to be noted that where the word *elder, elders,* and *fellow-elder* appear in translations of 1 Peter 5:1, the original Greek terms *presbyter, presbyters,* and *fellow-presbyter* are to be substituted.

Gospel Matthew 9:35–38, or John 10:11–18, or John 6:35–38

The Sermon

> The Congregation then says or sings the Nicene Creed.

The Examination

> All are seated except the Ordinand, who stands before the Bishop. The Bishop addresses him as follows:

My brother, the Church is the family of God, the body of Christ, and the temple of the Holy Spirit. All baptized people are called to make Christ known to men as Savior and Lord, and to share in the renewing of his world. Now you are being called to work, together with your Bishop and fellow-Presbyters, as a pastor, priest, and teacher in this ministry, and to take your share in the councils of the Church.

As Priest, it will be your task to proclaim the Gospel and to apply it, by your words and in your life. You are to love and serve the people among whom you work, caring alike for young and old, strong and weak, rich and poor. You are to preach, to declare God's forgiveness to penitent sinners, to baptize, to preside at the celebration of the mysteries of Christ's Body and Blood, and to perform the other ministrations entrusted to you.

In all that you do, you are to nourish Christ's people and strengthen them to glorify God in this life and in the life to come.

My brother, do you believe that you are truly called by God and his Church to this Priesthood?

Answer   I believe I am so called.

Bishop   Do you now in the presence of the Church commit yourself to this trust and responsibility?

Answer   I do.

Bishop   Will you be faithful in prayer, and in the reading and study of the Holy Scriptures?

Bishop   I will, for in God's Word is my trust.

Answer   Will you look for Christ, and serve him, in your fellow men?

Answer   I will.

Bishop   Will you do your best to pattern your life [and that of your *family**] in accordance with the teachings of Christ, so that you may be a wholesome example to your people?

Answer   I will, God being my helper.

Bishop   May the Lord who has given you the will to do these things, give you the grace and power to perform them.

* *or,* household; *or,* community

The Consecration of the Priest

All now stand except the Ordinand, who kneels facing the Bishop and the Presbyters who stand to the right and left of the Bishop.

The Hymn Veni Creator Spiritus, or the Hymn Veni Sancte Spiritus, is sung.

A period of silent prayer follows, the People still standing.

The Bishop then says this Prayer of Consecration:

God and Father of all, we praise you for your infinite love in calling us to be a holy people in the kingdom of your Son Jesus our Lord, who is the image of your eternal and invisible glory, the firstborn among many brethren, and the head of the Church. We thank you that by his death he has overcome death, and having ascended into heaven, has poured his gifts abundantly upon your people, making some Apostles, some Prophets, some Evangelists, some Pastors and Teachers, to equip the saints for the work of ministry and the building up of his body.

Here the Bishop lays his hands upon the head of the one being ordained, the Priests who are present also laying on their right hands. At the same time the Bishop prays

Therefore, O Father, through Jesus Christ your Son, give your Holy Spirit to *N.;* fill him with grace and power, and make him a Priest in your Church.

The Bishop then continues

May he glorify you in the midst of your people, and offer spiritual sacrifices acceptable to you. May he boldly proclaim the Gospel of salvation, and rightly administer the Sacraments of the new covenant. Make him a faithful pastor, a patient teacher, and a wise councilor. Grant that in all things he may serve without reproach, so that your people may be strengthened and your Name glorified; through Jesus Christ our Lord, who with you and the Holy Spirit lives and reigns, one God, for ever and ever.

The People in a loud voice respond **AMEN.**

The new Priest is then vested according to his Order.

The Bishop then gives him a Bible, saying

Receive this Bible as a sign of the authority given you to preach the Word of God and to administer his holy Sacraments. Forget not the trust committed to you as a Priest of the Church of God.

The Peace

The Bishop and the other Clergy present now greet the newly Ordained.

The new Priest then says to the Congregation

The Peace of the Lord be always with you.

Answer **And also with you.**

He may then greet his family, or others, as may be convenient. Meanwhile the People may greet one another.

At the Celebration of the Eucharist

The Liturgy continues with the Offertory. Standing at the Lord's Table with the Bishop and other Clergy, the newly Ordained joins in the celebration of the Holy Eucharist.

After Communion

In place of the usual post-communion Prayer, the following Prayer is said:

Almighty Father, we thank you for feeding us with the holy food of the Body and Blood of your Son, and for uniting us through him in the fellowship of your Holy Spirit. We thank you for raising up among us faithful servants for the ministry of your Word and Sacraments. We pray that *N.* may be to us an effective example in word and action, in love and patience, and in holiness of life. Grant that we, with him, may serve you now, and always rejoice in your glory; through Jesus Christ your Son our Lord, who lives and reigns with you and the Holy Spirit, one God, now and for ever. *Amen.*

The Bishop then asks the new Priest to bless the People.

The People kneel; and the new Priest says

The Peace of God, which passes all understanding, keep your hearts and minds in the knowledge and love of God, and of his Son Jesus Christ our Lord: And the Blessing of God Almighty, the Father, the Son, and the Holy Spirit, be among you, and remain with you always. *Amen.*

A Deacon (or a Priest) dismisses the assembly.

443

Additional Directions and Suggestions

The celebration of the Holy Eucharist at an Ordination may be according to the 1928 Liturgy, or any other Liturgy of this Church authorized for public worship. In the former case, the Prayer for the Whole State of Christ's Church and the General Confession are to be omitted, the service proceeding at once from the Offertory to "Lift up your hearts," and what follows. If another Liturgy is used, the Penitential Order and the Prayer of Intercession are omitted. In all cases, the Summary of the Law, the Gloria in excelsis, and the usual postcommunion Prayer are not to be used with this service of Ordination.

Provision is made herein for two Presenters; more may be appropriate on occasion, with the permission of the Bishop.

After the Old Testament Lesson, and after the Epistle, a Psalm, Hymn, or Canticle is sung or said.

The Hymn to the Holy Spirit before the Prayer of Consecration of the Priest may be sung responsively between the Bishop and the Congregation, or in some other convenient manner.

The stole worn about the neck, or other insignia of the Office of Priest, shall be placed upon the new Priest after the Ordination Prayer is completed, immediately before the Bible is presented.

After the Presentation of the Bible, other instruments and symbols of his office may be given him.

At the Offertory, it is appropriate that the bread and wine be brought to the Altar by the family or friends of the newly Ordained.

At the Eucharistic Consecration, the new Priest and other Priests shall stand at the Altar with the Bishop as associates and fellow-ministers of the Sacrament, and shall communicate with him. After the Lord's Prayer, the new Priest shall, and other Priests may, join the Bishop in breaking the consecrated Bread.

If two or more Candidates are to be ordained together, each shall have his own Presenters. They may be presented together, or in succession, as the Bishop may direct. Thereafter, references to the Ordinand in the singular shall be changed to the plural where necessary. The Ordinands are to be examined together. During the Ordination Prayer, the Bishop is to say over each Ordinand separately the words,

O Father, through Jesus Christ your Son, give your Holy Spirit to *N.*; fill him with grace and power, and make him a Priest in your Church.

Likewise the Bishop and Priests are to lay their hands on each Ordinand's head when these words are said. A Bible shall be given, and the words, "Receive this Bible", etc., shall also be said to each. All those newly ordained shall take part in the Peace, and shall join the Bishop and other Priests at the altar for the Consecration. Similarly, all the new Priests shall break the consecrated Bread and receive Holy Communion.

At the Ordination of a Deacon

When the Bishop is to confer Holy Orders, at least two Presbyters shall be present.

From the beginning of the service until the Offertory, it is desirable that a seat for the Bishop be placed close to the People, and facing them, so that all may see and hear what is done in the Ordination.

The Ordinand is to be vested in a surplice or alb, without tippet or other vesture distinctive of ecclesiastical or academic rank or office.

When the Candidate is presented, his full name (designated by the symbol *N.N.*) shall be used. Thereafter, it is appropriate to refer to him only by the Christian name by which he wishes to be known.

After receiving Holy Communion, the new Deacon shall assist in the distribution of the Sacrament, ministering either the consecrated Bread or Wine, or both.

The family of the newly Ordained may receive Communion before other members of the Congregation. And opportunity shall be given to the People to communicate.

Additional Directions and Suggestions are on pages 456–457.

THE ORDINATION OF A DEACON

A Psalm, or Hymn, or Anthem may be sung during the entrance of the Ministers.

The People being assembled, and all standing, the Bishop says

Blessed be God: Father, Son, and Holy Spirit.

People

And blessed be his Kingdom, now and for ever. Amen.

From Easter Day through the Day of Pentecost, he says instead

Alleluia! Christ is risen.

People

The Lord is risen indeed. Alleluia!

Bishop

Almighty God, to you all hearts are open, all desires known, and from you no secrets are hid; cleanse the thoughts of our hearts by the inspiration of your Holy Spirit, that we may perfectly love you, and worthily magnify your holy Name; through Christ our Lord. *Amen.*

The Presentation

The Bishop sits. A Priest and a Lay Person, standing before the Bishop, present to him the one proposed for ordination, saying

Reverend Father in God, on behalf of the Clergy and People of the Diocese of *N.*, we present to you *N.N.* to be ordained a Deacon in Christ's Holy Catholic Church.

Bishop

Has he been selected in accordance with the Canons of this Church? And do you believe his manner of life to be suitable to the exercise of this Ministry?

Presenters

We certify to you that he has satisfied the requirements of the Canons, and we believe him qualified for this Order.

The Bishop says to the Person presented

Will you be loyal to the Doctrine, Discipline, and Worship of Christ as this Church has received them? And will you, in accordance with the Canons of this Church, obey your Bishop and other Ministers who may have authority over you and your work?

Answer   I am willing and ready to do so.

THE ORDINATION OF A DEACON

The Bishop stands and says to the People

Dear friends in Christ, you know the importance of this Ministry, and the weight of your responsibility in presenting *N.N.* for ordination to the sacred Order of Deacons. Therefore, if any of you knows any impediment or crime because of which we should not proceed, let him come forward and make it known.

If no objection is made, the Bishop continues

I ask you then to declare your will that this Ministry be conferred on him. Is he worthy?

The People respond with a loud voice saying these or other words, several times:

He is worthy.

The Bishop then calls the People to prayer with these or similar words:

Let us pray to Almighty God for his blessing upon us and all men, and for the gift of his grace to those who are called to the ordained Ministry of his Church.

All kneel, and the Person appointed leads the Litany for the Ministry of the Church, or some other approved Litany. At the end of the Litany, after the Kyries, the Bishop stands and reads the Collect for the Day, or the following Collect, or both, first saying

The Lord be with you.

Answer   And also with you.

Bishop   Let us pray.

The Collect

Almighty God, the giver of all good gifts, who of your divine providence appointed various Orders in your Church: Give your grace, we humbly pray, to this person now called to the Order of Deacons: and so replenish him with the truth of your doctrine, and endue him with holiness of life, that he may faithfully serve before you to the glory of your great Name, and to the benefit of your holy Church; through Jesus Christ our Lord, who lives and reigns with you in the unity of the Holy Spirit, one God, now and ever. *Amen.*

At the Ministry of the Word

> Three Lessons are to be read. Lay persons read the Old Testament Lesson and the Epistle. A Deacon or Priest reads the Gospel. The readings are ordinarily selected from the following list, except that on a major Feast, or on a Sunday, the Bishop may select readings from the Proper of the Day if they are appropriate.

Old Testament	Jeremiah 1:4–9, or Ecclesiasticus (Sirach) 39:1–8.
Suggested Psalm	84, or 119:33–40
Epistle	2 Corinthians 4:1–2, or 1 Timothy 3:8–13, or Acts 6:2–7
Gospel	Luke 12:35–38, or Luke 22:24–27

The Sermon

> The Congregation then says or sings the Nicene Creed.

The Examination

All are seated except the Ordinand, who stands before the Bishop. The Bishop addresses him as follows:

My brother, every Christian is called to follow Jesus Christ, serving God the Father in his world, through the power of the Holy Spirit. God now calls you to a special ministry of servanthood directly under your Bishop. You are to serve all people, particularly the poor, the weak, the sick, and the lonely.

As Deacon in the Church, you are to study the Holy Scriptures and to model your life upon God's Word. You are to be ready to make him known to those among whom you live, and work, and worship. You are to interpret to the Church the needs, concerns, and hopes of the world. You are to assist the Bishop and Priests in public worship and in the ministration of the Sacraments. By your teaching and your life, you are to show Christ's people that in serving the helpless they are serving Christ himself.

My brother, do you believe that you are truly called by God and his Church to the life and work of a Deacon?

Answer   I believe I am so called.

Bishop   Do you now in the presence of the Church commit yourself to this trust and responsibility?

Answer   I do.

Bishop   Will you be faithful in prayer, and in the reading and study of the Holy Scriptures?

Answer   I will, for in God's Word is my trust.

Bishop   Will you look for Christ, and serve him, in your fellow men?

Answer   I will.

Bishop   Will you do your best to pattern your life [and that of your *family**] in accordance with the teachings of Christ, so that you may be a wholesome example to your people?

Answer   I will, God being my helper.

Bishop   May the Lord by his grace uphold you in the service he lays upon you.

The Consecration of the Deacon

All now stand except the Ordinand, who kneels facing the Bishop.

The Hymn *Veni Creator Spiritus,* or the Hymn *Veni Sancte Spiritus,* is sung.

A period of silent prayer follows, the People still standing.

The Bishop then says this Prayer of Consecration:

O God, most merciful Father, we praise you for sending your Son, Jesus Christ, who took on himself the form of a servant, and humbled himself, becoming

* *or,* household; *or,* community

452

obedient even to death on the Cross. We praise you that you have highly exalted him, and made him Lord of all; and that through him we know that he who would be great must be servant of all. We praise you for the many ministries in your Church, and for calling this your servant to the Order of Deacon.

Here the Bishop lays his hands upon the head of the one being ordained, and prays

Therefore, O Father, through Jesus Christ your Son, give your Holy Spirit to N.; fill him with grace and power, and make him a Deacon in your Church.

The Bishop then continues

Make him, O Lord, modest and humble, strong and constant to observe the discipline of Christ. Let his life and teaching so reflect your commandments, that through him many may come to know you and love you. As your Son came not to be served but to serve, may this Deacon share in his service, and come to the unending glory of him who, with you and the Holy Spirit, lives and reigns, one God, for ever and ever.

The People in a loud voice respond AMEN.

The new Deacon is then vested according to his Order.
The Bishop then gives him a Bible, saying

Receive this Bible as the sign of your authority to proclaim God's Word and to assist in the ministration of his holy Sacraments.

The Peace

The Bishop and the other Clergy present now greet the newly Ordained.

The Bishop then says to the Congregation

The Peace of the Lord be always with you.

Answer **And also with you.**

The new Deacon may then greet his family, or others, as may be convenient. Meanwhile the People may greet one another.

At the Celebration of the Eucharist

The Liturgy continues with the Offertory; the newly-ordained Deacon prepares the Bread, pours sufficient Wine (and a little water) into the Chalice, and places the vessels on the Holy Table. The Bishop, at the Table, proceeds to the Consecration and Communion, which the newly Ordained shall receive with him.

After Communion

In place of the usual post-communion Prayer, the following Prayer is said:

Almighty Father, we thank you for feeding us with the holy food of the Body and Blood of your Son, and for uniting us through him in the fellowship of your Holy Spirit. We thank you for raising up among us faithful servants for the ministry of your Word and Sacraments. We pray that *N*. may be to us an effective example in

word and action, in love and patience, and in holiness
of life. Grant that we, with him, may serve you now,
and always rejoice in your glory; through Jesus Christ
your Son our Lord, who lives and reigns with you and
the Holy Spirit, one God, now and for ever. *Amen.*

The Bishop then blesses the People, after which the new
Deacon dismisses them.

Deacon   **Go forth into the world**
          rejoicing in the power of the Spirit.
          Thanks be to God.

Additional Directions and Suggestions

The celebration of the Holy Eucharist at an Ordination may be according to the 1928 Liturgy, or any other Liturgy of this Church authorized for public worship. In the former case, the Prayer of the Whole State of Christ's Church and the General Confession are to be omitted, the service proceeding at once from the Offertory to "Lift up your hearts," and what follows. If another Liturgy is used, the Penitential Order and the Prayer of Intercession are omitted. In all cases, the Summary of the Law, the Gloria in excelsis, and the usual post-communion Prayer are not to be used with this service of Ordination.

Provision is made herein for two Presenters; more may be appropriate on occasion, with the permission of the Bishop.

After the Old Testament Lesson, and after the Epistle, a Psalm, Hymn, or Canticle is sung or said.

The Hymn to the Holy Spirit before the Prayer of Consecration of the Deacon may be sung responsively between the Bishop and the Congregation, or in some other convenient manner.

The stole worn over the left shoulder, or other insignia of the Office of Deacon, shall be placed upon the new Deacon after the Ordination Prayer is completed, immediately before the Bible is given.

At the Offertory, it is appropriate that the bread and wine be brought to the Altar by the family or friends of the newly Ordained.

If other Deacons are present, it is appropriate that they assist the new Deacon at the Offertory.

If two or more candidates are to be ordained together, each may have his own Presenters. They may be presented together, or in succession, as the Bishop may direct. Thereafter, references to the Ordinand in the singular shall be changed to the plural where necessary. The Ordinands are to be examined together. During the Ordination Prayer, the Bishop is to say over each Ordinand separately the words,

O Father, through Jesus Christ your Son, give your Holy Spirit to *N.*; fill him with grace and power, and make him a Deacon in your Church.

Likewise, he is to lay his hands on the head of each one while saying these words. A Bible shall be given, and the words "Receive this Bible", etc., shall also be said to each.

After participating in the Peace, the Deacons go to the altar for the Offertory. If there are many Deacons, some can assist in the Offertory, and others can administer Holy Communion. One appointed by the Bishop is to say the Dismissal.

It is appropriate for Deacons to consume the remaining Elements of the Sacrament and to cleanse the vessels. Also, when desired, Deacons may be appointed to carry the Sacrament and minister Holy Communion to communicants who, because of sickness or other grave cause, could not be present at the celebration.

A LITANY FOR THE MINISTRY

To be used at Ordinations as directed; or after the Collects at Morning or Evening Prayer; or separately.

God the Father,
Have mercy on us.

God the Son,
Have mercy on us.

God the Holy Spirit,
Have mercy on us.

Holy Trinity, one God,
Have mercy on us.

We humbly pray that you will hear us, O Lord; and that you will send peace to the whole world, which you have reconciled to yourself by the ministry of your Son, Jesus,
Lord, hear our prayer.

That you will guide all in civil authority to establish justice and maintain it for all men,
Lord, hear our prayer.

That you will heal the divisions of your visible Church, that all may be one,
Lord, hear our prayer.

That you will grant to your People the forgiveness of sins, and give us grace to amend our lives,
Lord, hear our prayer.

That you will lead every member of your Church in his particular vocation and ministry to serve you in a true and godly life,
Lord, hear our prayer.

That you will raise up able ministers for your Church, that the Gospel may be made known to all people,
Lord, hear our prayer.

That you will inspire all Bishops, Priests, and Deacons with your love, that they may hunger for truth, and thirst after righteousness,
Lord, hear our prayer.

That you will fill them with compassion, and move them to care for all your people,
Lord, hear our prayer.

At the ordination of a bishop the following is said:

That you will bless our brother *N.*, elected bishop in your Church, and pour your grace upon him, that he

may faithfully fulfill the duties of this Ministry, build up your Church, and glorify your Name,
> *Lord, hear our prayer.*

At the ordination of deacons or of priests is said:

That you will bless your servant(s), *N.* (*N.*), now to be admitted to the Order of Deacons (*or* Priests), and pour your grace upon *him,* that *he* may faithfully fulfill the duties of this Ministry, build up your Church, and glorify your Name,
> *Lord, hear our prayer.*

As appropriate, the following suffrage is added, adapted when necessary.

That you will bless his *family* [the members of his household *or* community], and adorn them with all Christian virtues,
> *Lord, hear our prayer.*

That by the indwelling of your Holy Spirit you will sustain those who have been called to the ministry of your Church, and encourage them to persevere to the end,
> *Lord, hear our prayer.*

That we, with [your blessed servant, St. ―――――, and] all your saints who have served you in the past, may be gathered into your unending kingdom,
> *Lord, hear our prayer.*

Lord, have mercy.

Christ, have mercy.

Lord, have mercy.

The Bishop stands and says

The Lord be with you.

Answer **And also with you.**

Bishop **Let us pray.**

The Bishop says the appointed Collect.

The Litany Noted for Chant

God the Fa-ther, *Have mer-cy on us.*

God the Son, *Have mer-cy on us.*

God the Ho-ly Spir-it, *Have mer-cy on us.*

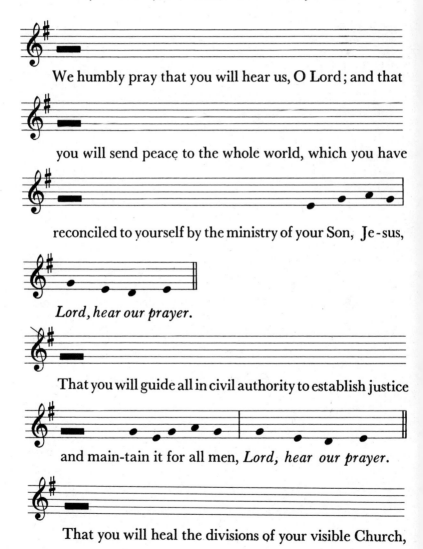

Ho-ly Trin-i-ty, one God, *Have mer-cy on us.*

We humbly pray that you will hear us, O Lord; and that

you will send peace to the whole world, which you have

reconciled to yourself by the ministry of your Son, Je-sus,

Lord, hear our prayer.

That you will guide all in civil authority to establish justice

and main-tain it for all men, *Lord, hear our prayer.*

That you will heal the divisions of your visible Church,

that all may be one, *Lord, hear our prayer.*

That you will grant to your People the forgiveness of sins,

and give us grace to a-mend our lives, *Lord, hear our prayer.*

That you will lead every member of your Church in his

particular vocation and ministry to serve you in a true and

god-ly life, *Lord, hear our prayer.*

That you will raise up able ministers for your Church,

that the Gospel may be made known to all peo-ple.

Lord, hear our prayer. That you will inspire all Bishops,

Priests, and Deacons with your love, that they may hunger

for truth, and thirst af-ter right - eous - ness.

Lord, hear our prayer.

That you will fill them with compassion, and move them to

care for all your peo-ple, *Lord, hear our prayer.*

At the ordination of a bishop the following is sung:

That you will bless our brother N., elected bishop in your

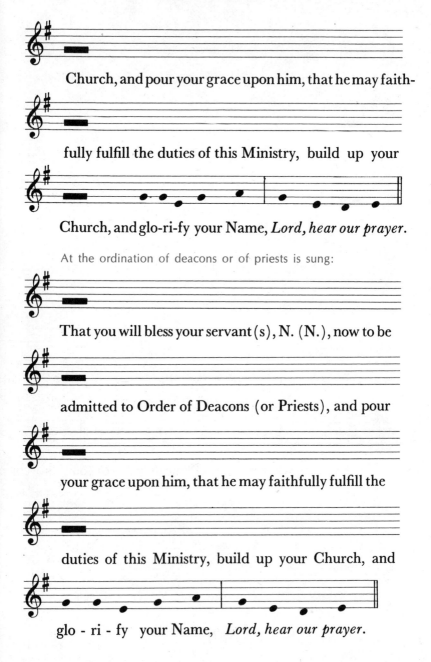

Church, and pour your grace upon him, that he may faith-

fully fulfill the duties of this Ministry, build up your

Church, and glo-ri-fy your Name, *Lord, hear our prayer.*

At the ordination of deacons or of priests is sung:

That you will bless your servant(s), N. (N.), now to be

admitted to Order of Deacons (or Priests), and pour

your grace upon him, that he may faithfully fulfill the

duties of this Ministry, build up your Church, and

glo - ri - fy your Name, *Lord, hear our prayer.*

As appropriate, the following suffrage is added,
adapted when necessary:

That you will bless { his family,
{ the members of his household

(community), and adorn them with all Christ-ian vir-tues,

Lord, hear our prayer.

That by the indwelling of your Holy Spirit you will sustain

those who have been called to the ministry of your Church,

and encourage them to per-se-vere to the end,

Lord, hear our prayer.   That we, with (your blessed

servant, St. _____, and) all your saints who have served

you in the past, may be gathered into your un-end-ing

king-dom, Lord, hear our prayer.

Lord, have mer-cy, Christ, have mer-cy. Lord, have mer-cy.

The Bishop stands and says:

The Lord be with you. *And also with you.* Let us pray.

The Bishop says the appointed Collect.

If he sings the Collect to the usual tone, the Conclusion is as follows:

... the Ho-ly Spir-it,   one God, now and ever. *A-men.*

THE PROPER

Of the Sundays and Other Holy Days
Throughout the Church Year

GENERAL DIRECTIONS

The Psalms or selections from Psalms appointed in the proper are for optional use at any place in the Liturgy where the rubrics allow the use of a Psalm, Hymn, or Anthem. They may be lengthened or shortened, at the discretion of the Minister, and may be used with or without the Gloria Patri.

The first Psalm listed in the proper has been chosen as especially suitable for use at the Entrance of the Ministers; the second one, as especially suitable for use between the Lessons.

Three Lessons have been provided in each set of proper. According to the rubrics of the Liturgy, the Minister may use all three Lessons, or he may omit either the first or the second Lesson. The Lesson from the Gospels is always read.

Year C of the three-year cycle of Lessons begins on the First Sunday in Advent, 1970.

The Proper Preface appointed with each set of proper is to be used according to the rubrics of the Liturgy. But the Priest may, at his discretion, omit the Proper Preface indicated in "The Common of Saints" and "Special Occasions," or use the Proper Preface of the Season.

In each proper, two forms of the Collect are given: The first is always in contemporary language, the second is in traditional wording.

THE FIRST SUNDAY IN ADVENT

THE COLLECT

ALMIGHTY GOD, give us grace to cast away the works of darkness, and put on the armor of light, now in the time of this mortal life, in which your Son Jesus Christ came to visit us in great humility; that in the last day, when he shall come again in his glorious majesty to judge the living and the dead, we may rise to the life immortal, through him who lives and reigns with you and the Holy Spirit, one God, now and ever. *Amen.*

ALMIGHTY GOD, give us grace to cast away the works of darkness, and put on us the armor of light, now in the time of this mortal life, in which thy Son Jesus Christ came to visit us in great humility; that in the last day, when he shall come again in his glorious majesty to judge both the living and the dead, we may rise to the life immortal, through him who liveth and reigneth with thee and the Holy Spirit, one God, now and ever. *Amen.*

THE PSALMS

50:1–6
25:1–6

THE LESSONS

A Isaiah 2:1–5
  Romans 13:11–14
  Matthew 24:37–44

B Isaiah 63:16b–64:8
  1 Corinthians 1:3–9
  Mark 13:33–37

C Jeremiah 33:14–16
  1 Thessalonians 3:9–13
  Luke 21:25–31

PROPER PREFACE OF ADVENT

THE SECOND SUNDAY IN ADVENT

THE COLLECT

MERCIFUL GOD, who sent your messengers the prophets, to preach repentance and prepare the way for our salvation: Give us grace to heed their warning and forsake our sins, that we may greet with joy the coming of our Redeemer, Jesus Christ our Lord, who lives and reigns with you and the Holy Spirit, one God, now and for ever. *Amen.*

MERCIFUL GOD, who hast sent thy messengers the prophets, to preach repentance and prepare the way for our salvation: Give us grace to heed their warning and forsake our sins, that we may greet with joy the coming of our Redeemer, Jesus Christ our Lord, who liveth and reigneth with thee and the Holy Spirit, one God, now and for ever. *Amen.*

THE PSALMS   80:1–7
                    85:4–9

THE LESSONS

A Isaiah 11:1–10   B Isaiah 40:1–5, 9–11
   Romans 15:4–13   2 Peter 3:8–14
   Matthew 3:1–12   Mark 1:1–8

              C Baruch 5:1–9
                Philippians 1:3–11
                Luke 3:1–6

PROPER PREFACE OF ADVENT

THE THIRD SUNDAY IN ADVENT

The Collect

RAISE UP your mighty power, O Lord, and come; and, because we are hindered and bound by our sins, let your plentiful grace and mercy speedily help and deliver us; through Jesus Christ our Lord, to whom with you and the Holy Spirit be honor and glory, one God, now and for ever. *Amen.*

RAISE UP thy mighty power, O Lord, and come; and, because we are hindered and bound by our sins, let thy plentiful grace and mercy speedily help and deliver us; through Jesus Christ our Lord, to whom with thee and the Holy Spirit be honor and glory, one God, now and for ever. *Amen.*

The Psalms

82
126

The Lessons

A Isaiah 35
   James 5:7–10
   Matthew 11:2–11

B Isaiah 61:1–3, 10–11
   1 Thessalonians 5:16–24
   John 1:6–8, 19–28

C Zephaniah 3:14–18a
  Philippians 4:4–7
  Luke 3:7–18

Proper Preface of Advent

THE FOURTH SUNDAY IN ADVENT

THE COLLECT

MIGHTY LORD, cleanse our consciences, we pray, and bring light to the darkness of our hearts by the visitation of our Savior Jesus Christ; that when he comes, he may find in us a mansion prepared for himself, who now lives and reigns with you in the unity of the Holy Spirit, one God, for ever and ever. *Amen.*

MIGHTY LORD, we beseech thee to cleanse our consciences, and bring light to the darkness of our hearts by the visitation of our Savior Jesus Christ; that when he comes, he may find in us a mansion prepared for himself, who now liveth and reigneth with thee in the unity of the Holy Spirit, one God, for ever and ever. *Amen.*

THE PSALMS 132:8–15
146:4–10

THE LESSONS

A Isaiah 7:10–14
Romans 9:1–5
Matthew 1:18–25

B 2 Samuel 7:1–5, 8b–11, 16
Romans 16:25–27
Luke 1:26–38

C Micah 5:2–5a
Hebrews 10:5–10
Luke 1:39–49

PROPER PREFACE OF ADVENT

THE NATIVITY OF OUR LORD JESUS CHRIST OR CHRISTMAS DAY

DECEMBER 25

When there is more than one celebration of the Liturgy on this day, any of the collects and lessons appointed may be used, at the discretion of the Priest; but the Gospel lesson from John 1:1–14 shall be read at one of them at least.

THE COLLECT

O GOD, in our joyful remembrance of the birth of your only Son Jesus Christ, grant us to receive him so faithfully as our Redeemer, that we may with sure confidence behold him when he shall come to be our Judge, who lives and reigns with you and the Holy Spirit, one God, now and for ever. *Amen.*

O GOD, who makest us glad with the yearly remembrance of the birth of thine only Son Jesus Christ: Grant that as we joyfully receive him for our Redeemer, so we may with sure confidence behold him when he shall come to be our Judge, who liveth and reigneth with thee and the Holy Spirit, one God, now and for ever. *Amen.*

THE PSALMS	19:1–6
	89:1–4, 27–30
THE LESSONS	Isaiah 9:2–4, 6–7
	Titus 2:11–14
	Luke 2:1–14

PROPER PREFACE OF CHRISTMAS

A SECOND PROPER FOR CHRISTMAS DAY

THE COLLECT

ALMIGHTY FATHER, by whom the world has been filled with the new light of your beloved Son, the incarnate Word: Grant, we pray, that as he kindles the flame of faith and love in our hearts, so his light may shine forth in our lives, who now lives and reigns with you in the unity of the Holy Spirit, one God, now and for ever. *Amen.*

ALMIGHTY FATHER, who hast filled the world with the new light of thy beloved Son, the incarnate Word: Grant, we beseech thee, that as he enkindles the flame of faith and love in our hearts, so his light may shine forth in our lives, the same thy Son, Jesus Christ our Lord, who liveth and reigneth with thee in the unity of the Holy Spirit, one God, now and for ever. *Amen.*

THE PSALMS 96
113

THE LESSONS
Isaiah 62:10–12
Titus 3:4–7
Luke 2:15b–20

PROPER PREFACE OF CHRISTMAS

A THIRD PROPER FOR CHRISTMAS DAY

THE COLLECT

ALMIGHTY GOD, who gave us your only-begotten Son to take our nature upon him, and to be born of a pure virgin: Grant that we, who have been born again in him, and made your children by adoption and grace, may daily be renewed by your Holy Spirit; through our Lord Jesus Christ, to whom with you and the Spirit be all honor and glory, one God, now and for ever. *Amen.*

ALMIGHTY GOD, who hast given us thine only-begotten Son to take our nature upon him, and to be born of a pure virgin: Grant that we, being born again in him and made thy children by adoption and grace, may daily be renewed by thy Holy Spirit; through the same our Lord Jesus Christ, who liveth and reigneth with thee and the same Spirit, one God, now and for ever. *Amen.*

THE PSALMS   98
                    145:1–9

THE LESSONS   Isaiah 52:7–10
                    Hebrews 1:1–6
                    John 1:1–14

PROPER PREFACE OF CHRISTMAS

THE FIRST SUNDAY AFTER CHRISTMAS DAY

THE COLLECT

ALMIGHTY GOD, who revealed in the incarnation of your eternal Word, our Savior Jesus Christ, the source and perfection of all true religion: Grant that we may entrust our lives to him, on whom is built the whole salvation of mankind, and who now lives and reigns with you and the Holy Spirit, one God, in glory evermore. *Amen.*

ALMIGHTY GOD, who hast revealed in the incarnation of thine eternal Word, our Savior Jesus Christ, the source and perfection of all true religion: Grant that we may entrust our lives to him, on whom is built the whole salvation of mankind, the same Jesus Christ our Lord, who now liveth and reigneth with thee and the Holy Spirit, one God, in glory evermore. *Amen.*

| THE PSALMS | 97:1–6 |
| | 97:8–12 |

THE LESSONS	Isaiah 60:13–21
	Galatians 4:4–7
	John 1:1–18

PROPER PREFACE OF CHRISTMAS

THE HOLY NAME
OF OUR LORD JESUS CHRIST

JANUARY 1

THE COLLECT

ETERNAL FATHER, who gave to your incarnate Son the name of Jesus, to be the sign of our salvation: Plant in every heart, we pray, the love of him who is the Savior of the world, and who now lives and reigns with you and the Holy Spirit, one God, in glory everlasting. *Amen.*

ETERNAL FATHER, who didst give to thine incarnate Son the name of Jesus, to be the sign of our salvation: Plant in every heart, we beseech thee, the love of him who is the Savior of the world, even our Lord Jesus Christ, who now liveth and reigneth with thee and the Holy Spirit, one God, in glory everlasting. *Amen.*

THE PSALMS   85:1–3, 10–13
                   8

THE LESSONS   Isaiah 9:2–4, 6–7
                   Romans 1:1–7
                   Luke 2:15–21

PROPER PREFACE OF CHRISTMAS

THE SECOND SUNDAY
AFTER CHRISTMAS DAY

THE COLLECT

O GOD, who wonderfully created us in the dignity of your own image, and yet more wonderfully restored us after the likeness of your Son Jesus Christ: Make us worthy, we pray, to partake of his divine life, who for our sake came to share our human nature, and who now lives and reigns with you in the unity of the Holy Spirit, one God, for ever and ever. *Amen.*

O GOD, who hast wonderfully created us in the dignity of thine own image, and hast yet more wonderfully restored us after the likeness of thy Son Jesus Christ: Make us worthy, we beseech thee, to partake of his divine life, who for our sake came to share our human nature, the same Jesus Christ our Lord, who now liveth and reigneth with thee in the unity of the Holy Spirit, one God, for ever and ever. *Amen.*

THE PSALMS   84:1–7
                  128

THE LESSONS   Isaiah 61:10—62:3
                  Ephesians 1:3–6, 15–18
                  Matthew 2:13–15, 19–23
                    or Luke 2:41–52

PROPER PREFACE OF CHRISTMAS

THE EPIPHANY, OR THE MANIFESTATION OF CHRIST TO THE GENTILES

JANUARY 6

THE COLLECT

O GOD, who guided by a star the wise men of the Gentiles to the worship of your only Son: Lead all peoples of the earth to know him now by faith, and in the world to come to see him in the splendor of his glory, where he lives and reigns with you and the Holy Spirit, one God, now and ever. *Amen.*

O GOD, who by a star didst guide the wise men of the Gentiles to the worship of thine only Son: Lead all the peoples of the earth to know him now by faith, and in the world to come to see him in the splendor of his glory, where he liveth and reigneth with thee and the Holy Spirit, one God, now and ever. *Amen.*

THE PSALMS   72:1–8
                              72:10–17

THE LESSONS   Isaiah 60:1–6
                              Ephesians 3:1–12
                              Matthew 2:1–12

PROPER PREFACE OF EPIPHANY

THE FIRST SUNDAY AFTER THE EPIPHANY, THE BAPTISM OF OUR LORD JESUS CHRIST

THE COLLECT

FATHER IN HEAVEN, who at the baptism of our Savior Jesus Christ declared him to be your beloved Son, and endowed him with the mighty power of the Holy Spirit: Grant that all who are baptized into his Name may be found worthy of their calling to be your adopted sons, and heirs with him of everlasting life, who lives and reigns with you and the Holy Spirit, one God, now and ever. *Amen.*

FATHER IN HEAVEN, who at the baptism of our Savior Jesus Christ didst declare him to be thy beloved Son, and didst endow him with the mighty power of the Holy Spirit: Grant, we beseech thee, that all who are baptized into his Name may be found worthy of their calling to be thine adopted sons, and heirs with him of everlasting life, the same thy Son Jesus Christ our Lord, who liveth and reigneth with thee and the Holy Spirit, one God, now and ever. *Amen.*

THE PSALMS   93
                                       29

THE LESSONS

Isaiah 42:1–7   A Matthew 3:13–17
Acts 10:34–38   B Mark 1:7–11
                                 C Luke 3:15–16, 21–22

PROPER PREFACE OF EPIPHANY

THE SECOND SUNDAY AFTER
THE EPIPHANY

THE COLLECT

O GOD, the giver of all grace: Set us free from the bondage of our sins; and give us, we pray, that abundant life and liberty of sonship which you have made known in your Son our Savior Jesus Christ, who lives and reigns with you in the unity of the Holy Spirit, one God, now and for ever. *Amen.*

O GOD, the giver of all grace: Set us free from the bondage of our sins; and give us, we pray, that abundant life and liberty of sonship which thou hast manifested to us in thy Son our Savior Jesus Christ, who liveth and reigneth with thee in the unity of the Holy Spirit, now and for ever. *Amen.*

THE PSALMS   63:1–8
                    36:5–10

THE LESSONS

A Isaiah 49:1–7   B 1 Samuel 3:1–10
  1 Corinthians 4:9–16   1 Corinthians 6:13b–20
  John 1:29–41   John 1:43–51

      C Isaiah 62:2–5
       1 Corinthians 12:4–11
       John 2:1–12

PROPER PREFACE OF EPIPHANY

THE THIRD SUNDAY
AFTER THE EPIPHANY

THE COLLECT

GIVE US GRACE, heavenly Father, to answer readily the call of our Savior Jesus Christ to follow him in his service, that, in proclaiming to all men the good news of his salvation, we may perceive the glory of his marvelous works; through Jesus Christ our Lord, who lives and reigns with you and the Holy Spirit, one God, for ever and ever. *Amen.*

GIVE US GRACE, heavenly Father, to answer readily the call of our Savior Jesus Christ to follow him in his service, that, in proclaiming to all men the good news of his salvation, we may perceive the glory of his marvelous works; through the same Jesus Christ our Lord, who liveth and reigneth with thee and the Holy Spirit, one God, for ever and ever. *Amen.*

THE PSALMS

84:8–13
65:4–8

THE LESSONS

A Isaiah 9:1–4
  1 Corinthians 1:10–13, 17
  Matthew 4:12–23

B Jonah 3:1–5, 10
  1 Corinthians 7:17–23
  Mark 1:14–20

C Isaiah 61:1–6
  1 Corinthians 12:12–27
  Luke 4:14–21

PROPER PREFACE OF EPIPHANY

486

THE FOURTH SUNDAY
AFTER THE EPIPHANY

BLESSED LORD, who caused all holy Scriptures to be written for our learning: Grant us so to hear them, read, mark, learn, and inwardly digest them, that we may embrace and ever hold fast the hope of everlasting life, which you have given us in our Savior Jesus Christ, who lives and reigns with you and the Holy Spirit, one God, now and ever. *Amen.*

BLESSED LORD, who hast caused all holy Scriptures to be written for our learning: Grant that we may in such wise hear them, read, mark, learn, and inwardly digest them, that by patience and comfort of thy holy Word, we may embrace, and ever hold fast, the blessed hope of everlasting life, which thou hast given us in our Savior Jesus Christ, who liveth and reigneth with thee and the Holy Spirit, one God, now and ever. *Amen.*

THE PSALMS   112:1–7
                                   19:7–14

THE LESSONS

A Zephaniah 3:9–13   B Deuteronomy 18:15–20
  1 Corinthians 1:26–31   1 Corinthians 8:1b–13
  Matthew 5:1–12a   Mark 1:21–28

        C Jeremiah 1:4–10
          1 Corinthians 14:12b–17, 33, 40
         Luke 4:21–30

PROPER PREFACE OF EPIPHANY

THE FIFTH SUNDAY AFTER THE EPIPHANY

THE COLLECT

ALMIGHTY GOD, who gave your Son our Savior Jesus Christ to be the light of the world: Nourish us, your people, by your Word and Sacraments, that we may be strengthened to serve all men with the immeasurable riches of Christ, so that he may be known, worshiped, and obeyed to the ends of the earth; through Jesus Christ our Lord, who lives and reigns with you and the Holy Spirit, one God, now and for ever. *Amen.*

ALMIGHTY GOD, who didst give thy Son our Savior Jesus Christ to be the light of the world: Nourish thy people, we beseech thee, by thy Word and Sacraments, that we may be strengthened to serve all men with the immeasurable riches of Christ, so that he may be known, worshiped, and obeyed to the ends of the earth; through the same Jesus Christ our Lord, who liveth and reigneth with thee and the Holy Spirit, one God, now and for ever. *Amen.*

THE PSALMS   67
                           15

THE LESSONS

A Isaiah 58:8–12   B Zephaniah 3:14–20
     1 Corinthians 2:1–5   1 Corinthians 9:16–23
     Matthew 5:13–24   Mark 1:29–39

               C Isaiah 6:1–8
                  1 Corinthians 15:1–11
                  Luke 5:1–11

PROPER PREFACE OF EPIPHANY

THE SIXTH SUNDAY
AFTER THE EPIPHANY

THE COLLECT

O GOD, the strength of all who put their trust in you: Mercifully accept our prayers; and because, through the weakness of our nature, we can do nothing that is good without you, grant us the help of your grace, that in keeping your commandments we may please you both in will and deed; through Jesus Christ our Lord, who lives and reigns with you and the Holy Spirit, one God, now and for ever. *Amen.*

O GOD, the strength of all those who put their trust in thee: Mercifully accept our prayers; and because, through the weakness of our mortal nature, we can do no good thing without thee, grant us the help of thy grace, that in keeping thy commandments we may please thee both in will and deed; through Jesus Christ our Lord, who liveth and reigneth with thee and the Holy Spirit, one God, now and for ever. *Amen.*

THE PSALMS   33:1–6
                   102:15–22

THE LESSONS

A Ecclesiasticus 15:14–20   B 2 Kings 5:1–14
  1 Corinthians 2:6–10   2 Corinthians 4:16b–18
  Matthew 5:27–37   Mark 1:40–45

          C Jeremiah 17:5–10
            1 Corinthians 15:12, 16–20
            Luke 6:20–26

PROPER PREFACE OF EPIPHANY

THE SEVENTH SUNDAY
AFTER THE EPIPHANY

THE COLLECT

O LORD, who taught us in your holy Word that anything we do without love is worth nothing: Pour into our hearts that most excellent gift of love, the true bond of peace and all virtues, without which whoever lives is counted dead before you. Grant this for the sake of your only Son Jesus Christ, who lives and reigns with you and the Holy Spirit, one God, now and ever. *Amen.*

O LORD, who hast taught us in thy holy Word that all our doings without charity are nothing worth: Send thy Holy Spirit, and pour into our hearts that most excellent gift of charity, the very bond of peace and of all virtues, without which whosoever liveth is counted dead before thee. Grant this for thine only Son Jesus Christ's sake, who liveth and reigneth with thee and the same Spirit, one God, now and ever. *Amen.*

THE PSALMS   103:1–6

                      37:4–9

THE LESSONS

A Leviticus 19:1–2, 15–18   B Isaiah 43:18–19, 22,
  1 Corinthians 3:16–23   24b–25
  Matthew 5:38–48   2 Corinthians 1:18–22
                               Mark 2:1–12

            C Genesis 45:1–7
            1 Corinthians 15:44b–49
            Luke 6:27–38

PROPER PREFACE OF EPIPHANY

490

THE EIGHTH SUNDAY
AFTER THE EPIPHANY

The Collect

Most loving Father, whose will it is for us to cast all our care on you, who care for us: Preserve us from faithless fears and worldly anxieties, that no clouds of this mortal life may hide from us the light of that love which you have made known to us in your Son, Jesus Christ our Lord, who lives and reigns with you in the unity of the Holy Spirit, one God, now and ever. *Amen.*

Most loving Father, who willest us to cast all our care on thee, who carest for us: Preserve us from faithless fears and worldly anxieties, and grant that no clouds of this mortal life may hide from us the light of that love which thou hast manifested unto us in thy Son, Jesus Christ our Lord, who liveth and reigneth with thee in the unity of the Holy Spirit, one God, now and ever. *Amen.*

The Psalms

34:11–19
37:23–28

The Lessons

A Isaiah 49:13–15
　1 Corinthians 4:1–5
　Matthew 6:24–34

B Hosea 2:14–23
　2 Corinthians 3:17—4:2
　Mark 2:18–22

C Isaiah 55:10–13
　1 Corinthians 15:54–58
　Luke 6:39–45

Proper Preface of Epiphany

THE LAST SUNDAY
AFTER THE EPIPHANY

The proper for this Sunday is always to be used on the Sunday before the beginning of Lent on Ash Wednesday, whether the Sundays
after the Epiphany be four or more in number.

THE COLLECT

O GOD, who before the passion of your only-begotten Son
revealed his glory upon the holy mountain: Grant to us
your servants that, in faith beholding the light of his countenance, we may be strengthened to bear the cross, and be
changed into his likeness from glory to glory; through Jesus
Christ your Son our Lord, who lives and reigns with you
and the Holy Spirit, one God, for ever and ever. *Amen.*

O GOD, who before the passion of thine only-begotten Son
didst reveal his glory upon the holy mount: Grant unto us
thy servants that, in faith beholding the light of his countenance, we may be strengthened to bear the cross, and be
changed into his likeness from glory to glory; through the
same thy Son Jesus Christ our Lord, who liveth and reigneth with thee and the Holy Spirit, one God, for ever and
ever. *Amen.*

THE PSALMS

99
27:1–7

THE LESSONS

A Exodus 24:12, 15–18
  1 Corinthians 12:31—13:13
  Matthew 17:1–9

B 1 Kings 19:4–12
  2 Corinthians 4:3–6
  Mark 9:2–9

C Deuteronomy 8:1–3, 5–6
  Philippians 3:7–15
  Luke 9:28–36

PROPER PREFACE OF EPIPHANY

THE FIRST DAY OF LENT, OR ASH WEDNESDAY

On this day, the Liturgy begins with the Collect of the Day, the Minister first saying

The Lord be with you.

Answer   **And also with you.**

Minister   **Let us pray.**

THE COLLECT

ALMIGHTY AND EVERLASTING GOD, who hate nothing that you have made, and forgive the sins of all who are penitent, create and make in us new and contrite hearts, that we, worthily lamenting our sins and acknowledging our wretchedness, may obtain of you, God of all mercy, perfect forgiveness and peace; through Jesus Christ our Lord. *Amen.*

ALMIGHTY AND EVERLASTING GOD, who hatest nothing that thou hast made, and dost forgive the sins of all those who are penitent: Create and make in us new and contrite hearts, that we, worthily lamenting our sins, and acknowledging our wretchedness, may obtain of thee, the God of all mercy, perfect forgiveness and peace; through Jesus Christ our Lord. *Amen.*

THE PSALMS   86:1–7
103:8–14

THE LESSONS   Joel 2:12–19
2 Corinthians 5:20b—6:10
Matthew 6:1–6, 16–21

493

After the Sermon, all stand, and the Priest or Minister appointed invites the People to the observance of a Holy Lent, saying

DEAR PEOPLE OF GOD: The first Christians observed with great devotion the days of our Lord's Passion and Resurrection; and it became the custom of the Church to prepare for them by a season of penitence and fasting. This season of Lent provided a time in which converts to the faith were prepared for holy Baptism. It was also a time when those who, because of notorious sins, had been separated from the body of the faithful were reconciled by penitence and forgiveness, and restored to the fellowship of the Church. Thereby the whole congregation was put in mind of the message of pardon and absolution set forth in the gospel of our Savior, and of the need which all Christians continually have to renew their repentance and faith.

I invite you, therefore, in the name of the Church, to the observance of a holy Lent, by self-examination and repentance; by prayer, fasting, and self-denial; and by reading and meditating on God's holy Word. And, to make a right beginning of repentance and as a mark of our mortal nature, let us now kneel before the Lord, our Maker and Redeemer.

Silence is then kept for a time, all kneeling, after which the Minister may say

> Remember, O man, that dust you are,
>   and to dust shall you return.

The following Psalm is then sung or said [PSALM 51:1–18]:

Have mercy on me, O God,
according to your loving-kindness;
    in your great compassion blot out my offences.

Wash me through and through from my wickedness,
and cleanse me from my sin.

For I know my transgressions only too well,
and my sin is ever before me.

Against you only have I sinned,
and done what is evil in your sight.

And so you are justified when you speak,
and upright in your judgment.

Indeed, I have been wicked from my birth,
a sinner from my mother's womb.

For behold, you look for truth in the inward parts,
and shall make me understand wisdom secretly.

Take away my sin, and I shall be pure;
wash me, and I shall be cleaner than snow.

Make me hear of joy and gladness,
that the body you have broken may rejoice.

Hide your face from my sins,
and blot out all my iniquities.

Create in me a clean heart, O God,
and renew a right spirit within me.

Cast me not away from your presence,
and take not your holy Spirit from me.

Give me the joy of your saving help again,
and sustain me with your bountiful spirit.

I shall teach your ways to the wicked,
    and sinners shall return unto you.

Deliver me from death, O God,
    and my tongue shall sing of your righteousness,
    O God of my salvation.

Open my lips, O Lord,
    and my mouth shall show forth your praise.

Had you desired it, I would have offered sacrifice;
    but you take no delight in burnt-offerings.

The sacrifice of God is a troubled spirit;
    a broken and contrite heart, O God, you will not despise.

The Minister then leads the People, all kneeling, in the following

LITANY OF PENITENCE

All say together

Most holy and merciful Father:
We confess to you and to one another,
    and to the whole communion of saints
    in heaven and earth,
    that we have sinned in thought, word, and deed,
    by what we have done, and by what we have left undone.

Minister

We have not loved you with our whole heart
and mind and strength;
    We have not loved our neighbors as ourselves;
    We have not forgiven others, as we have been forgiven.
                    Have mercy on us, Lord.

We have been deaf to your call to serve, as Christ served us;
  We have not had in us the mind of Christ;
  We have grieved your Holy Spirit.
          Have mercy on us, Lord.

We confess to you, Lord, all our past unfaithfulness:
  The pride, hypocrisy, and impatience of our lives,
          We confess to you, Lord.

  Our negligence in prayer and worship, and our failure
  to commend the faith that is in us,
          We confess to you, Lord.

  Our dishonesty in daily life and work, and our intemperate love of worldly goods and comforts,
          We confess to you, Lord.

Accept our repentance, Lord, for the wrongs we have done
to our fellow men:
  For our blindness to human need and suffering, and our
  indifference to injustice and cruelty,
          Accept our repentance, Lord.

  For all false judgments, and uncharitable thoughts toward our neighbors, and for our prejudice and contempt
  toward those who differ from us,
          Accept our repentance, Lord.

  For our waste and pollution of your creation, and our lack
  of concern for those who come after us,
          Accept our repentance, Lord.

Restore us, good Lord, and let your anger depart from us.
  Favorably hear us, for your mercy is great.
Accomplish in us the work of your salvation,
  That we may show forth your glory in the world.

By the cross and passion of your Son our Lord,
Bring us and all men to the joy of his resurrection.

The Minister then says

MAY THE ALMIGHTY and merciful God, the Father of our Lord Jesus Christ, who desires not the death of sinners, but rather that we turn from our wickedness and live, accept our repentance, forgive us our sins, and restore us by his Holy Spirit to newness of life. *Amen.*

The Ministers and People then exchange the Peace.

In the absence of a Priest or Deacon, all that precedes may be led by a Lay Reader.

When Communion follows, the service continues with the Offertory.

PROPER PREFACE OF LENT

Note: The Litany of Penitence may be used at other times and may be preceded by an appropriate invitation and a penitential Psalm.

THE FIRST SUNDAY IN LENT

THE COLLECT

ALMIGHTY GOD, whose blessed Son our Savior was in every way tempted as we are, yet did not sin: Strengthen us, we pray, to withstand the assaults of our many temptations; and as you know our weaknesses, so may we find you mighty to save; through Jesus Christ your Son our Lord, who lives and reigns with you and the Holy Spirit, one God, now and for ever. *Amen.*

ALMIGHTY GOD, whose blessed Son our Savior was in every way tempted as we are, yet did not sin: Strengthen us, we pray, to withstand the assaults of our manifold temptations; and, as thou knowest our weaknesses, so may we find thee mighty to save; through the same Jesus Christ thy Son our Lord, who liveth and reigneth with thee and the Holy Spirit, one God, now and for ever. *Amen.*

THE PSALMS   91:1–8
                    91:9–16

THE LESSONS

A Genesis 2:7–9, 15–17; 3:1–7a B Genesis 22:1–14
   Romans 5:12–19   Romans 4:2–3, 20–25
   Matthew 4:1–11   Mark 1:9–13

                 C Deuteronomy 26:5–10
                   James 1:12–18
                   Luke 4:1–13

PROPER PREFACE OF LENT

499

THE SECOND SUNDAY IN LENT

THE COLLECT

HEAVENLY FATHER, whose glory it is always to have mercy: Be gracious, we pray, to all who have erred and gone astray from your holy Word, and bring them again in steadfast faith, to receive and hold fast your unchangeable truth; through Jesus Christ our Lord, who lives and reigns with you and the Holy Spirit, one God, now and for ever. *Amen.*

HEAVENLY FATHER, whose glory it is always to have mercy: Be gracious, we beseech thee, to all who have erred and gone astray from thy holy Word, and bring them again in steadfast faith, to receive and hold fast thine unchangeable truth; through Jesus Christ our Lord, who liveth and reigneth with thee and the Holy Spirit, one God, now and for ever. *Amen.*

THE PSALMS

25:5–10
42:1–7

THE LESSONS

A Genesis 12:1–8
  Romans 5:1–10
  John 4:5–26

B Genesis 28:11–17
  Romans 10:8–13
  John 2:13–22

C Ezekiel 36:22–28
  1 Corinthians 10:1–13
  Mark 10:32–45

PROPER PREFACE OF LENT

THE THIRD SUNDAY IN LENT

THE COLLECT

ALMIGHTY GOD, since we have no power of ourselves to help ourselves, keep us, we pray, both outwardly in our bodies and inwardly in our souls, that we may be defended from all adversities which may happen to the body, and from all evil thoughts which may assault and hurt the soul; through Jesus Christ our Lord, who lives and reigns with you in the unity of the Holy Spirit, one God, for ever and ever. *Amen.*

ALMIGHTY GOD, who seest that we have no power of ourselves to help ourselves: Keep us both outwardly in our bodies, and inwardly in our souls; that we may be defended from all adversities which may happen to the body, and from all evil thoughts which may assault and hurt the soul; through Jesus Christ our Lord, who liveth and reigneth with thee in the unity of the Holy Spirit, one God, for ever and ever. *Amen.*

THE PSALMS   27:8–16
                           25:14–21

THE LESSONS

A Deuteronomy 5:1, 6–21   B Exodus 3:1–8b, 10–15
  Romans 8:1–10   Ephesians 5:8–14
  John 9:1–13, 24–28   John 3:14–21

                    C 1 Samuel 16:1–13
                      2 Corinthians 5:17–21
                      Luke 13:1–9

PROPER PREFACE OF LENT

501

THE FOURTH SUNDAY IN LENT

THE COLLECT

GRACIOUS FATHER, whose blessed Son came down from heaven to be the true bread of life for the world: Feed us continually, we pray, with this bread, that he may evermore live in us, and we in him, our Savior Jesus Christ, who lives and reigns with you and the Holy Spirit, one God, now and for ever. *Amen.*

GRACIOUS FATHER, whose blessed Son came down from heaven to be the true bread of life for the world: Feed us continually, we beseech thee, with this bread; that he may evermore live in us, and we in him, even our Savior Jesus Christ, who liveth and reigneth with thee and the Holy Spirit, one God, now and for ever. *Amen.*

THE PSALMS   34:1–10
                    145:15–21

THE LESSONS

A Deuteronomy 8:7–18   B Exodus 16:2–8, 13–15
   Romans 8:11–19   Galatians 4:26—5:1
   John 6:4–15   Mark 8:12–21

            C Isaiah 12
              Ephesians 2:4–10
              Luke 15:11–32

PROPER PREFACE OF LENT

THE FIFTH SUNDAY IN LENT

THE COLLECT

ALMIGHTY GOD, who alone can order the unruly wills and affections of sinful men: Grant your people grace to love what you command and desire what you promise; that among the swift and varied changes of the world, our hearts may surely there be fixed, where true joys are to be found; through Jesus Christ our Lord, who lives and reigns with you and the Holy Spirit, one God, now and for ever. *Amen.*

ALMIGHTY GOD, who alone canst order the unruly wills and affections of sinful men: Grant unto thy people, that they may love the thing which thou commandest, and desire that which thou dost promise; that so, among the sundry and manifold changes of the world, our hearts may surely there be fixed, where true joys are to be found; through Jesus Christ our Lord, who liveth and reigneth with thee and the Holy Spirit, one God, now and for ever. *Amen.*

THE PSALMS   142
                     28:1–3, 7–10

THE LESSONS

A Ezekiel 37:1–3, 11–14   B Jeremiah 31:31–34
   Romans 8:31b–39   Hebrews 5:5–9
   John 11:18–44   John 12:20–33

                 C Isaiah 43:16–21
                    Philippians 2:12–15
                    Mark 12:1–11

PROPER PREFACE OF LENT

503

THE SUNDAY OF THE PASSION
OR PALM SUNDAY

AT THE BLESSING OF PALMS AND PROCESSION

The branches of palm or of other trees to be carried in the Procession may be distributed to the People immediately after the Prayer of Blessing, or before the Service.

The following Anthem is sung or said, the People standing:

Blessed is the King who comes in the name of the Lord.
Peace in heaven and glory in the highest.

THE COLLECT

Minister **Let us pray.**

ASSIST US mercifully with *your* help, O Lord God of our salvation, that we may enter with joy upon the meditation of those mighty acts, whereby *you have* given us eternal life; through Jesus Christ our Lord. *Amen.*

Here may be read one of the following lessons:

> Matthew 21:1–11
> Mark 11:1–11a
> Luke 19:29–40

When it is desired to ask God's blessing on the branches to be carried in the Procession, the following form may be used:

Minister **Let us give thanks to the Lord our God.**
Answer **It is right to give him thanks and praise.**

Minister

We praise *you,* almighty and everlasting God, whose Son our Savior Jesus Christ before his passion entered the holy city of Jerusalem, and was triumphantly acclaimed as King by those who spread their garments and branches of palm along his way. Bless, we pray, these branches, and those who bear them in his Name, and grant that we may ever hail him as our King, and follow him in the way that leads to eternal life, who *lives* and *reigns* in glory with *you* and the Holy Spirit, one God, now and for ever. *Amen.*

The following anthem may be sung or said at the distribution of the branches.

Blessed is he who comes in the name of the Lord: *Hosanna in the highest.*

The Procession

Minister   Let us go forth in peace.

People   In the name of Christ. *Amen.*

During the Procession, appropriate Hymns, Psalms, or Anthems are sung, such as the Hymn "All glory, laud, and honor" and Psalm 118:19–29.

The following Collect may be said, either in the course of the Procession, or at its conclusion.

ALMIGHTY GOD, who showed us in your Son the true way of blessedness: Give us grace to take up our cross and follow him, in the strength of patience and in constancy of faith; and grant us such fellowship with him in his suffering, that we may know the secret of his strength and peace; who now *lives* and *reigns* with *you* in the unity of the Holy Spirit, one God, for ever and ever. *Amen.*

In the absence of a Priest or Deacon, the preceding Service may be led by a Lay Reader.

When the Blessing of Palms and Procession immediately precede the celebration of the Holy Eucharist, the Liturgy begins at once with the Salutation and Collect of the Day.

THE COLLECT

ALMIGHTY AND EVERLIVING GOD, who of your tender love towards mankind sent your Son, our Savior Jesus Christ, to take upon him our nature, and to suffer death upon the cross, that all should follow the example of his great humility: Mercifully grant that we may follow the example of his patience, and become partakers of his resurrection; through Jesus Christ our Lord, who lives and reigns with you and the Holy Spirit, one God, for ever and ever. *Amen.*

ALMIGHTY AND EVERLASTING GOD, who, of thy tender love towards mankind, hast sent thy Son our Savior Jesus Christ, to take upon him our flesh, and to suffer death upon the cross, that all mankind should follow the example of his great humility: Mercifully grant, that we may both follow the example of his patience, and also may be made partakers of his resurrection; through the same Jesus Christ our Lord, who liveth and reigneth with thee and the Holy Spirit, one God, for ever and ever. *Amen.*

THE PSALMS   118:19–29
                    22:23–28

THE LESSONS   Zechariah 9:9–12
                    Philippians 2:5–11

For the Gospel, the Minister or Ministers appointed read

The passion of our Lord Jesus Christ according to _____.

A Matthew 26:36—27:54

B Mark 14:32—15:39

C Luke 22:39—23:49

When desired, the Passion Gospel may be read or chanted by lay persons.

PROPER PREFACE OF HOLY WEEK

MONDAY IN HOLY WEEK

THE COLLECT

ALMIGHTY GOD, whose most dear Son went not up to joy but first he suffered pain, and entered not into glory before he was crucified: Mercifully grant that we, walking in the way of the cross, may find it none other than the way of life and peace; through Jesus Christ your Son our Lord. *Amen.*

ALMIGHTY GOD, whose most dear Son went not up to joy but first he suffered pain, and entered not into glory before he was crucified: Mercifully grant that we, walking in the way of the cross, may find it none other than the way of life and peace; through Jesus Christ thy Son our Lord. *Amen.*

THE PSALMS 55:1–8
56:1–11

THE LESSONS Isaiah 42:1–7
Hebrews 11:39—12:3
John 12:1–11,
or Mark 14:3–9

PROPER PREFACE OF HOLY WEEK

508

TUESDAY IN HOLY WEEK

THE COLLECT

O GOD, who in the passion of your blessed Son made an instrument of shameful death to be to us the sign of life: Grant us so to glory in the cross of Christ that we may gladly suffer shame and loss for the sake of his Name, your Son our Savior Jesus Christ. *Amen.*

O GOD, who in the passion of thy blessed Son didst make an instrument of shameful death to be unto us the sign of life: Grant us so to glory in the cross of Christ, that we may gladly suffer shame and loss for the sake of his Name, even thy Son our Savior Jesus Christ. *Amen.*

THE PSALMS   59:1–4, 8–9
                   60:1–5

THE LESSONS   Isaiah 49:1–9a
                   1 Corinthians 1:18–31
                   John 12:37–38, 42–50

PROPER PREFACE OF HOLY WEEK

WEDNESDAY IN HOLY WEEK

THE COLLECT

LORD GOD, whose blessed Son our Savior gave his back to the smiters and hid not his face from shame: Give us grace to take joyfully the sufferings of the present time, in full assurance of the glory that shall be revealed; through Jesus Christ your Son our Lord. *Amen.*

LORD GOD, whose blessed Son our Savior gave his back to the smiters and hid not his face from shame: Give us grace to take joyfully the sufferings of the present time, in full assurance of the glory that shall be revealed; through Jesus Christ thy Son our Lord. *Amen.*

THE PSALMS   61:1–5, 8
                       62:1–8

THE LESSONS   Isaiah 50:4–9a
                       Hebrews 9:11–15, 24–28
                       John 13:21–35,
                          or Matthew 26:1–5, 14–25

PROPER PREFACE OF HOLY WEEK

510

MAUNDY THURSDAY

The Collect

ALMIGHTY FATHER, whose dear Son, on the night before he suffered, instituted the Sacrament of his Body and Blood: Mercifully grant that we may thankfully receive it in remembrance of him, who in these holy mysteries gives us a pledge of life eternal, even Jesus Christ your Son our Lord, who lives and reigns with you and the Holy Spirit, one God, now and for ever. *Amen.*

ALMIGHTY FATHER, whose dear Son, on the night before he suffered, didst institute the Sacrament of his Body and Blood: Mercifully grant that we may thankfully receive the same in remembrance of him, who in these holy mysteries giveth us a pledge of life eternal; the same thy Son Jesus Christ our Lord, who liveth and reigneth with thee and the Holy Spirit, one God, now and for ever. *Amen.*

The Psalms	43
	78:14–21, 24–26

The Lessons	Exodus 12:1–14a
	1 Corinthians 11:23–26
	John 13:1–15,
	or Luke 22:14–30

PROPER PREFACE OF HOLY WEEK

GOOD FRIDAY

On this day, the Liturgy begins with the Collect of the Day, the Minister first saying

> The Lord be with you.

Answer   **And also with you.**

Minister   **Let us pray.**

THE COLLECT

ALMIGHTY GOD, we pray you graciously to behold this your family, for whom our Lord Jesus Christ was content to be betrayed, and given up into the hands of sinful men, and to suffer death upon the Cross; who now lives and reigns with you and the Holy Spirit, one God, for ever and ever. *Amen.*

ALMIGHTY GOD, we beseech thee graciously to behold this thy family, for which our Lord Jesus Christ was contented to be betrayed, and given up into the hands of wicked men, and to suffer death upon the Cross; who now liveth and reigneth with thee and the Holy Spirit, one God, for ever and ever. *Amen.*

THE PSALMS   22:1–11, *or* 1–19
                         69:1–9, 13–22

THE LESSONS   Isaiah 52:13—53:12
                         Hebrews 10:1–25

For the Gospel, the Minister or Ministers appointed read

The Passion of our Lord Jesus Christ according to John.

> John 18:1—19:37, *or* 19:1–37

When desired, the Passion Gospel may be read or chanted by lay persons.

After the Sermon, the Nicene Creed may be said.

Then, all standing, the Priest or Minister appointed says to the People

DEAR PEOPLE OF GOD: Our heavenly Father sent his Son into the world, not to condemn the world, but that the world through him might be saved; that all who believe in him might be delivered from the power of sin and death, and become heirs with him of everlasting life.

We pray, therefore, for all men according to their needs, and for the people of God in every place.

In the biddings which follow, the indented petitions may be adapted by addition or omission, as appropriate, at the discretion of the Minister. The People stand or kneel.

LET US PRAY for the holy Catholic Church of Christ throughout the world; especially,

> For its unity in witness and service
> For all Bishops and other Ministers
>   and the people whom they serve
> For N., our Bishop, and all the people of this Diocese
> For all Christians in this community
> For those preparing to be baptized (particularly, ...)

that God will confirm his Church in faith, increase it in love, and preserve it in peace.

SILENCE

Almighty and everlasting God, by whose Spirit the whole company of your faithful people is governed and sanctified: Receive our prayers which we now offer before you for all members of your holy Church, that in their vocation and ministry they may truly and devoutly serve you, to the glory of your Name; through our Lord and Savior Jesus Christ. *Amen.*

Almighty and everlasting God, by whose Spirit the whole body of the Church is governed and sanctified: Receive our supplications and prayers, which we offer before thee for all members of thy holy Church, that every member of the same, in his vocation and ministry, may truly and godly serve thee; through our Lord and Savior Jesus Christ. *Amen.*

LET US PRAY for all nations and peoples of the earth, and for those in authority among them; especially,

For *N.,* the President of the United States
For the Congress and the Supreme Court
For the Members and representatives of the United Nations
For all who serve the common good of men

that by God's help they may seek justice and truth, and live in peace and concord.

Almighty God, from whom all thoughts of truth and peace proceed: We pray you to kindle in the hearts of all men the true love of peace; and guide with your pure and peaceable wisdom those who take counsel for the nations of the earth, that in tranquillity your kingdom may go forward, until the earth is filled with the knowledge of your love; through Jesus Christ our Lord. *Amen.*

Almighty God, from whom all thoughts of truth and peace proceed: Kindle, we pray thee, in the hearts of all men the true love of peace; and guide with thy pure and peaceable wisdom those who take counsel for the nations of the earth; that in tranquillity thy kingdom may go forward, till the earth is filled with the knowledge of thy love; through Jesus Christ our Lord. *Amen.*

Lᴇᴛ ᴜs ᴘʀᴀʏ for all who suffer, and are afflicted in body or in mind; especially,

For the hungry and the homeless, the destitute and the oppressed
For the sick, the wounded, and the crippled
For those in loneliness, fear, and anguish
For those who face temptation, doubt, and despair
For prisoners and captives, and those in mortal danger
For the sorrowful and bereaved

that God in his mercy will comfort and relieve them, and grant them the knowledge of his love, and stir up in us the will and patience to minister to their needs.

SILENCE

Gracious God, you see all the suffering, injustice, and misery which abound in this world. We implore you to look mercifully upon the poor, the oppressed, and all who are burdened with pain and sorrow. Fill our hearts with your compassion, and give us strength to serve them in their need, for the sake of him who suffered for us, our Savior Jesus Christ. *Amen.*

Gracious God, who seest all the suffering, injustice, and misery which abound in this world: We beseech thee to look mercifully upon the poor, the oppressed, and all who are burdened with pain and sorrow. Fill our hearts with thy compassion, and give us strength to serve them in their need, for the sake of him who suffered for us, our Savior Jesus Christ. *Amen.*

LET US PRAY for all who, whether in ignorance or in disbelief, have not received the gospel of Christ; especially,

> For those who have never heard the word of Christ
> For those who have lost their faith
> For those hardened by sin or indifference
> For the contemptuous and the scornful
> For those who are enemies of the Cross of Christ, and persecutors of his disciples

that God will open their hearts to the truth, and lead them to faith and obedience.

SILENCE

Merciful God, who made all men and hate nothing that you have made; nor do you desire the death of a sinner, but rather that he should be converted and live: Have mercy upon all who know you not as you are revealed in the Gospel of your Son. Take from them all ignorance, hardness of heart, and contempt of your Word. Bring all men home, good Lord, to your fold, so that they may be one flock under the one shepherd, your Son Jesus Christ our Lord. *Amen.*

Merciful God, who hast made all men, and hatest nothing that thou hast made, nor desirest the death of a sinner, but rather that he should be converted and live: Have mercy upon all who know thee not as thou art revealed in the Gospel of thy Son. Take from them all ignorance, hardness of heart, and contempt of thy Word; and so bring them home, blessed Lord, to thy fold, that they may be made one flock under one shepherd, Jesus Christ our Lord. *Amen.*

LET US COMMIT ourselves to our God, and pray for the grace of a holy life, that, with all who have departed this world and have died in the faith, we may be accounted worthy to enter into the fullness of the joy of our Lord, and receive the crown of life in the day of resurrection.

SILENCE

O God of unchangeable power and eternal light: Look favorably on your whole Church, that wonderful and sacred mystery. By the tranquil operation of your providence, carry out the work of man's salvation. Let the whole world see and know that things which were cast down are being raised up, and things which had grown old are being made new, and that all things are being renewed to the perfection of him through whom all things were made, your Son our Lord Jesus Christ, who lives and reigns with you, in the unity of the Holy Spirit, one God, for ever and ever. *Amen.*

O God of unchangeable power and eternal light: Look favorably upon thy whole Church, that wonderful and sacred mystery; and by the tranquil operation of thy providence, carry out the work of man's salvation. Let the whole world see and know that things which were cast down are being raised up, and things which had grown old are being made new, and that all things are being renewed unto the perfection of him through whom all things were made, thy Son our Lord Jesus Christ, who liveth and reigneth with thee in the unity of the Holy Spirit, one God, for ever and ever. *Amen.*

Here, at his discretion, the Minister may add other appropriate devotions set forth by authority.

One or both of the following Anthems may be sung or said:

O Savior of the world, who by your Cross and precious blood have redeemed us:
Save us, and help us, we humbly beseech you, O Lord.

We adore you, O Christ, and we bless you,
Because by your holy Cross you have redeemed the world.

The Minister may conclude the Service with the following Prayer:

LORD JESUS CHRIST, Son of the living God, set, we pray, your passion, cross, and death between your judgment and our souls, now and in the hour of death. Give mercy and grace to the living, and pardon and rest to the dead. Grant peace and concord to your holy Church, and to us sinners everlasting life and glory; who with the Father and the Holy Spirit live and reign, one God, now and for ever. *Amen.*

The Service ends with an Anthem, or with a Dismissal.

In the absence of a Priest or Deacon, all that precedes may be led by a Lay Reader.

In places where Holy Communion is to be administered from the Reserved Sacrament, the following order is observed before the dismissal of the People:

THE LORD'S PRAYER

A CONFESSION OF SIN

THE COMMUNION

A PRAYER AFTER COMMUNION

O Savior of the world, who by thy Cross and precious blood
hast redeemed us:
Save us, and help us, we humbly beseech thee, O Lord.

We adore thee, O Christ and we bless thee:
Because by thy holy Cross thou hast redeemed the world.

LORD JESUS CHRIST, Son of the living God, we beseech thee
to set thy passion, cross, and death between thy judgment
and our souls, now and in the hour of death. Give mercy
and grace to the living, and pardon and rest to the dead.
Grant peace and concord to thy holy Church, and to us
sinners everlasting life and glory; who with the Father and
the Holy Spirit livest and reignest, one God, now and for
ever. *Amen.*

HOLY SATURDAY

There is no celebration of the Eucharist on this day, until after the Vigil of Easter Eve.

When there is a Ministry of the Word, the following proper is used:

THE COLLECT

MOST GRACIOUS GOD, as we have been baptized into the death of your Son our Savior Jesus Christ, so in your mercy may we be dead to sin and buried with him; that from the grave and gate of death, we may be raised up with him to newness of life; through Jesus Christ our Lord. *Amen.*

MOST GRACIOUS GOD, who hast baptized us into the death of thy Son our Savior Jesus Christ: Grant in thy mercy that we, being dead to sin, may be buried with him; that through the grave and gate of death, we may be raised up with him unto newness of life; through the same Jesus Christ our Lord. *Amen.*

THE PSALMS   31:1–6
                     130

THE LESSONS   Job 14:1–14
                    1 Peter 4:1–8
                    Matthew 27:57–66, *or*
                      John 19:38–42

EASTER SEASON

EASTER EVE

AT THE LIGHTING OF THE PASCHAL CANDLE

The lighting of the Paschal Candle may take place at the beginning of the Vigil, or at some other convenient time before the Liturgy of Easter Day, all standing.

The Deacon or other Minister appointed, standing near the Paschal Candle, sings or says the *Exultet,* as follows. (The Music of the *Exultet* will be found in the Altar Book edition.)

When a shorter form is desired, any of the bracketed sections may be omitted.

REJOICE NOW, heavenly hosts and choirs of angels,
    and let your trumpets shout Salvation
    for the victory of our mighty King.
Rejoice and sing now, all the round earth,
    bright with a glorious splendor,
    for darkness has been vanquished by our eternal King.
Rejoice and be glad now, Mother Church,
    and let your holy courts in radiant light
    resound with the praises of your people.

[All you who stand near this marvelous holy flame,
    pray with me to God the Almighty
    for the grace to sing the worthy praise of this great light;
    through Jesus Christ his Son our Lord,
    who lives and reigns with him,
    in the unity of the Holy Spirit,
    one God, for ever and ever. *Amen.*]

The Lord be with you.

Answer   And also with you.

Minister   Let us give thanks to the Lord our God.

Answer   It is right to give him thanks and praise.

Minister

It is truly right and good, always and everywhere, with our whole heart and mind and voice, to praise you, the invisible, almighty, and eternal God, and your only-begotten Son, our Lord Jesus Christ: For he is the true Paschal Lamb, who at the Feast of the Passover paid for us the debt of Adam's sin, and delivered by his blood your faithful people.

This is the night, when you brought our fathers,
    the children of Israel, out of bondage in Egypt,
    and led them through the Red Sea on dry land.
This is the night, when all who believe in Christ
    are delivered from the shade of sin,
    and are restored to grace and holiness of life.
This is the night, when Christ broke the bonds
                            of death and hell,
    and rose victorious from the grave.

[How wonderful and beyond our knowing, O God,
    is your mercy and loving-kindness to us,
    that to redeem a slave, you gave a Son.
How holy is this night, when wickedness is put to flight,
    and sin is washed away. It restores innocence to the fallen,
    and joy to those who mourn. It casts out pride and hatred,
    and brings peace and concord.
How blessed is this night,
    when earth and heaven are joined,
    and man is reconciled to God.]

522

If the Paschal Candle was not lit earlier, the Deacon or Minister now lights it; and from its flame other candles and lamps in the church may be lighted; after which he continues

Holy Father, accept our evening sacrifice,
the offering of this Candle in your honor.

[May it shine continually to drive away all darkness.
May Christ, the Morning Star who knows no setting,
find it ever burning—he who gives his light
to all creation.]

We pray you, Lord, to direct, sanctify, and govern us your servants, and all your faithful family, with your continual grace; that we may pass our time in peace and gladness, in the festival of our redemption;

Through Jesus Christ your Son our Lord, who lives and reigns with you in the unity of the Holy Spirit, one God, for ever and ever. *Amen.*

Note: It is customary that the Paschal Candle be burning at all services during the Easter Season.

AT THE VIGIL

At least two of the following Lessons are read, one of which is always the lesson from the Book of Exodus. After each Lesson, an appropriate Psalm, Canticle, or Hymn may be sung; a period of silence may be kept, and an appropriate Collect may be said.

> Genesis 1:1—2:2
> Genesis 22:1–18
> Exodus 14:15—15:1
> Isaiah 4:2–6
> Isaiah 55:1–11
> Ezekiel 36:24–28
> Zephaniah 3:14–17, 19–20

SUGGESTED PSALMS AND CANTICLES

Psalms 19:1–6; 30:1–13; 33:1–11 *or* 12–21; 42:1–7; 98; 113.

The Song of Moses, Exodus 15:1b–2, 11–13, [17–18]
The First Song of Isaiah, Isaiah 12:2–6

The Litany may then be sung or said.

Holy Baptism [and the Laying on of Hands] may be administered either before or after the Litany; or after the Gospel (and Sermon) in the Eucharist.

In the absence of a Priest or Deacon, all that precedes (except for the ministration of Baptism) may be led by a Lay Reader. He may conclude the Service in the manner described in the following rubric.

If the Eucharist is not immediately to follow, the Minister may conclude the service with what follows through the Collect of the Day.

AT THE EUCHARIST

When the celebration of the Eucharist immediately follows the Vigil, the Liturgy begins with one of the Canticles listed below. Immediately before the Canticle, the Minister may say to the People

> Alleluia! Christ is risen.

Answer The Lord is risen indeed, Alleluia!

THE CANTICLES

> Gloria in excelsis
> Te Deum laudamus
> Christ our Passover

The Minister then says

> The Lord be with you.

Answer And also with you.

Minister Let us pray.

THE COLLECT

ALMIGHTY GOD, who for our redemption gave your only-begotten Son to the death of the Cross, and by his glorious Resurrection delivered us from the power of our enemy: Grant us so to die daily to sin, that we may evermore live with him in the joy of his resurrection; through Jesus Christ your Son our Lord, who lives and reigns with you and the Holy Spirit, one God, now and ever. *Amen.*

ALMIGHTY GOD, who for our redemption didst give thine only-begotten Son to the death of the Cross, and by his glorious Resurrection hast delivered us from the power of our enemy: Grant us so to die daily from sin, that we may evermore live with him in the joy of his resurrection; through the same thy Son Jesus Christ our Lord, who liveth and reigneth with thee and the Holy Spirit, one God, now and ever. *Amen.*

THE PSALMS   2:1–8
                     114

THE LESSONS   Romans 6:3–11
                     Matthew 28:1–10

PROPER PREFACE OF EASTER

THE SUNDAY OF THE RESURRECTION, OR EASTER DAY

The Collect

ALMIGHTY GOD, who through your only-begotten Son Jesus Christ overcame death, and opened to us the gate of everlasting life: Grant that we, who celebrate with joy the solemnity of the Lord's resurrection, may arise from the death of sin through the renewal of your Holy Spirit; through Jesus Christ our Lord, who now lives and reigns with you and the Holy Spirit, one God, for ever and ever. *Amen.*

ALMIGHTY GOD, who through thine only-begotten Son Jesus Christ hast overcome death, and opened to us the gate of everlasting life: Grant that we, who celebrate with joy the solemnity of the Lord's resurrection, may arise from the death of sin through the renewal of thy Holy Spirit; through Jesus Christ our Lord, who liveth and reigneth with thee and the same Spirit, one God, now and for ever. *Amen.*

The Psalms
118:1–6, 14–18
66:1–11

The Lessons

Isaiah 25:6–9,
   or Acts 10:34–43
Colossians 3:1–4

A John 20:1–9,
   or Matthew 28:1–10
B Mark 16:1–8
C Luke 24:1–10

Proper Preface of Easter

MONDAY IN EASTER WEEK

THE COLLECT

GRANT, we pray, Almighty God, that we, who celebrate with reverence the Paschal feast, may be found worthy to attain to everlasting joys; through Jesus Christ our Lord, who lives and reigns with you and the Holy Spirit, one God, now and ever. *Amen.*

GRANT, we beseech thee, Almighty God, that we, who celebrate with reverence the Paschal feast, may be found worthy to attain to everlasting joys; through Jesus Christ our Lord, who liveth and reigneth with thee and the Holy Spirit, one God, now and ever. *Amen.*

THE PSALMS   118:19–24
                     16:9–12

THE LESSONS   Acts 2:14, 22–32
                     Matthew 28:9–15

PROPER PREFACE OF EASTER

TUESDAY IN EASTER WEEK

THE COLLECT

O GOD, who by the glorious resurrection of your Son Jesus
Christ destroyed death, and brought life and immortality to
light: Grant that we, being raised together with him, may
know the strength of his presence, and rejoice in the hope
of his eternal glory; through Jesus Christ our Lord, to whom
with you and the Holy Spirit, be dominion and praise for
ever and ever. *Amen.*

O GOD, who by the glorious resurrection of thy Son Jesus
Christ hast destroyed death, and brought life and immortality to light: Grant that we, being raised together with him,
may know the strength of his presence, and rejoice in the
hope of his eternal glory; through the same Jesus Christ our
Lord, to whom with thee and the Holy Spirit, be dominion
and praise for ever and ever. *Amen.*

THE PSALMS   118:19–24
                    33:17–21

THE LESSONS   Acts 2:36–41
                    John 20:11–18

PROPER PREFACE OF EASTER

WEDNESDAY IN EASTER WEEK

O GOD, whose blessed Son made himself known to his disciples in the breaking of bread: Open the eyes of our faith, that we may behold him in all his redeeming work; through Jesus Christ your Son our Lord, who lives and reigns with you in the unity of the Holy Spirit, one God, now and ever. *Amen.*

O GOD, whose blessed Son did manifest himself to his disciples in the breaking of bread: Open, we pray thee, the eyes of our faith, that we may behold him in all his redeeming work; through the same thy Son Jesus Christ our Lord, who liveth and reigneth with thee in the unity of the Holy Spirit, one God, now and ever. *Amen.*

THE PSALMS   118:19–24
                   105:1–8

THE LESSONS   Acts 3:1–10
                   Luke 24:13–35

PROPER PREFACE OF EASTER

THURSDAY IN EASTER WEEK

THE COLLECT

ALMIGHTY AND EVERLASTING GOD, who established the new covenant of reconciliation in the Paschal mystery of Christ: Grant that all who have been reborn into the fellowship of his Body, may show forth in their lives what they profess by their faith; through Jesus Christ our Lord, who lives and reigns in eternal glory with you and the Holy Spirit, one God, for ever and ever. *Amen.*

ALMIGHTY AND EVERLASTING GOD, who hast established the new covenant of reconciliation in the Paschal mystery of Christ: Grant that all who have been reborn into the fellowship of his Body, may show forth in their lives what they profess by their faith; through Jesus Christ our Lord, who liveth and reigneth in eternal glory with thee and the Holy Spirit, one God, for ever and ever. *Amen.*

THE PSALMS   118:19–24
                       8, *or* 114

THE LESSONS   Acts 3:11–26
                       Luke 24:36b–48

PROPER PREFACE OF EASTER

FRIDAY IN EASTER WEEK

THE COLLECT

ALMIGHTY FATHER, who gave your only Son to die for our sins and to rise for our justification: Give us grace so to put away the leaven of malice and wickedness, that we may always serve you in pureness of living and truth; through Jesus Christ your Son our Lord, who lives and reigns with you and the Holy Spirit, one God, now and ever. *Amen.*

ALMIGHTY FATHER, who didst give thine only Son to die for our sins and to rise for our justification: Give us grace so to put away the leaven of malice and wickedness, that we may always serve thee in pureness of living and truth; through Jesus Christ our Lord, who liveth and reigneth with thee and the Holy Spirit, one God, now and ever. *Amen.*

THE PSALMS   118:19–24
                    116:1–9

THE LESSONS   Acts 4:1–12
                    John 21:1–14

PROPER PREFACE OF EASTER

SATURDAY IN EASTER WEEK

The Collect

WE THANK YOU, heavenly Father, for delivering us from the power of darkness, and bringing us into the kingdom of your Son; and we pray that, as by his death he has recalled us to life, so by his presence abiding in us he may raise us to joys eternal; through Jesus Christ your Son our Lord, who lives and reigns with you in the unity of the Holy Spirit, one God, now and for ever. *Amen.*

WE THANK THEE, heavenly Father, for delivering us from the power of darkness, and bringing us into the kingdom of thy Son; and we pray that, as by his death he hath recalled us to life, so by his presence abiding in us he may raise us to joys eternal; through the same thy Son Jesus Christ our Lord, who liveth and reigneth with thee in the unity of the Holy Spirit, one God, now and for ever. *Amen.*

THE PSALMS — 118:19–24
118:14–18

THE LESSONS — Acts 4:13–21
Mark 16:9–15. 20

PROPER PREFACE OF EASTER

THE SECOND SUNDAY OF EASTER

The Collect

ALMIGHTY AND EVERLASTING GOD, who established in the Paschal mystery the new covenant of reconciliation: Grant to all who have been reborn into the fellowship of Christ's Body, that they may show forth in their lives what they profess by their faith; through Jesus Christ our Lord, who lives and reigns in eternal glory with you and the Holy Spirit, one God, now and ever. *Amen.*

ALMIGHTY AND EVERLASTING GOD, who hast established the new covenant of reconciliation in the Paschal mystery of Christ: Grant that all who have been reborn into the fellowship of his Body, may show forth in their lives what they profess by their faith; through Jesus Christ our Lord, who liveth and reigneth in eternal glory with thee and the Holy Spirit, one God, for ever and ever. *Amen.*

The Psalms

124
126

The Lessons

A Acts 2:42–47
1 Peter 1:3–9
John 20:19–31

B Acts 4:32–35
1 John 5:1–6
John 20:19–31

C Acts 5:12–16
Revelation 1:4–10a, 12–18
John 20:19–31

Proper Preface of Easter

THE THIRD SUNDAY OF EASTER

The Collect

O GOD, whose blessed Son made himself known to his disciples in the breaking of bread: Open the eyes of our faith, that we may behold him in all his redeeming work; through Jesus Christ your Son our Lord, who lives and reigns with you in the unity of the Holy Spirit, one God, now and ever. *Amen.*

O GOD, whose blessed Son did manifest himself to his disciples in the breaking of bread: Open, we pray thee, the eyes of our faith, that we may behold him in all his redeeming work; through the same thy Son Jesus Christ our Lord, who liveth and reigneth with thee in the unity of the Holy Spirit, one God, now and ever. *Amen.*

The Psalms

71:18–23
116:11–16

The Lessons

A Acts 2:22–32
  1 Peter 1:17–23
  Luke 24:13–35

B Acts 3:13–15, 17–21
  1 John 1:3—2:5a
  Luke 24:35–48

C Acts 5:27–35
  Revelation 5:6–14
  John 21:1–14

Proper Preface of Easter

THE FOURTH SUNDAY OF EASTER

THE COLLECT

HEAVENLY FATHER, whose Son our Savior is the good shepherd of your people: Grant that we, who are guarded by his continual care, may daily be nourished and led by his risen presence, who lives and reigns with you and the Holy Spirit, one God, now and ever. *Amen.*

HEAVENLY FATHER, whose Son our Savior is the good shepherd of thy people: Grant that we, who are guarded by his continual care, may daily be nourished and led by his risen presence, the same thy Son Jesus Christ our Lord, who liveth and reigneth with thee and the Holy Spirit, one God, now and ever. *Amen.*

THE PSALMS   116:1–9
                                        23

THE LESSONS

A Acts 2:14a, 36–41   B Acts 4:5, 7–12
   1 Peter 2:19–25   1 John 3:1–8
   John 10:1–10   John 10:11–16

          C Acts 13:16, 26–33
             Revelation 7:9–17
             John 10:22–30

PROPER PREFACE OF EASTER

536

THE FIFTH SUNDAY OF EASTER

THE COLLECT

ALMIGHTY GOD, whom truly to know is everlasting life: Grant us perfectly to know your Son Jesus Christ to be the way, the truth, and the life; that we may steadfastly follow his steps in the way that leads to eternal life; through Jesus Christ your Son our Lord, who lives and reigns with you in the unity of the Holy Spirit, one God, for ever and ever. *Amen.*

ALMIGHTY GOD, whom truly to know is everlasting life: Grant us perfectly to know thy Son Jesus Christ to be the way, the truth, and the life; that, following in his steps, we may steadfastly walk in the way that leadeth to eternal life; through the same thy Son Jesus Christ our Lord, who liveth and reigneth with thee in the unity of the Holy Spirit, one God, for ever and ever. *Amen.*

THE PSALMS   108:1–6
                      67

THE LESSONS

A Acts 6:1–7a   B Acts 9:26–31
  1 Peter 2:1–10   1 John 3:18–24
  John 14:1–12   John 15:1–11

        C Acts 13:44–52
          Revelation 19:1, 4–9
          John 13:31–35

PROPER PREFACE OF EASTER

537

THE SIXTH SUNDAY OF EASTER

The Collect

O God, who prepared for those who love you such good things as pass man's understanding: Pour into our hearts such love towards you, that we, loving you in all things and above all things, may obtain your promises; through Jesus Christ our Lord, who lives and reigns with you and the Holy Spirit, one God, for ever and ever. *Amen.*

O God, who hast prepared for those who love thee such good things as pass man's understanding: Pour into our hearts such love towards thee, that we, loving thee in all things and above all things, may obtain thy promises, which exceed all that we can desire; through Jesus Christ our Lord, who liveth and reigneth with thee and the Holy Spirit, one God, for ever and ever. *Amen.*

The Psalms   20
144:9–15

The Lessons

A Acts 8:5–8, 14–17   B Acts 11:5a, 11–18
  1 Peter 3:13–18   1 John 4:7–21
  John 14:15–21   John 15:9–17

C Acts 15:1–6, 22–29
Revelation 21:2–4, 14, 22–24
John 14:23–29

Proper Preface of Easter

538

ASCENSION DAY

The Collect

GRANT, we pray, Almighty God, that as we believe your only-begotten Son our Lord Jesus Christ to have ascended into heaven, so we may also in heart and mind there ascend, and with him continually dwell; through Jesus Christ our Lord, who lives and reigns with you and the Holy Spirit, one God, for ever and ever. *Amen.*

GRANT, we beseech thee, Almighty God, that like as we do believe thine only-begotten Son our Lord Jesus Christ to have ascended into the heavens; so we may also in heart and mind thither ascend, and with him continually dwell, who liveth and reigneth with thee and the Holy Spirit, one God, for ever and ever. *Amen.*

THE PSALMS	110:1–4
	24:7–10

THE LESSONS	Acts 1:1–11
	Ephesians 1:16–23
	Luke 24:49–53

PROPER PREFACE OF ASCENSION

THE SEVENTH SUNDAY OF EASTER

THE COLLECT

ALMIGHTY GOD, whose blessed Son our Savior Jesus Christ ascended far above all heavens, that he might fill all things: Mercifully give us faith to perceive that according to his promise he abides with his Church on earth, even to the end of the world; through Jesus Christ our Lord, who lives and reigns with you and the Holy Spirit, one God, for ever and ever. *Amen.*

ALMIGHTY GOD, whose blessed Son our Savior Jesus Christ ascended far above all heavens, that he might fill all things: Mercifully give us faith to perceive that according to his promise he abides with his Church on earth, even unto the end of the world; through the same Jesus Christ our Lord, who liveth and reigneth with thee and the Holy Spirit, one God, for ever and ever. *Amen.*

THE PSALMS
48:8–13
47

THE LESSONS

A Acts 1:8–14
    1 Peter 4:12–19
    John 17:1–11a

B Acts 1:15–26
    1 John 5:9–15
    John 17:11b–19

C Acts 7:55–60
    Revelation 22:12–14, 16–17, 20
    John 17:20–26

PROPER PREFACE OF ASCENSION

540

THE DAY OF PENTECOST, OR WHITSUNDAY

When there is more than one celebration of the Liturgy on this day, the following proper may be used:

THE COLLECT

ALMIGHTY GOD, who gave us the abiding presence of the Holy Spirit: Increase in us daily, we pray, the manifold gifts of his grace, that we may know the freedom of the children of God, and bear witness boldly for the Name of our Lord Jesus Christ, who now lives and reigns with you and the Holy Spirit, one God, for ever and ever. *Amen.*

ALMIGHTY GOD, who hast given to us the abiding presence of the Holy Spirit: Increase in us, we beseech thee, the manifold gifts of his grace, that we may know the freedom of the children of God, and bear witness boldly for the Name of our Lord Jesus Christ, who now liveth and reigneth with thee and the same Holy Spirit, one God, for ever and ever. *Amen.*

THE PSALMS   68:1–4, 18–20
                         68:32–35

THE LESSONS   Joel 2:28–32
                          Romans 8:14–17, 22–27
                          Luke 11:9–13

PROPER PREFACE OF PENTECOST

At the principal celebration, this proper is used:

The Collect

O God, who taught the hearts of your faithful people by sending to them the light of your Holy Spirit: Grant us by the Spirit to have a right judgment in all things, and evermore to rejoice in his strength; through Jesus Christ your Son our Lord, who lives and reigns with you in the unity of the Spirit, one God, now and for ever. *Amen.*

O God, who didst teach the hearts of thy faithful people by sending to them the light of thy Holy Spirit: Grant us by the same Spirit to have a right judgment in all things, and evermore to rejoice in his holy strength; through Jesus Christ our Lord, who liveth and reigneth with thee and the same Holy Spirit, one God, now and for ever. *Amen.*

The Psalms   122
                          33:12–14, 17–21

The Lessons   Acts 2:1–11
                          1 Corinthians 12:4–13
                          John 20:19–23

Proper Preface of Pentecost

THE FIRST SUNDAY AFTER PENTECOST, OR TRINITY SUNDAY

The Collect

ALMIGHTY AND EVERLASTING GOD, who gave to us your servants grace, by the confession of a true faith, to acknowledge the glory of the eternal Trinity, and in the power of your divine Majesty to worship the Unity: We humbly pray you to keep us steadfast in this faith, and evermore defend us from all adversities, who live and reign, one God, for ever and ever. *Amen.*

ALMIGHTY AND EVERLASTING GOD, who hast given unto us thy servants grace, by the confession of a true faith, to acknowledge the glory of the eternal Trinity, and in the power of the Divine Majesty to worship the Unity: We beseech thee that thou wouldest keep us steadfast in this faith, and evermore defend us from all adversities, who livest and reignest, one God, for ever and ever. *Amen.*

The Psalms

148
150

The Lessons

A Isaiah 6:1–8
  Revelation 4:1–11
  Matthew 28:16–20

B Exodus 3:1–6
  Acts 2:32–39
  John 3:1–16

C Numbers 6:22–27
  Romans 8:12–17
  John 14:8–17

PROPER PREFACE OF TRINITY SUNDAY

543

THE SECOND SUNDAY AFTER PENTECOST

THE COLLECT

ALMIGHTY AND EVERLASTING GOD: Give us the increase of faith, hope, and charity; and, that we may obtain what you promise, make us love what you command; through Jesus Christ our Lord, who lives and reigns with you in the unity of the Holy Spirit, one God, now and for ever. *Amen.*

ALMIGHTY AND EVERLASTING GOD: Give unto us the increase of faith, hope, and charity; and, that we may obtain that which thou dost promise, make us to love that which thou dost command; through Jesus Christ our Lord, who liveth and reigneth with thee in the unity of the Holy Spirit, one God, now and for ever. *Amen.*

THE PSALMS 81:1–10
15

THE LESSONS

A Deuteronomy 11:18–21, 26–28
Romans 3:21–25a, 28
Matthew 7:21–27

B Deuteronomy 5:6–21; *or* verses 12–15
2 Corinthians 4:7–11
Mark 2:23–28

C 1 Kings 8:41–43
Galatians 1:1–10
Luke 7:1–10

PROPER PREFACE OF THE LORD'S DAY

544

THE THIRD SUNDAY AFTER PENTECOST

The Collect

ALMIGHTY AND EVERLASTING GOD, ever more ready to hear than we to pray, and to give more than we desire or deserve: Pour upon us the abundance of your mercy; forgiving us those things of which our conscience is afraid, and giving us those good things which we are not worthy to ask, but for the sake of our Savior Jesus Christ, who lives and reigns with you and the Holy Spirit, one God, now and for ever. *Amen.*

ALMIGHTY AND EVERLASTING GOD, who art always more ready to hear than we to pray, and art wont to give more than either we desire or deserve: Pour down upon us the abundance of thy mercy; forgiving us those things whereof our conscience is afraid, and giving us those good things which we are not worthy to ask, but through the merits and mediation of Jesus Christ thy Son our Lord, who liveth and reigneth with thee and the Holy Spirit, one God, now and for ever. *Amen.*

The Psalms

50:7–15
30:6–13

The Lessons

A Hosea 6:3–6
  Romans 4:18–25
  Matthew 9:9–13

B Genesis 3:9–15
  2 Corinthians 4:13—5:1
  Mark 3:20–35

C 1 Kings 17:17–24
  Galatians 1:11–19
  Luke 7:11–17

Proper Preface of the Lord's Day

THE FOURTH SUNDAY
AFTER PENTECOST

THE COLLECT

KEEP, O LORD, your household the Church in your stead-fast faith and love; that, by the help of your grace, we may proclaim your truth with courage, and minister your love with compassion; for the sake of our Savior Jesus Christ, your Son our Lord, who lives and reigns with you and the Holy Spirit, one God, for ever and ever. *Amen.*

KEEP, O LORD, we beseech thee, thy household the Church in thy steadfast faith and love; that, by the help of thy grace, it may proclaim thy truth with courage, and minister thy love with compassion; for the sake of our Savior Jesus Christ, thy Son our Lord, who liveth and reigneth with thee and the Holy Spirit, one God, for ever and ever. *Amen.*

THE PSALMS

94:8–15
94:16–22

THE LESSONS

A Exodus 19:2–6a
  Romans 5:6–11
  Matthew 9:35—10:8

B Ezekiel 17:22–24
  2 Corinthians 5:6–10
  Mark 4:26–34

C 2 Samuel 12:7–10, 13
  Galatians 2:11–21
  Luke 7:36–50

PROPER PREFACE OF THE LORD'S DAY

546

THE FIFTH SUNDAY AFTER PENTECOST

THE COLLECT

ALMIGHTY FATHER, whose blessed Son laid down his life for us that we might live in him: Grant us so perfectly, and without any doubt, to commit our lives to him, that our faith may never be found wanting in your sight; through Jesus Christ our Lord, who lives and reigns with you and the Holy Spirit, one God, now and evermore. *Amen.*

ALMIGHTY FATHER, whose blessed Son laid down his life for us that we might live in him: Grant us so perfectly, and without any doubt, to commit our lives to him, that our faith may never be found wanting in thy sight; through Jesus Christ our Lord, who liveth and reigneth with thee and the Holy Spirit, one God, now and evermore. *Amen.*

THE PSALMS   69:30–37
                        107:23–32

THE LESSONS

A Jeremiah 20:7–13   B Job 38:1–11, 16–18
  Romans 5:12–15   2 Corinthians 5:14–17
  Matthew 10:26–33   Mark 4:35–41

          C Zechariah 12:9–11
            Galatians 3:23–29
            Luke 9:18–24

PROPER PREFACE OF THE LORD'S DAY

547

THE SIXTH SUNDAY AFTER PENTECOST

THE COLLECT

O GOD, whose almighty power is made known chiefly in showing mercy and pity: Stir our hearts with such desire for your gracious promises, that we may become partakers of your heavenly treasure; through Jesus Christ our Lord, who lives and reigns with you and the Holy Spirit, one God, now and ever. *Amen.*

O GOD, who declarest thy almighty power chiefly in showing mercy and pity: Mercifully grant unto us such a measure of thy grace, that we, running the way of thy commandments, may obtain thy gracious promises, and be made partakers of thy heavenly treasure; through Jesus Christ our Lord, who liveth and reigneth with thee and the Holy Spirit, one God, now and ever. *Amen.*

THE PSALMS

89:1–2, 16–19
16

THE LESSONS

A Isaiah 2:10–17
  Romans 6:3–11
  Matthew 10:34–42

B Wisdom 1:13–15; 2:23–24
  2 Corinthians 8:1–9, 13–15
  Mark 5:21–24, 35b–43

C 1 Kings 19:15–16, 19–21
  Galatians 4:31—5:1, 13–18
  Luke 9:51–62

PROPER PREFACE OF THE LORD'S DAY

THE SEVENTH SUNDAY
AFTER PENTECOST

THE COLLECT

O GOD, who taught us to keep all your commandments by loving you and our neighbor: Grant us the grace of your Holy Spirit, that we may be devoted to you with our whole heart, and united to one another with pure affection; through Jesus Christ our Lord, who lives and reigns with you and the Holy Spirit, one God, for ever and ever. *Amen.*

O GOD, who hast taught us to keep all thy commandments by loving thee and our neighbor: Grant unto us the grace of thy Holy Spirit, that we may be devoted to thee with our whole heart, and united to one another with pure affection; through Jesus Christ our Lord, who liveth and reigneth with thee and the Holy Spirit, one God, for ever and ever. *Amen.*

THE PSALMS 138
123

THE LESSONS

A Zechariah 9:9–10
   Romans 8:9–17
   Matthew 11:25–30

B Ezekiel 2:2–5
   2 Corinthians 12:7–10
   Mark 6:1–6

C Isaiah 66:10–14
   Galatians 6:14–18
   Luke 10:1–9, 16–20

PROPER PREFACE OF THE LORD'S DAY

549

THE EIGHTH SUNDAY
AFTER PENTECOST

The Collect

Lord, we pray that your grace may always go before us and follow us, that by your continual help we may accomplish those good works which are pleasing to you; through Jesus Christ our Lord, who lives and reigns with you and the Holy Spirit, one God, now and for ever. *Amen.*

Lord, we pray thee that thy grace may always go before us and follow us, that by thy continual help we may accomplish those good works which are pleasing to thee; through Jesus Christ our Lord, who liveth and reigneth with thee and the Holy Spirit, one God, now and for ever. *Amen.*

The Psalms

65:9–14
85:8–13

The Lessons

A Isaiah 55:10–11
   Romans 8:18–23
   Matthew 13:1–9, 18–23

B Amos 7:10–15
   Ephesians 1:3–14
   Mark 6:7–13

C Deuteronomy 30:10–14
   Colossians 1:1–12
   Luke 10:25–37

Proper Preface of the Lord's Day

THE NINTH SUNDAY AFTER PENTECOST

THE COLLECT

GRANT, O LORD, we pray, that the course of this world may be so peaceably ordered by your governance, that your Church may serve you in all joy and peace; through Jesus Christ our Lord, who lives and reigns with you and the Holy Spirit, one God, now and for ever. *Amen.*

GRANT, O LORD, we beseech thee, that the course of this world may be so peaceably ordered by thy governance, that thy Church may joyfully serve thee in all godly quietness; through Jesus Christ our Lord, who liveth and reigneth with thee and the Holy Spirit, one God, now and for ever. *Amen.*

THE PSALMS 86:11–17
23

THE LESSONS

A Wisdom 12:13, 16–19   B Jeremiah 23:1–6
  Romans 8:26–27   Ephesians 2:11–18
  Matthew 13:24–34   Mark 6:30–34

              C Genesis 18:1–10a
                Colossians 1:21–28
                Luke 10:38–42

PROPER PREFACE OF THE LORD'S DAY

551

THE TENTH SUNDAY AFTER PENTECOST

THE COLLECT

O LORD, we pray, mercifully receive the prayers of your people who call upon you, and grant that they may know and understand what things they ought to do, and may have grace and power faithfully to accomplish them; through Jesus Christ our Lord, who lives and reigns with you in the unity of the Holy Spirit, one God, now and ever. *Amen.*

O LORD, we beseech thee, mercifully to receive the prayers of thy people who call upon thee; and grant that they may both perceive and know what things they ought to do, and also may have grace and power faithfully to fulfill the same; through Jesus Christ our Lord, who liveth and reigneth with thee in the unity of the Holy Spirit, one God, now and ever. *Amen.*

THE PSALMS

145:14–21
119:129–136

THE LESSONS

A 1 Kings 3:5–12
  Romans 8:28–30
  Matthew 13:44–49a

B 2 Kings 4:42–44
  Ephesians 4:1–6
  Mark 6:35–44

C Genesis 18:20–32
  Colossians 2:6–15
  Luke 11:1–13

PROPER PREFACE OF THE LORD'S DAY

THE ELEVENTH SUNDAY
AFTER PENTECOST

THE COLLECT

ALMIGHTY GOD, the fountain of all wisdom, as you know our necessities before we ask, and our ignorance in asking: Have compassion on our weakness; and mercifully give us those things which for our unworthiness we dare not, and for our blindness we cannot ask, for the sake of your Son Jesus Christ our Lord, who lives and reigns with you and the Holy Spirit, one God, now and for ever. *Amen.*

ALMIGHTY GOD, the fountain of all wisdom, who knowest our necessities before we ask, and our ignorance in asking: We beseech thee to have compassion upon our infirmities; and those things which for our unworthiness we dare not, and for our blindness cannot ask, mercifully give us, for the sake of thy Son Jesus Christ our Lord, who liveth and reigneth with thee and the Holy Spirit, one God, now and for ever. *Amen.*

THE PSALMS   95:1–7
                    36:5–12

THE LESSONS

A Isaiah 55:1–3   B Exodus 16:2–4, 12–15
   Romans 8:35–39   Ephesians 4:17–24
   Matthew 14:13–21   John 6:24–35

            C Ecclesiastes 1:2, 2:18–23
               Colossians 3:1–5, 9–11
               Luke 12:13–21

PROPER PREFACE OF THE LORD'S DAY

THE TWELFTH SUNDAY AFTER PENTECOST

THE COLLECT

O LORD, we pray, let your continual mercy cleanse and defend your Church; and, because it cannot continue in safety without your aid, preserve and govern it always by your help and goodness; through Jesus Christ our Lord, who lives and reigns with you and the Holy Spirit, one God, for ever and ever. *Amen.*

O LORD, we beseech thee, let thy continual pity cleanse and defend thy Church; and, because it cannot continue in safety without thy succor, preserve it evermore by thy help and goodness; through Jesus Christ our Lord, who liveth and reigneth with thee and the Holy Spirit, one God, for ever and ever. *Amen.*

THE PSALMS

34:1–8
27:1–7

THE LESSONS

A 1 Kings 19:9–12
   Romans 9:1–5
   Matthew 14:22–33

B 1 Kings 19:4–8
   Ephesians 4:30—5:2
   John 6:41–51

C Genesis 15:1–6
   Hebrews 11:1–2, 8–16
   Luke 12:32–40

PROPER PREFACE OF THE LORD'S DAY

554

THE THIRTEENTH SUNDAY AFTER PENTECOST

THE COLLECT

GRANT TO US, LORD, we pray, the spirit to think and do always such things as are right; that we, who cannot exist without you, may by your strength live according to your will; through Jesus Christ our Lord, who lives and reigns with you and the Holy Spirit, one God, now and ever. *Amen.*

GRANT TO US, LORD, we beseech thee, the spirit to think and do always such things as are right; that we, who cannot exist without thee, may by thee be enabled to live according to thy will; through Jesus Christ our Lord, who liveth and reigneth with thee and the Holy Spirit, one God, now and ever. *Amen.*

THE PSALMS

147:1–7
62:1–8

THE LESSONS

A Isaiah 56:1, 6–7
  Romans 11:13–15, 29–32
  Matthew 15:21–28

B Proverbs 9:1–6
  Ephesians 5:15–20
  John 6:53–58

C Jeremiah 23:23–29
  Hebrews 12:1–4
  Luke 12:49–56

PROPER PREFACE OF THE LORD'S DAY

THE FOURTEENTH SUNDAY AFTER PENTECOST

THE COLLECT

ALMIGHTY GOD, who built your Church upon the foundation of the apostles and prophets, Jesus Christ himself being the head corner-stone: Grant us so to be joined together in unity of spirit by their teaching, that we may be made a holy temple acceptable to you; through Jesus Christ our Lord, who lives and reigns with you and the Holy Spirit, one God, now and for ever. *Amen.*

ALMIGHTY GOD, who hast built thy Church upon the foundation of the apostles and prophets, Jesus Christ himself being the head corner-stone: Grant us so to be joined together in unity of spirit by their doctrine, that we may be made a holy temple, acceptable unto thee; through the same Jesus Christ our Lord, who liveth and reigneth with thee and the Holy Spirit, one God, now and for ever. *Amen.*

THE PSALMS   71:1–7
                       125

THE LESSONS

A Isaiah 22:15–16, 19–23   B Joshua 24:1–2a, 14–18
  Romans 11:33–36   Ephesians 5:21–32
  Matthew 16:13–20   John 6:60–69

         C Isaiah 66:18b–23
           Hebrews 12:5–7, 11–13
           Luke 13:22–30

PROPER PREFACE OF THE LORD'S DAY

556

THE FIFTEENTH SUNDAY
AFTER PENTECOST

The Collect

ALMIGHTY GOD, who gave your only Son to be for us both a sacrifice for sin, and also an example of godly life: Give us grace always to receive thankfully his incomparable benefit, and also daily endeavor to follow the blessed steps of his most holy life; through Jesus Christ your Son our Lord, who lives and reigns with you and the Holy Spirit, one God, now and ever. *Amen.*

ALMIGHTY GOD, who hast given thine only Son to be unto us both a sacrifice for sin, and also an example of godly life: Give us grace that we may always most thankfully receive that his inestimable benefit, and also daily endeavor ourselves to follow the blessed steps of his most holy life; through the same thy Son Jesus Christ our Lord, who liveth and reigneth with thee and the Holy Spirit, one God, now and ever. *Amen.*

The Psalms

112
113

The Lessons

A Jeremiah 20:7–9
  Romans 12:1–2
  Matthew 16:21–26

B Deuteronomy 4:1–2, 6b–8
  James 1:17–18, 21b–22, 27
  Mark 7:1–8, 14–15, 21–23

C Ecclesiasticus 3:17–18, 20, 28–29
  Hebrews 12:18–19, 22–24
  Luke 14:1, 7–14

Proper Preface of the Lord's Day

THE SIXTEENTH SUNDAY
AFTER PENTECOST

THE COLLECT

GRANT, we pray, merciful God, that your Church, being gathered together in unity by your Holy Spirit, may show forth your power among all peoples, to the glory of your Name; through Jesus Christ our Lord, who lives and reigns with you and the Holy Spirit, one God, now and for ever. *Amen.*

GRANT, we beeseech thee, merciful God, that thy Church, being gathered together in unity by thy Holy Spirit, may manifest thy power among all peoples, to the glory of thy Name; through Jesus Christ our Lord, who liveth and reigneth with thee and the same Spirit, one God, now and for ever. *Amen.*

THE PSALMS

146
82

THE LESSONS

A Ezekiel 33:7–9
  Romans 13:8–10
  Matthew 18:15–20

B Isaiah 35:4–7a
  James 2:1–5
  Mark 7:31–37

C Wisdom 9:13–18
  Philemon 1, 7–17
  Luke 14:25–33

PROPER PREFACE OF THE LORD'S DAY

558

THE SEVENTEENTH SUNDAY
AFTER PENTECOST

The Collect

GRANT US, O LORD, we pray, to trust in you with all our heart; for since you always resist the proud who confide in their own strength, so you never forsake those who make their boast in your mercy; through Jesus Christ our Lord, who lives and reigns with you and the Holy Spirit, one God, now and for ever. *Amen.*

GRANT UNTO US, O LORD, we beseech thee, to trust in thee with all our heart; seeing that, as thou dost always resist the proud who confide in their own strength, so thou dost not forsake those who make their boast in thy mercy; through Jesus Christ our Lord, who liveth and reigneth with thee and the Holy Spirit, one God, now and for ever. *Amen.*

The Psalms

103:1–12
103:13–22

The Lessons

A Ecclesiasticus 27:29—28:7
  Romans 14:7–9
  Matthew 18:21–35

B Isaiah 50:5–9a
  James 2:14–18
  Mark 8:27–38

C Exodus 32:7–11, 13–14
1 Timothy 1:12–17
Luke 15:1–10

Proper Preface of the Lord's Day

559

THE EIGHTEENTH SUNDAY AFTER PENTECOST

THE COLLECT

O GOD, since without you we are not able to please you: Mercifully grant that your Holy Spirit may in all things direct and rule our hearts; through Jesus Christ our Lord, who lives and reigns with you and the Holy Spirit, one God, now and ever. *Amen.*

O GOD, forasmuch as without thee we are not able to please thee: Mercifully grant that thy Holy Spirit may in all things direct and rule our hearts; through Jesus Christ our Lord, who liveth and reigneth with thee and the same Spirit, one God, now and ever. *Amen.*

THE PSALMS   80:7–14
                    54

THE LESSONS

A Isaiah 55:6–9   B Wisdom 2:1, 12–20
  Philippians 1:20c–24, 27a   James 3:16—4:3
  Matthew 20:1–16   Mark 9:30–37

              C Amos 8:4–7
                1 Timothy 2:1–8
                Luke 16:10–13

PROPER PREFACE OF THE LORD'S DAY

THE NINETEENTH SUNDAY
AFTER PENTECOST

THE COLLECT

REMEMBER, O LORD, what you have wrought in us and not what we deserve; and as you have called us to your service, make us worthy of our calling; through Jesus Christ our Lord, who lives and reigns with you and the Holy Spirit, one God, now and for ever. *Amen.*

REMEMBER, O LORD, what thou hast wrought in us and not what we deserve; and as thou hast called us to thy service, make us worthy of our calling; through Jesus Christ our Lord, who liveth and reigneth with thee and the Holy Spirit, one God, now and for ever. *Amen.*

THE PSALMS 18:21–29
19:7–14

THE LESSONS

A Ezekiel 18:25–28
  Philippians 2:1–11
  Matthew 21:28–32

B Numbers 11:25–29
  James 5:1–6
  Mark 9:38–43, 45, 47–48

C Amos 6:1, 3–7
  1 Timothy 6:11–16
  Luke 16:19–31

PROPER PREFACE OF THE LORD'S DAY

561

THE TWENTIETH SUNDAY
AFTER PENTECOST

THE COLLECT

O GOD, the protector of all who trust in you, without whom nothing is strong, nothing is holy: Increase and multiply upon us your mercy, that we may so pass through things temporal, that we lose not the things eternal; through Jesus Christ our Lord, who lives and reigns with you and the Holy Spirit, one God, now and ever. *Amen.*

O GOD, the protector of all that trust in thee, without whom nothing is strong, nothing is holy: Increase and multiply upon us thy mercy; that, thou being our ruler and guide, we may so pass through things temporal, that we lose not the things eternal; through Jesus Christ our Lord, who liveth and reigneth with thee and the Holy Spirit, one God, now and ever. *Amen.*

THE PSALMS   80:14–19
      128

THE LESSONS

A Isaiah 5:1–7   B Genesis 2:18–24
  Philippians 4:4–8   Hebrews 2:9–18
  Matthew 21:33–43   Mark 10:2–9

    C Habakkuk 1:2–3; 2:2–4
     2 Timothy 1:6–14
     Luke 17:5–10

PROPER PREFACE OF THE LORD'S DAY

THE TWENTY–FIRST SUNDAY
AFTER PENTECOST

THE COLLECT

GRANT US, O LORD, not to be anxious about earthly things, but to love things heavenly; and even now, while we are placed among things that are passing away, to cleave to those that shall abide; through Jesus Christ our Lord, who lives and reigns with you and the Holy Spirit, one God, now and for ever. *Amen.*

GRANT US, O LORD, not to mind earthly things, but to love things heavenly; and even now, while we are placed among things that are passing away, to cleave to those that shall abide; through Jesus Christ our Lord, who liveth and reigneth with thee and the Holy Spirit, one God, now and for ever. *Amen.*

THE PSALMS   92:1–5, 11–14
                    84:1–7

THE LESSONS

A Isaiah 25:6–10a   B Wisdom 7:7–11
  Philippians 4:10–13   Hebrews 3:1–6
  Matthew 22:1–14   Mark 10:17–27

              C Ruth 1:8–19a
                2 Timothy 2:8–13
                Luke 17:11–19

PROPER PREFACE OF THE LORD'S DAY

563

THE TWENTY–SECOND SUNDAY AFTER PENTECOST

THE COLLECT

O GOD OF HOPE, fill us with all joy and peace in believing, that we may ever abound in hope by the power of your Holy Spirit, and show forth our thankfulness to you in trustful and courageous lives; through Jesus Christ our Lord, who lives and reigns with you and the Holy Spirit, one God, now and for ever. *Amen.*

O GOD OF HOPE, fill us, we beseech thee, with all joy and peace in believing, that we may ever abound in hope by the power of thy Holy Spirit, and show forth our thankfulness to thee in trustful and courageous lives; through Jesus Christ our Lord, who liveth and reigneth with thee and the same Spirit, one God, now and for ever. *Amen.*

THE PSALMS 96:1–8
121

THE LESSONS

A Isaiah 45:1, 4–6
1 Thessalonians 1:1–5b
Matthew 22:15–21

B Isaiah 53:10–11
Hebrews 4:12–16
Mark 10:35–45

C Exodus 17:8–12
2 Timothy 3:14—4:2
Luke 18:1–8a

PROPER PREFACE OF THE LORD'S DAY

564

THE TWENTY–THIRD SUNDAY AFTER PENTECOST

The Collect

LORD OF ALL POWER AND MIGHT, the author and giver of all good things: Graft in our hearts the love of your Name; increase in us true religion; and nourish us with all goodness; through Jesus Christ our Lord, who lives and reigns with you and the Holy Spirit, one God, now and for ever. *Amen.*

LORD OF ALL POWER AND MIGHT, who art the author and giver of all good things: Graft in our hearts the love of thy Name, increase in us true religion, nourish us with all goodness, and of thy great mercy keep us in the same; through Jesus Christ our Lord, who liveth and reigneth with thee and the Holy Spirit, one God, now and for ever. *Amen.*

The Psalms   1
17:1–7

The Lessons

A Exodus 22:21–27
  1 Thessalonians 1:5c–10
  Matthew 22:34–40

B Jeremiah 31:7–9
  Hebrews 5:1–9
  Mark 10:46–52

C Ecclesiasticus 35:12–14, 16–19
  2 Timothy 4:6–8, 16–18
  Luke 18:9–14

Proper Preface of the Lord's Day

THE TWENTY–FOURTH SUNDAY
AFTER PENTECOST

THE COLLECT

O GOD, from whom all good things come: Grant to us your servants, that by your holy inspiration we may think those things which are good, and by your merciful guidance may bring them to good effect; through Jesus Christ our Lord, who lives and reigns with you and the Holy Spirit, one God, now and for ever. *Amen.*

O GOD, from whom all good things do come: Grant to us thy humble servants, that by thy holy inspiration we may think those things that are good, and by thy merciful guiding may perform the same; through Jesus Christ our Lord, who liveth and reigneth with thee and the Holy Spirit, one God. now and for ever. *Amen.*

THE PSALMS

4
32:1–8

THE LESSONS

A Malachi 1:14b—2:2b, 8–10
  1 Thessalonians 2:7–13
  Matthew 23:1–12

B Deuteronomy 6:1–6
  Hebrews 7:23–28
  Mark 12:28b–34

C Wisdom 11:23—12:2
  2 Thessalonians 1:1–5, 11–12
  Luke 19:1–10

PROPER PREFACE OF THE LORD'S DAY

THE TWENTY–FIFTH SUNDAY
AFTER PENTECOST

THE COLLECT

ALMIGHTY AND EVERLASTING GOD, who revealed your glory by Christ among all nations: Preserve the works of your mercy, that your Church, which is spread throughout the world, may persevere with steadfast faith in the confession of your Name; through Jesus Christ our Lord, who lives and reigns with you in the unity of the Holy Spirit, one God, now and ever. *Amen.*

ALMIGHTY AND EVERLASTING GOD, who hast revealed thy glory by Christ among the nations: Preserve the works of thy mercy, that thy Church, which is spread throughout the world, may persevere with steadfast faith in the confession of thy Name; through Jesus Christ our Lord, who liveth and reigneth with thee in the unity of the Holy Spirit, one God, now and ever. *Amen.*

THE PSALMS   105:1–8
                              111

THE LESSONS

A Jeremiah 26:1–9   B 1 Kings 17:10–16
   1 Thessalonians 3:7–13   Hebrews 9:24–28
   Matthew 24:4–14   Mark 12:38–44

          C Job 19:23–27
             2 Thessalonians 2:15—3:5
             Luke 20:27, 34–38

PROPER PREFACE OF THE LORD'S DAY

567

THE TWENTY–SIXTH SUNDAY
AFTER PENTECOST

THE COLLECT

ALMIGHTY GOD, whose sovereign purpose none can make void: Give us faith to be steadfast amid the tumults of the world, knowing that your kingdom shall come and your will be done, to the eternal glory of your Name; through Jesus Christ our Lord, who lives and reigns with you and the Holy Spirit, one God, now and for ever. *Amen.*

ALMIGHTY GOD, whose sovereign purpose none can make void: Give us faith to be steadfast amidst the tumults of the world, knowing that thy kingdom shall come and thy will be done, to the eternal glory of thy Name; through Jesus Christ our Lord, who liveth and reigneth with thee and the Holy Spirit, one God, now and for ever. *Amen.*

THE PSALMS   57:8–12
                         40:1–7

THE LESSONS

A Wisdom 6:12–16   B Daniel 7:9–12
  1 Thessalonians 4:12–17   Hebrews 10:11–14, 18
  Matthew 25:1–13   Mark 13:14–23

          C Malachi 4:1–2a
            2 Thessalonians 3:7–12
            Luke 21:5–19

PROPER PREFACE OF THE LORD'S DAY

THE TWENTY–SEVENTH SUNDAY AFTER PENTECOST

THE COLLECT

O GOD, whose blessed Son came into the world that he might destroy the works of the devil, and make us the sons of God, and heirs of eternal life: Grant us, we pray, that, having this hope, we may purify ourselves, even as he is pure; that, when he shall appear again with power and great glory, we may be made like him in his eternal and glorious kingdom, where he lives and reigns with you and the Holy Spirit, one God, now and for ever. *Amen.*

O GOD, whose blessed Son was manifested that he might destroy the works of the devil, and make us the sons of God, and heirs of eternal life: Grant us, we pray, that, having this hope, we may purify ourselves, even as he is pure; that, when he shall appear again with power and great glory, we may be made like unto him in his eternal and glorious kingdom, where he liveth and reigneth with thee and the Holy Spirit, one God, now and for ever. *Amen.*

THE PSALMS

90:1–8, 12
90:13–17

THE LESSONS

A Proverbs 31:10–13, 19–20, 30–31
1 Thessalonians 5:1–10
Matthew 25:14–15, 19–30

B Daniel 12:1–3
Hebrews 10:31–33, 35–39
Mark 13:24–32

C Malachi 3:1–5, 4:5–6
1 Peter 4:17–19
Luke 21:32–36

PROPER PREFACE OF THE LORD'S DAY

569

THE LAST SUNDAY AFTER PENTECOST, OR THE SUNDAY BEFORE ADVENT

The proper for this Sunday is always to be used on the Sunday before the First Sunday in Advent, whether the Sundays after Pentecost be twenty-three or more in number.

THE COLLECT

ALMIGHTY AND EVERLASTING GOD, whose will it is to restore all things in your well-beloved Son, the King of kings and Lord of lords: Mercifully grant that all the peoples of the earth, being set free from the captivity of sin and death, may be brought under his gracious rule, who lives and reigns with you and the Holy Spirit, one God, now and for ever. *Amen.*

ALMIGHTY AND EVERLASTING GOD, who didst will to restore all things in thy well-beloved Son, the King of kings, and Lord of lords: Mercifully grant that all the peoples of the earth, being set free from the captivity of sin and death, may be brought under his gracious rule, who liveth and reigneth with thee and the Holy Spirit, one God, now and for ever. *Amen.*

THE PSALMS   24, 46

THE LESSONS

A Ezekiel 34:11–17   B Daniel 7:13–14
  1 Corinthians 15:20–26, 28   Revelation 1:4b–8
   Matthew 25:31–46   John 18:33b–37

         C Jeremiah 23:2–6
           Colossians 1:12–20
           Luke 23:35–43

PROPER PREFACE OF THE LORD'S DAY

SAINT ANDREW THE APOSTLE

NOVEMBER 30

THE COLLECT

ALMIGHTY GOD, who gave such grace to your apostle Andrew, that he readily obeyed the calling of your son Jesus Christ, and followed him without delay: Grant, we pray, that we, who are called by your holy Word, may offer ourselves in glad obedience to your service; through Jesus Christ our Lord, who lives and reigns with you and the Holy Spirit, one God, now and ever. *Amen.*

ALMIGHTY GOD, who didst give such grace to thine apostle Andrew, that he readily obeyed the calling of thy Son Jesus Christ, and followed him without delay: Grant, we beseech thee, that we, who are called by thy holy Word, may offer ourselves in glad obedience to thy service; through Jesus Christ our Lord, who liveth and reigneth with thee and the Holy Spirit, one God, now and ever. *Amen.*

THE PSALMS 117
102:15—22

THE LESSONS Deuteronomy 30:11—14
Romans 10:8—18
Matthew 4:18—22

PROPER PREFACE OF APOSTLES

571

SAINT THOMAS THE APOSTLE

DECEMBER 21

THE COLLECT

ETERNAL GOD, who strengthened Thomas your apostle, being doubtful, with firm and certain faith in the resurrection of your Son our Lord: Grant to us your people, that we may be not faithless but believing, until we come to see our Savior in his glory face to face; through Jesus Christ your Son our Lord, who lives and reigns with you and the Holy Spirit, one God, now and for ever. *Amen.*

O ETERNAL GOD, who didst strengthen thine apostle Thomas, being doubtful, with firm and certain faith in the resurrection of thy Son our Lord: Grant unto us thy people, that we may be not faithless but believing, until we come to see our Savior in his glory face to face; through the same thy Son Jesus Christ our Lord, who liveth and reigneth with thee and the Holy Spirit, one God, now and for ever. *Amen.*

THE PSALMS   48:1–7
                        126

THE LESSONS   Habakkuk 2:1–4
                        Hebrews 10:35—11:1
                        John 20:24–29

PROPER PREFACE OF APOSTLES

SAINT STEPHEN, DEACON AND MARTYR
DECEMBER 26

When this feast falls on the First Sunday after Christmas, it is transferred to the Monday following.

THE COLLECT

GRANT, O FATHER, that in all our sufferings here on earth in witness to your truth, we may follow the example of our Lord and of his first martyr Saint Stephen, and learn to love our enemies and forgive our persecutors; through Jesus Christ our Savior, who lives and reigns with you and the Holy Spirit, one God, in glory everlasting. *Amen.*

GRANT, O FATHER, that in all our sufferings here on earth in witness to thy truth, we may follow the example of our Lord and of his first martyr Saint Stephen, and learn to love our enemies and forgive our persecutors; through Jesus Christ our Savior, who liveth and reigneth with thee and the Holy Spirit, one God, in glory everlasting. *Amen.*

THE PSALMS   30:1–5
                    31:1–6

THE LESSONS   2 Chronicles 24:17–22
                    Acts 7:55–60
                    Matthew 23:34–39

PROPER PREFACE OF CHRISTMAS

SAINT JOHN, APOSTLE AND EVANGELIST

DECEMBER 27

When this feast falls on the First Sunday after Christmas, it is transferred to the Monday following; but if Saint Stephen's Day has been transferred to the Monday, this feast is observed on the Tuesday following.

THE COLLECT

MERCIFUL LORD, pour upon your Church, we pray, the brightness of your light, that we, being illumined by the teaching of your apostle and evangelist Saint John, may so live by the light of your truth that we may obtain eternal life; through our Lord Jesus Christ, who lives and reigns with you and the Holy Spirit, one God, for ever and ever. *Amen.*

MERCIFUL LORD, we beseech thee to cast thy bright beams of light upon thy Church, that we, being illumined by the doctrine of thy blessed apostle and evangelist Saint John, may so walk in the light of thy truth that we may at length attain to life everlasting; through Jesus Christ our Lord, who liveth and reigneth with thee and the Holy Spirit, one God, for ever and ever. *Amen.*

THE PSALMS   92:11–14
                  23

THE LESSONS   Proverbs 8:22–30
                  1 John 1:1–5
                  John 21:19–24

PROPER PREFACE OF CHRISTMAS

574

THE HOLY INNOCENTS

DECEMBER 28

This feast is observed on the day following the feast of Saint John; but if that day is the First Sunday after Christmas, this feast is transferred to the Monday following.

THE COLLECT

GRANT, most merciful Father, that, as we remember the slaughter of innocent babes by the order of a tyrant, when our Lord was born in Bethlehem, so we may be firm to defend all helpless people from cruelty and oppression, for the sake of our Savior Jesus Christ, who also suffered death though he had done no wrong, and who now lives and reigns with you and the Holy Spirit, one God, for ever and ever. *Amen.*

GRANT, most merciful Father, that, as we remember the slaughter of innocent children by the order of a tyrant, when our Lord was born in Bethlehem, so we may be firm to defend all helpless people from cruelty and oppression, for the sake of our Savior Jesus Christ, who also suffered death though he had done no wrong, and who now liveth and reigneth with thee and the Holy Spirit, one God, for ever and ever. *Amen.*

THE PSALMS	9:11–14
	9:16–20
THE LESSONS	Jeremiah 31:15–20
	Revelation 21:3–5
	Matthew 2:13–18

PROPER PREFACE OF CHRISTMAS

THE CONFESSION
OF SAINT PETER THE APOSTLE

JANUARY 18

THE COLLECT

ALMIGHTY FATHER, who inspired Simon Peter, first among the apostles, to confess Jesus as the Messiah and Son of the living God: Keep your Church steadfast upon the rock of this faith, that in unity and peace it may proclaim one truth and follow one Lord, your Son our Savior Jesus Christ, who lives and reigns with you and the Holy Spirit, one God, now and for ever. *Amen.*

ALMIGHTY FATHER, who didst inspire Simon Peter, first among the apostles, to confess Jesus as the Messiah and Son of the living God: Keep thy Church steadfast upon the rock of this faith, that in unity and peace it may proclaim one truth and follow one Lord, thy Son our Savior Jesus Christ, who liveth and reigneth with thee and the Holy Spirit, one God, now and for ever. *Amen.*

THE PSALMS   89:9–18
                        133

THE LESSONS   Ezekiel 3:4–11
                       Acts 4:8–13
                       Matthew 16:13–19

PROPER PREFACE OF APOSTLES

THE CONVERSION
OF SAINT PAUL THE APOSTLE

JANUARY 25

THE COLLECT

O GOD, who caused the light of the gospel to shine throughout the world by the preaching of your apostle Saint Paul: Grant that we may ever hold in remembrance his wonderful conversion, and show our thanksgiving by following his holy teaching; through Jesus Christ our Lord, who lives and reigns with you in the unity of the Holy Spirit, one God, now and ever. *Amen.*

O GOD, who hast caused the light of the gospel to shine throughout the world by the preaching of thy blessed apostle Saint Paul: Grant that we may ever hold in remembrance his wonderful conversion, and show our thanksgiving unto thee for the same by following the holy doctrine which he taught; through Jesus Christ our Lord, who liveth and reigneth with thee in the unity of the Holy Spirit, one God, now and ever. *Amen.*

THE PSALMS   66:1–8
                     67

THE LESSONS   Acts 26:9–20
                     Galatians 1:11–24
                     Luke 21:10–19

PROPER PREFACE OF APOSTLES

THE PRESENTATION
OF OUR LORD JESUS CHRIST
IN THE TEMPLE,
also called
THE PURIFICATION
OF SAINT MARY THE VIRGIN

FEBRUARY 2

THE COLLECT

ALMIGHTY AND EVERLIVING GOD, we humbly pray, that, as your only Son our Savior was presented in the temple of the old covenant, so we, who are the temple of his Holy Spirit, may come before you with pure and clean hearts; through Jesus Christ our Lord, who lives and reigns with you and the Holy Spirit, one God, for ever and ever. *Amen.*

ALMIGHTY AND EVERLIVING GOD, we humbly beseech thee, that, as thine only Son our Savior was presented in the temple of the old covenant, so wc, who are the temple of his Holy Spirit, may come before thee with pure and clean hearts; through Jesus Christ our Lord, who liveth and reigneth with thee and the same Spirit, one God, for ever and ever. *Amen.*

THE PSALMS　　　　84:1–5
　　　　　　　　　48:8–13

THE LESSONS　　　Malachi 3:1–4
　　　　　　　　　1 John 3:1–8
　　　　　　　　　Luke 2:22–40

PROPER PREFACE OF THE INCARNATION

SAINT MATTHIAS THE APOSTLE

FEBRUARY 24

THE COLLECT

ALMIGHTY GOD, who in the place of a traitor chose your faithful servant Matthias to be counted in the number of the Twelve: Grant that your Church may ever be preserved in loyalty to your Son, and also be ordered and guided by faithful and true pastors; through Jesus Christ your Son our Lord, who lives and reigns with you in the unity of the Holy Spirit, one God, now and ever. *Amen.*

ALMIGHTY GOD, who in the place of a traitor didst choose thy faithful servant Matthias to be counted in the number of the Twelve: Grant that thy Church may ever be preserved in loyalty to thy Son, and also be ordered and guided by faithful and true pastors; through the same thy Son Jesus Christ our Lord, who liveth and reigneth with thee in the unity of the Holy Spirit, one God, now and ever. *Amen.*

THE PSALMS   15
                    11:1–6

THE LESSONS   Acts 1:15–26
                    Philippians 3:13–21
                    John 15:1, 6–16

PROPER PREFACE OF APOSTLES

579

SAINT JOSEPH

MARCH 19

THE COLLECT

O GOD, who called blessed Joseph to be the guardian of your only Son, and the spouse of his virgin mother: Give us grace to follow his faithfulness and obedience to your commands, that our homes may be blessed by your presence and peace; through Jesus Christ our Lord, who lives and reigns with you and the Holy Spirit, one God, now and for ever. *Amen.*

O GOD, who didst call blessed Joseph to be the guardian of thine only Son, and the spouse of his virgin mother: Give us grace to follow his faithfulness and obedience to thy commands, that our homes may be blessed by thy presence and peace; through Jesus Christ our Lord, who liveth and reigneth with thee and the Holy Spirit, one God, now and for ever. *Amen.*

THE PSALMS   127:1–4
                       119:57–64

THE LESSONS   Isaiah 63:7–9, 16
                       Philippians 4:5–8, 9b
                       Luke 2:41–51a

PROPER PREFACE OF ALL SAINTS

THE ANNUNCIATION
OF OUR LORD JESUS CHRIST
TO THE BLESSED VIRGIN MARY

MARCH 25

THE COLLECT

O LORD, we pray, pour your grace into our hearts, that, as we have known the birth of your son Jesus Christ by the message of an angel, so by his cross and passion we may be brought to the glory of his resurrection; through Jesus Christ our Lord, who lives and reigns with you in the unity of the Holy Spirit, one God, now and for ever. *Amen.*

O LORD, we beseech thee, pour thy grace into our hearts; that, as we have known the incarnation of thy Son Jesus Christ by the message of an angel, so by his cross and passion we may be brought unto the glory of his resurrection; through the same Jesus Christ our Lord, who liveth and reigneth with thee in the unity of the Holy Spirit, one God, now and for ever. *Amen.*

THE PSALMS   113
                  131

THE LESSONS   Isaiah 7:10–14; 8:10c
                  Hebrews 10:4–10
                  Luke 1:26–38

PROPER PREFACE OF THE INCARNATION

581

SAINT MARK THE EVANGELIST

APRIL 25

THE COLLECT

ALMIGHTY GOD, we thank you for the gospel of your Son Jesus Christ, committed to his Church by the hand of your evangelist Saint Mark; and we pray that, being firmly grounded in its truth, we may be faithful to its teaching both in word and deed; through Jesus Christ our Lord, who lives and reigns with you and the Holy Spirit, one God, now and evermore. *Amen.*

ALMIGHTY GOD, we thank thee for the gospel of thy Son Jesus Christ, committed to his Church by the hand of thine evangelist Saint Mark; and we pray that, being firmly grounded in its truth, we may be faithful to its teaching both in word and deed; through the same Jesus Christ our Lord, who liveth and reigneth with thee and the Holy Spirit, one God, now and evermore. *Amen.*

THE PSALMS   19:1–6
                        119:9–16

THE LESSONS   Isaiah 62:6–8, 10–12
                        Ephesians 4:7–8, 11–16
                        Mark 13:1–10

PROPER PREFACE OF ALL SAINTS

582

SAINT PHILIP AND SAINT JAMES, APOSTLES

MAY 1

THE COLLECT

ALMIGHTY GOD, who gave to your apostles Saint Philip and Saint James grace and strength fearlessly to bear testimony to the truth: Grant that we, being always mindful of their victory of faith, may learn like them to overcome the world, and glorify the Name of our Lord Jesus Christ, who lives and reigns with you and the Holy Spirit, one God, now and ever. *Amen.*

ALMIGHTY GOD, who didst give to thine apostles Saint Philip and Saint James grace and strength fearlessly to bear testimony to the truth: Grant that we, being ever mindful of their victory of faith, may learn like them to overcome the world, and glorify the Name of our Lord Jesus Christ, who liveth and reigneth with thee and the Holy Spirit, one God, now and ever. *Amen.*

THE PSALMS   25:1–4
                  119:41–48

THE LESSONS   Isaiah 30:18–21
                  2 Corinthians 4:1–6
                  John 14:6–13a

PROPER PREFACE OF APOSTLES

583

THE VISITATION
OF THE BLESSED VIRGIN MARY

MAY 31

The Collect

FATHER IN HEAVEN, who chose in wondrous grace the blessed Virgin Mary to be the mother of your incarnate Son: Grant that, as we honor the exaltation of her lowliness, so we may follow the example of her humble obedience to your will; through Jesus Christ your Son our Lord, who now lives and reigns with you and the Holy Spirit, one God, in glory everlasting. *Amen.*

FATHER IN HEAVEN, who didst choose in wondrous grace the blessed Virgin Mary to be the mother of thine incarnate Son: Grant that, as we honor the exaltation of her lowliness, so we may follow the example of her humble obedience to thy will; through Jesus Christ our Lord, who now liveth and reigneth with thee and the Holy Spirit, one God, in glory everlasting. *Amen.*

The Psalms   121
                         23

The Lessons   Zephaniah 3:14–17
                      Ephesians 5:18b–20
                      Luke 1:39–49

PROPER PREFACE OF THE INCARNATION

SAINT BARNABAS THE APOSTLE

JUNE 11

THE COLLECT

O GOD, whose Son Jesus Christ has taught us that it is more blessed to give than to receive: Help us, by the example of your apostle and servant Barnabas, to be generous in our judgments and unselfish in our service; through Jesus Christ our Lord, who lives and reigns with you and the Holy Spirit, one God, now and for ever. *Amen.*

O GOD, whose Son Jesus Christ hath taught us that it is more blessed to give than to receive: Help us, by the example of thine apostle and servant Barnabas, to be generous in our judgments and unselfish in our service; through Jesus Christ our Lord, who liveth and reigneth with thee and the Holy Spirit, one God, now and for ever. *Amen.*

THE PSALMS
112:1–6
37:23–28

THE LESSONS
Job 29:11–16
Acts 11:22–30
Mark 10:23–31

PROPER PREFACE OF APOSTLES

585

THE NATIVITY OF SAINT JOHN THE BAPTIST

JUNE 24

THE COLLECT

ALMIGHTY GOD, by whose providence your servant John the Baptist was wonderfully born to be the forerunner of our Savior Jesus Christ: Give us grace to repent according to his preaching, and turn to you with all our hearts, that we may be ready for that day when the glory of the Lord shall be revealed; through Jesus Christ our Lord, who lives and reigns with you in the unity of the Holy Spirit, one God, now and ever. *Amen.*

ALMIGHTY GOD, by whose providence thy servant John the Baptist was wonderfully born to be the forerunner of our Savior Jesus Christ: Give us grace to repent according to his preaching, and to turn to thee with all our hearts, that we may be ready for that day when the glory of the Lord shall be revealed; through Jesus Christ our Lord, who liveth and reigneth with thee in the unity of the Holy Spirit, one God, now and ever. *Amen.*

| THE PSALMS | 85:7–13 |
| | 81:9–15 |

THE LESSONS	Isaiah 40:1–11
	Acts 13:14b–26
	Luke 1:57–80

PROPER PREFACE OF ADVENT

SAINT PETER AND SAINT PAUL, APOSTLES

JUNE 29

THE COLLECT

ALMIGHTY GOD, who made this day holy by the martyrdom of your blessed apostles Peter and Paul: Grant that your household the Church, being instructed by their teaching and example, and knit together in unity by your Spirit, may ever stand firm upon the one foundation, which is Jesus Christ our Lord, who lives and reigns with you and the Holy Spirit, one God, for ever and ever. *Amen.*

ALMIGHTY GOD, who hast made this day holy by the martyrdom of thy blessed apostles Peter and Paul: Grant that thy household the Church, being instructed by their teaching and example, and knit together in unity by thy Spirit, may ever stand firm upon the one foundation, which is Jesus Christ our Lord, who liveth and reigneth with thee and the same Spirit, one God, for ever and ever. *Amen.*

| THE PSALMS | 18:1–7 |
| | 87 |

THE LESSONS	Ezekiel 34:11–16
	2 Timothy 4:1–8
	John 21:15–19

PROPER PREFACE OF APOSTLES

587

INDEPENDENCE DAY

JULY 4

THE COLLECT

ETERNAL GOD, through whose mighty power our fathers won their liberties of old: Grant, we pray, that we and all the people of this land may have grace to maintain these liberties in righteousness and peace; through Jesus Christ our Lord, who lives and reigns with you and the Holy Spirit, one God, in glory everlasting. *Amen.*

ETERNAL GOD, through whose mighty power our fathers won their liberties of old: Grant, we beseech thee, that we and all the people of this land may have grace to maintain these liberties in righteousness and peace; through Jesus Christ, our Lord, who liveth and reigneth with thee and the Holy Spirit, one God, in glory everlasting. *Amen.*

THE PSALMS   145:1–9
                145:14–21

THE LESSONS   Micah 4:1–5
                Hebrews 11:8–16
                Matthew 5:43–48

PROPER PREFACE OF TRINITY SUNDAY

SAINT MARY MAGDALENE

JULY 22

THE COLLECT

ALMIGHTY GOD, whose blessed Son restored Mary Magdalene to health of body and of mind, and called her to be a witness of his resurrection: Mercifully grant that by your grace we may be healed of all our infirmities, and serve you in the power of his endless life, who with you and the Holy Spirit lives and reigns, one God, now and for ever. *Amen.*

ALMIGHTY GOD, whose blessed Son restored Mary Magdalene to health of body and mind, and called her to be a witness of his resurrection: Mercifully grant that by thy grace we may be healed of all our infirmities, and serve thee in the power of his endless life, who with thee and the Holy Spirit liveth and reigneth, one God, now and for ever. *Amen.*

THE PSALMS   138:1–5
                  116:5–9

THE LESSONS   Acts 13:27–31
                  2 Corinthians 5:14–18
                  John 20:11–18

PROPER PREFACE OF ALL SAINTS

589

SAINT JAMES THE APOSTLE

JULY 25

THE COLLECT

ALMIGHTY GOD, who gave to your apostle Saint James a ready will to obey the calling of your Son, and strength to suffer for his Name: Mercifully grant that no worldly affections may draw our hearts away from steadfast devotion to his service; through Jesus Christ your Son our Lord, who lives and reigns with you and the Holy Spirit, one God, now and evermore. *Amen.*

ALMIGHTY GOD, who didst give to thine apostle Saint James a ready will to obey the calling of thy Son, and strength to suffer for his Name: Mercifully grant that no worldly affections may draw our hearts away from steadfast devotion to his service; through the same thy Son Jesus Christ our Lord, who liveth and reigneth with thee and the Holy Spirit, one God, now and evermore. *Amen.*

THE PSALMS   75:1–8
                  33:13–18

THE LESSONS   Jeremiah 45
                  Acts 11:27—12:2
                  Matthew 20:20–28

PROPER PREFACE OF APOSTLES

590

THE TRANSFIGURATION OF OUR LORD JESUS CHRIST

AUGUST 6

THE COLLECT

O GOD, who on the holy mount revealed to chosen witnesses your well-beloved Son, wonderfully transfigured with your sublime glory: Mercifully grant that we, being delivered from the disquiet of this world, may by faith behold the King in his beauty, who with you and the Holy Spirit now lives and reigns, one God, for ever and ever. *Amen.*

O GOD, who on the holy mount didst reveal to chosen witnesses thy well-beloved Son, wonderfully transfigured with thy sublime glory: Mercifully grant that we, being delivered from the disquiet of this world, may by faith behold the King in his beauty, who with thee and the Holy Spirit now liveth and reigneth, one God for ever and ever. *Amen.*

THE PSALMS	99:5–9
	27:4–7

THE LESSONS	Exodus 34:29–35
	2 Peter 1:13–21
	Luke 9:28–26

PROPER PREFACE OF THE INCARNATION

SAINT MARY THE VIRGIN

AUGUST 15

THE COLLECT

O GOD, who received to yourself the blessed Virgin Mary, mother of your only Son: Grant that we, who have been redeemed by his blood, may share with her the glory of your eternal kingdom; through Jesus Christ your Son our Lord, who lives and reigns with you in the unity of the Holy Spirit, one God, for ever and ever. *Amen.*

O GOD, who hast taken to thyself the blessed Virgin Mary, mother of thine only Son: Grant that we, who have been redeemed by his blood, may share with her the glory of thine eternal kingdom; through the same thy Son Jesus Christ our Lord, who liveth and reigneth with thee in the unity of the Holy Spirit, one God, for ever and ever. *Amen.*

| THE PSALMS | 34:1–4 |
| | 66:14–18 |

THE LESSONS	Isaiah 61:7–11
	Galatians 4:4–7
	Luke 1:46–55

PROPER PREFACE OF ALL SAINTS

SAINT BARTHOLOMEW THE APOSTLE

AUGUST 24

THE COLLECT

ALMIGHTY AND EVERLASTING GOD, who gave to your apostle
Bartholomew grace truly to believe and to preach your
Word: Grant, we pray, that your Church may love the Word
which he believed, and both preach it and obey it; through
Jesus Christ our Lord, who lives and reigns with you and
the Holy Spirit, one God, now and ever. *Amen.*

ALMIGHTY AND EVERLASTING GOD, who didst give to thine
apostle Bartholomew grace truly to believe and to preach
thy Word: Grant, we beseech thee, that thy Church may love
the Word which he believed, and both preach and obey the
same; through Jesus Christ our Lord, who liveth and
reigneth with thee and the Holy Spirit, one God, now and
ever. *Amen.*

THE PSALMS   91:1–4
                  119:161–168

THE LESSONS   Deuteronomy 18:15–18
                  1 Corinthians 4:9–15
                  Luke 22:24–30

PROPER PREFACE OF APOSTLES

HOLY CROSS DAY

SEPTEMBER 14

THE COLLECT

ALMIGHTY GOD, whose Son our Savior Jesus Christ was lifted high upon the cross that he might draw all men to himself: Mercifully grant that we, who glory in his death for our salvation, may also glory in his call to take up our cross and follow him, who now lives and reigns with you and the Holy Spirit, one God, in glory everlasting. *Amen.*

ALMIGHTY GOD, whose Son our Savior Jesus Christ was lifted high upon the cross that he might draw all men unto himself: Mercifully grant that we, who glory in his death for our salvation, may also glory in his call to take up our cross and follow him, who now liveth and reigneth with thee and the Holy Spirit, one God, in glory everlasting. *Amen.*

THE PSALMS   27:1–6
                  98:1–4

THE LESSONS   Isaiah 45:21–25
                  Philippians 2:5–11
                      or Galatians 6:14–18
                  John 12:31–36

PROPER PREFACE OF HOLY WEEK

594

SAINT MATTHEW, APOSTLE AND EVANGELIST

SEPTEMBER 21

THE COLLECT

WE THANK YOU, heavenly Father, for the witness of your apostle and evangelist Matthew to the gospel of your Son our Savior; and we pray that, after his example, we may with ready wills and hearts obey the calling of our Lord to follow him; through Jesus Christ our Lord, who lives and reigns with you and the Holy Spirit, one God, now and ever. *Amen.*

WE THANK THEE, heavenly Father, for the witness of thine apostle and evangelist Matthew to the gospel of thy Son our Savior; and we pray that, after his example, we may with ready wills and hearts obey the calling of our Lord to follow him; through Jesus Christ our Lord, who liveth and reigneth with thee and the Holy Spirit, one God, now and ever. *Amen.*

THE PSALMS   65:1–5
                   119:33–40

THE LESSONS   Proverbs 3:1–6
                   2 Timothy 3:14–17
                   Matthew 9:9–13

PROPER PREFACE OF APOSTLES

595

SAINT MICHAEL AND ALL ANGELS

SEPTEMBER 29

THE COLLECT

EVERLASTING GOD, by whom the ministries of angels and men have been ordained and constituted in a wonderful order: Mercifully grant that, as your holy angels always serve and worship you in heaven, so by your appointment they may help and defend us on earth; through Jesus Christ our Lord, who lives and reigns with you and the Holy Spirit, one God, now and ever. *Amen.*

EVERLASTING GOD, who hast ordained and constituted the ministries of angels and men in a wonderful order: Mercifully grant that, as thy holy angels always serve and worship thee in heaven, so by thy appointment they may help and defend us on earth; through Jesus Christ our Lord, who liveth and reigneth with thee and the Holy Spirit, one God, now and ever. *Amen.*

THE PSALMS   148:1–5
103:19–22

THE LESSONS   Genesis 28:10–17
Revelation 12:7–11
John 1:47–51

PROPER PREFACE OF TRINITY SUNDAY

SAINT LUKE THE EVANGELIST

OCTOBER 18

THE COLLECT

ALMIGHTY GOD, who inspired your servant Saint Luke, the physician, to set forth in the gospel the love and healing power of your Son: Graciously continue in your Church the like love and power to heal, to the praise and glory of your Name; through Jesus Christ our Lord, who lives and reigns with you in the unity of the Holy Spirit, one God, now and forever. *Amen.*

ALMIGHTY GOD, who didst inspire thy servant Saint Luke, the physician, to set forth in the gospel the love and healing power of thy Son: Graciously continue in thy Church the like love and power to heal, to the praise and glory of thy Name; through Jesus Christ our Lord, who liveth and reigneth with thee in the unity of the Holy Spirit, one God, now and for ever. *Amen.*

THE PSALMS	68:4–6
	37:38–41

THE LESSONS	Ecclesiasticus, 38:1–4, 6–10, 12–14
	2 Timothy 4:5–13
	Luke 4:14–21

PROPER PREFACE OF ALL SAINTS

SAINT JAMES OF JERUSALEM
BROTHER OF OUR LORD JESUS CHRIST AND MARTYR

OCTOBER 23

THE COLLECT

GRANT, we pray, O God, that after the example of your servant James, the brother of our Lord, your Church may give itself continually to prayer, and to the reconciliation of all who are at variance and enmity; through Jesus Christ our Lord, who lives and reigns with you in the unity of the Holy Spirit, one God, now and for ever. *Amen.*

GRANT, we beseech thee, O God, that after the example of thy servant James, the brother of our Lord, thy Church may give itself continually to prayer, and to the reconciliation of all who are at variance and enmity; through Jesus Christ our Lord, who liveth and reigneth with thee in the unity of the Holy Spirit, one God, now and for ever. *Amen.*

THE PSALMS   1

119:145–152

THE LESSONS   Acts 15:12–22

1 Corinthians 15:1–11

Mark 3:31–35,

or Matthew 13:54–58

PROPER PREFACE OF ALL SAINTS

SAINT SIMON AND SAINT JUDE, APOSTLES
OCTOBER 28

THE COLLECT

O GOD, we thank you for the glorious company of the apostles, and especially on this day for Saint Simon and Saint Jude; and we pray that, as they were faithful and zealous in their mission, so we may with ardent devotion make known among the nations the love and mercy of our Lord and Savior Jesus Christ, who lives and reigns with you in the unity of the Holy Spirit, one God, now and for ever. *Amen.*

O GOD, we thank thee for the glorious company of the apostles, and especially on this day for Saint Simon and Saint Jude; and we pray that, as they were faithful and zealous in their mission, so we may with ardent devotion make known among the nations the love and mercy of our Lord and Savior Jesus Christ, who liveth and reigneth with thee in the unity of the Holy Spirit, one God, now and for ever. *Amen.*

THE PSALMS   62:7–12
                            119:137–144

THE LESSONS   Deuteronomy 32:1–4
                              Ephesians 2:13–22
                              John 14:21–27

PROPER PREFACE OF APOSTLES

599

ALL SAINTS' DAY

NOVEMBER 1

THE COLLECT

ALMIGHTY GOD, whose elect are knit together in one communion and fellowship, in the mystical body of your Son Christ our Lord: Grant us grace so to follow your blessed saints in all virtuous and holy living, that we may come to those inexpressible joys that you have prepared for those who truly love you; through Jesus Christ our Lord, who lives and reigns with you and the Holy Spirit, one God, in glory everlasting. *Amen.*

ALMIGHTY GOD, who hast knit together thine elect in one communion and fellowship, in the mystical body of thy Son Christ our Lord: Grant us grace so to follow thy blessed saints in all virtuous and godly living, that we may come to those unspeakable joys which thou hast prepared for those who unfeignedly love thee; through Jesus Christ our Lord, who liveth and reigneth with thee and the Holy Spirit, one God, in glory everlasting. *Amen.*

THE PSALMS   149
                34:4–9

THE LESSONS   Ecclesiasticus 44:1–10, 13–14
                Revelation 7:9–17
                Matthew 5:1–12

PROPER PREFACE OF ALL SAINTS

THANKSGIVING DAY

The Collect

ALMIGHTY AND GRACIOUS FATHER, we give you thanks for the fruits of the earth in their season, and for the labors of those who harvest them. Make us, we pray, faithful stewards of your great bounty, in the provision for our necessities, and the relief of all who are in need, to the glory of your Name; through Jesus Christ our Lord, who lives and reigns with you and the Holy Spirit, one God, now and for ever. *Amen.*

ALMIGHTY AND GRACIOUS FATHER, we give thee thanks for the fruits of the earth in their season, and for the labors of those who harvest them. Make us, we beseech thee, faithful stewards of thy great bounty, in the provision for our necessities, and the relief of all who are in need, to the glory of thy Name; through Jesus Christ our Lord, who liveth and reigneth with thee and the Holy Spirit, one God, now and for ever. *Amen.*

THE PSALMS   147:7–11
                      65:9–14

THE LESSONS   Deuteronomy 8:6–11
                      James 1:16–21
                      Matthew 6:25–33

PROPER PREFACE OF TRINITY SUNDAY

At the celebration of the Holy Eucharist, the following Litany of Thanksgiving may be used in place of the Prayer of Intercession:

LET US GIVE THANKS to God our Father for all his gifts so freely bestowed upon us:

For the beauty and wonder of his creation, in earth and sky and sea,

We thank you, Lord.

For all that is gracious in the lives of men and women, revealing the image of Christ,

We thank you, Lord.

For our daily food and drink, our homes and families, and our friends,

We thank you, Lord.

For minds to think, and hearts to love, and hands to serve,

We thank you, Lord.

For health and strength to work, and leisure to rest and play,

We thank you, Lord.

For the brave and courageous who are patient in suffering, and faithful in adversity,

We thank you, Lord.

For all valiant seekers after truth, liberty, and justice.

We thank you, Lord.

For the communion of saints, in all times and places,

We thank you, Lord.

Above all, let us give thanks for the great promises and mercies given to us in Christ Jesus our Lord:

To him be praise and glory, with the Father and the Holy Spirit, now and for ever. Amen.

THE COMMON OF SAINTS

The festival of a saint is observed according to the rules of precedence set forth in The Calendar of the Church Year (pages 3–6). At the discretion of the Priest, and as appropriate, any of the prayers and lessons following may be used:

a) in the commemoration of a saint listed in the Calendar for which this Book provides no proper collect or lessons, or for which no other provision is made by authority of this Church.
b) for the patronal festival of a saint not listed in the Calendar.

1. OF A MARTYR

THE COLLECT

ALMIGHTY GOD, by whose grace and power your holy martyr
N. triumphed over suffering, and was faithful even to death:
Grant us, who now remember *him* in thanksgiving, to be so
faithful in our witness to you in this world, that we may receive with *him* the crown of everlasting life; through Jesus
Christ our Lord, who lives and reigns with you and the
Holy Spirit, one God, now and ever. *Amen.*

ALMIGHTY GOD, by whose grace and power thy holy martyr
N. triumphed over suffering, and was faithful unto death:
Grant us, who now remember *him* in thanksgiving, to be so
faithful in our witness to thee in this world, that we may
receive with *him* the crown of everlasting life; through
Jesus Christ our Lord, who liveth and reigneth with thee
and the Holy Spirit, one God, now and ever. *Amen.*

or this Collect:

ALMIGHTY AND ETERNAL GOD, who kindled the fire of faith and love in the heart of your blessed martyr *N.:* Grant, we pray, that as we rejoice in *his* triumph, we may have courage to bear with him reproach for the Name of our Lord Jesus Christ, who lives and reigns with you and the Holy Spirit, one God, now and for ever. *Amen.*

ALMIGHTY AND ETERNAL GOD, who didst enkindle the fire of faith and love in the heart of thy blessed martyr *N.:* Grant, we beseech thee, that as we rejoice in *his* triumph, so we may have courage to bear with *him* reproach for the Name of our Lord Jesus Christ, who liveth and reigneth with thee and the Holy Spirit, one God, now and for ever. *Amen.*

THE PSALMS   126
                    121

THE LESSONS

2 Esdras 2:42–48   Ecclesiasticus 51:1–12
1 Peter 3:12–18   *or* Revelation 7:13–17
Matthew 10:16–22   Luke 12:2–12

PROPER PREFACE OF ALL SAINTS

2. OF A MISSIONARY

THE COLLECT

ALMIGHTY AND EVERLASTING GOD, we thank you for your servant *N.*, whom you called to preach the gospel to the people of _____. Raise up, we pray, in this and every land, heralds and evangelists of your kingdom, that your Church may make known the immeasurable riches of our Savior Jesus Christ, who lives and reigns with you and the Holy Spirit, one God, now and for ever. *Amen.*

ALMIGHTY AND EVERLASTING GOD, we thank thee for thy servant *N.*, whom thou didst call to preach the gospel to the people of _____. Raise up, we pray, in this and every land, heralds and evangelists of thy kingdom, that thy Church may make known the immeasurable riches of our Savior Jesus Christ, who liveth and reigneth with thee and the Holy Spirit, one God, now and for ever. *Amen.*

THE PSALMS   96:1–7
                   96:8–13

THE LESSONS   Isaiah 52:7–10
                   Acts 1:1–9
                   Luke 10:1–9

PROPER PREFACE OF ALL SAINTS

3. OF A PASTOR

THE COLLECT

FATHER IN HEAVEN, the good shepherd of your people, we thank you for your servant N., who was faithful in the care and nurture of your flock; and we pray that we, following his example and the teaching of his holy life, may by your grace grow into the full manhood and stature of our Lord and Savior Jesus Christ, who lives and reigns with you and the Holy Spirit, one God, for ever and ever. *Amen.*

FATHER IN HEAVEN, good shepherd of thy people, we thank thee for thy servant N., who was faithful in the care and nurture of thy flock; and we pray that we, following his example and the teaching of his holy life, may by thy grace grow into the full manhood and stature of our Lord and Savior Jesus Christ, who liveth and reigneth, with thee and the Holy Spirit, one God, for ever and ever. *Amen.*

THE PSALMS   112:1–9
                    23

THE LESSONS   Ezekiel 34:11–16
                    1 Peter 5:1–4
                    John 21:15–17

PROPER PREFACE OF ALL SAINTS

4. OF A THEOLOGIAN OR TEACHER

THE COLLECT

O GOD, by whose Holy Spirit is given to one the word of wisdom, and to another the word of knowledge, and to another the word of faith: We praise your Name for the gifts of grace imparted to your servant *N.*, and pray that by his teaching we may know you, the only true God, and Jesus Christ whom you have sent, and who now lives and reigns with you and the Holy Spirit, one God, for evermore. *Amen.*

O GOD, who by thy Holy Spirit dost give to one the word of wisdom, and to another the word of knowledge, and to another the word of faith: We praise thy Name for the gifts of grace imparted to thy servant *N.*, and we pray that by his teaching we may know thee, the only true God, and Jesus Christ whom thou hast sent, and who now liveth and reigneth with thee and the Holy Spirit, one God, for evermore. *Amen.*

THE PSALMS   119:33–40
             119:97–104

THE LESSONS Wisdom 7:7–14
             1 Corinthians 2:6–10, 13–16
             John 17:18–23

PROPER PREFACE OF ALL SAINTS, OR OF TRINITY SUNDAY

607

5. OF A MONASTIC

THE COLLECT

O GOD, whose blessed Son became poor that we through his poverty might be rich: Deliver us, we pray, from an inordinate love of this world, that, following the example of your servant *N.*, we may serve you with singleness of heart, and attain to the riches of the world to come; through Jesus Christ our Lord, who lives and reigns with you in the unity of the Holy Spirit, one God, now and for ever. *Amen.*

O GOD, whose blessed Son became poor that we through his poverty might be rich: Deliver us, we beseech thee, from an inordinate love of this world, that, following the example of thy servant *N.*, we may serve thee with singleness of heart, and attain to the riches of the world to come; through Jesus Christ our Lord, who liveth and reigneth with thee in the unity of the Holy Spirit, one God, now and for ever. *Amen.*

| THE PSALMS | 134 |
| | 139:13–18 |

THE LESSONS	Song of Songs 8:6–7
	Philippians 3:7–15
	Luke 12:33–37

PROPER PREFACE OF ALL SAINTS

6. OF A SAINT

I

THE COLLECT

ALMIGHTY GOD, by whose grace we are surrounded with so great a cloud of witnesses: Grant that we, encouraged by the good example of your servant *N.*, may persevere in running the race that is set before us, until at last, through your mercy, we with them attain to your eternal joy, through him who is the author and perfecter of our faith, your Son Jesus Christ our Lord, who lives and reigns with you and the Holy Spirit, one God, now and ever. *Amen.*

ALMIGHTY GOD, who hast surrounded us with so great a cloud of witnesses: Grant that we, encouraged by the good example of thy servant *N.*, may persevere in running the race that is set before us, until at length, through thy mercy, we with them attain to thine eternal joy; through him who is the author and finisher of our faith, thy Son Jesus Christ our Lord, who liveth and reigneth with thee and the Holy Spirit, one God, now and ever. *Amen.*

THE PSALMS   1
                             15

THE LESSONS

Micah 6:6–8   Wisdom 3:1–9
Hebrews 12:1–2   *or*   Philippians 4:4–9
Matthew 25:31–40   Luke 6:17–23

PROPER PREFACE OF ALL SAINTS

609

6. OF A SAINT

II

The Collect

O God, you have brought us near to an innumerable company of angels, and to the spirits of just men made perfect: Grant us during our earthly pilgrimage to abide in their fellowship, and in our heavenly country to become partakers of their joy; through Jesus Christ our Lord, who lives and reigns in glory with you and the Holy Spirit, one God, now and for ever. *Amen.*

O God, who hast brought us near to an innumerable company of angels, and to the spirits of just men made perfect: Grant us during our earthly pilgrimage to abide in their fellowship, and in our heavenly country to become partakers of their joy; through Jesus Christ our Lord, who liveth and reigneth in glory with thee and the Holy Spirit, one God, now and for ever. *Amen.*

The Psalms

1

15

The Lessons

Micah 6:6–8
Hebrews 12:1–2   *or*
Matthew 25:31–40

Wisdom 3:1–9
Philippians 4:4–9
Luke 6:17–23

Proper Preface of All Saints

6. OF A SAINT

III

THE COLLECT

ALMIGHTY AND EVERLASTING GOD, who enkindled the flame of your love in the heart of your servant *N.:* Grant to us, your humble servants, a like faith and power of love; that, as we rejoice in *her* triumph, we may profit by *her* example; through Jesus Christ our Lord, who lives and reigns with you and the Holy Spirit, one God, now and for ever. *Amen.*

ALMIGHTY AND EVERLASTING GOD, who didst enkindle the flame of thy love in the heart of thy servant *N.:* Grant to us, thy humble servants, the same faith and power of love; that, as we rejoice in *her* triumph, we may profit by *her* example; through Jesus Christ our Lord, who liveth and reigneth with thee and the Holy Spirit, one God, now and for ever. *Amen.*

THE PSALMS   63:1–8
                   34:3–10

THE LESSONS   Ecclesiasticus 2:7–11
                   1 Corinthians 1:26–31
                   Matthew 25:1–13

PROPER PREFACE OF ALL SAINTS

611

SPECIAL OCCASIONS

The following are provided for special celebrations of the Holy Eucharist, in accordance with the rules set forth in The Calendar of the Church Year.

1. OF THE HOLY TRINITY

THE COLLECT

ALMIGHTY GOD, whose eternal Being of glorious majesty and perfect love has been revealed to your Church as one God in Trinity of Persons: Give us grace to abide steadfast in the confession of this faith, and constant in our worship of you, in spirit and in truth, who live and reign, one God, Father, Son, and Holy Spirit, now and for ever. *Amen.*

ALMIGHTY GOD, who hast revealed to thy Church thine eternal Being of glorious majesty and perfect love as one God in Trinity of Persons: Give us grace to abide steadfast in the confession of this faith, and constant in our worship of thee in spirit and in truth, who livest and reignest, one God, Father, Son, and Holy Spirit, now and for ever. *Amen.*

THE PSALMS 148:1–6
             148:7–13

THE LESSONS Exodus 3:11–15
             Romans 11:33–36
             Matthew 28:18–20

PROPER PREFACE OF TRINITY SUNDAY

612

2. OF THE HOLY SPIRIT

THE COLLECT

ALMIGHTY AND MOST MERCIFUL GOD, grant that the indwelling of your Holy Spirit in our hearts may enlighten us by your truth and strengthen us for your service; through Jesus Christ our Lord, who lives and reigns with you in the unity of the Spirit, one God, now and for ever. *Amen.*

ALMIGHTY AND MOST MERCIFUL GOD, grant, we beseech thee, that by the indwelling of the Holy Spirit, we may be enlightened and strengthened for thy service; through Jesus Christ our Lord, who liveth and reigneth with thee in the unity of the same Spirit, one God, now and for ever. *Amen.*

THE PSALMS   139:6–11
                 51:10–13

THE LESSONS   Isaiah 61:1–3
                 1 Corinthians 12:4–14
                 Luke 11:9–13

PROPER PREFACE OF PENTECOST

3. OF THE HOLY ANGELS

THE COLLECT

EVERLASTING GOD, by whom the ministries of angels and men have been ordained and constituted in a wonderful order: Mercifully grant that, as your holy angels always serve and worship you in heaven, so by your appointment they may help and defend us on earth; through Jesus Christ our Lord, who lives and reigns with you and the Holy Spirit, one God, now and ever. *Amen.*

EVERLASTING GOD, who hast ordained and constituted the ministries of angels and men in a wonderful order: Mercifully grant that, as thy holy angels always serve and worship thee in heaven, so by thy appointment they may help and defend us on earth; through Jesus Christ our Lord, who liveth and reigneth with thee and the Holy Spirit, one God, now and ever. *Amen.*

THE PSALMS   103:19–22
                 104:1–4

THE LESSONS   Daniel 7:9–10a
                 Revelation 5:11–14
                 John 1:47–51

PROPER PREFACE OF TRINITY SUNDAY

4. OF THE INCARNATION

THE COLLECT

ALMIGHTY FATHER, by whom the world has been filled with the new light of your beloved Son, the incarnate Word: Grant, we pray, that as he kindles the flame of faith and love in our hearts, so his light may shine forth in our lives, who now lives and reigns with you in the unity of the Holy Spirit, one God, now and for ever. *Amen.*

ALMIGHTY FATHER, who hast filled the world with the new light of thy beloved Son, the incarnate Word: Grant, we beseech thee, that as he enkindles the flame of faith and love in our hearts, so his light may shine forth in our lives; the same thy Son, Jesus Christ our Lord, who liveth and reigneth with thee in the unity of the Holy Spirit, one God, now and for ever. *Amen.*

THE PSALMS   113
                      111:1–4, 8–9

THE LESSONS   Isaiah 11:1–10
                      1 John 4:1–11
                      Luke 1:26–38

PROPER PREFACE OF THE INCARNATION

5. OF THE HOLY EUCHARIST

Especially suitable for Thursdays.

THE COLLECT

GOD OUR FATHER, whose Son our Lord Jesus Christ gave us in this wonderful sacrament the memorial of his passion: Grant us so to reverence the sacred mysteries of his Body and Blood, that we may always discern within ourselves the fruit of his redemption, who now lives and reigns with you in the unity of the Holy Spirit, one God, for ever and ever. *Amen.*

O GOD OUR FATHER, whose Son our Lord Jesus Christ hath given us in this wonderful sacrament the memorial of his passion: Grant us so to reverence the sacred mysteries of his Body and Blood, that we may ever perceive within ourselves the fruit of his redemption, who now liveth and reigneth with thee in the unity of the Holy Spirit, one God, for ever and ever. *Amen.*

THE PSALMS   145:14–18
                         116:11–16

THE LESSONS   Deuteronomy 8:2–3
                         Revelation 19:1–2a, 4–9
                         John 6:47–59

PROPER PREFACE OF THE INCARNATION

6. OF THE HOLY CROSS

Especially suitable for Fridays.

THE COLLECT

ALMIGHTY GOD, whose beloved Son for our sake willingly endured the agony and shame of the Cross: Give us courage and patience to take up our cross and follow him, who lives and reigns with you and the Holy Spirit, one God, now and for ever. *Amen.*

ALMIGHTY GOD, whose beloved Son for our sake willingly endured the agony and shame of the Cross: Give us courage and patience to take up our cross and follow him, who liveth and reigneth with thee and the Holy Spirit, one God, now and for ever. *Amen.*

THE PSALMS   56:1–4
                40:5–10

THE LESSONS   Isaiah 52:12–15; 53:10–12
                1 Corinthians 1:18–24
                John 12:23–33

PROPER PREFACE OF HOLY WEEK

7. FOR ALL BAPTIZED CHRISTIANS

Especially suited for Saturdays.

THE COLLECT

GRANT, LORD GOD, to all who have been baptized into the death and resurrection of your Son our Savior Jesus Christ, that, as we have put away the old life of sin, so we may be renewed in the spirit of our minds, and live in righteousness and true holiness; through Jesus Christ our Lord, who now lives and reigns with you in the unity of the Holy Spirit, one God, for ever and ever. *Amen.*

GRANT, O LORD GOD, to all who have been baptized into the death and resurrection of thy Son our Savior Jesus Christ, that, as we have put away the old life of sin, so we may be renewed in the spirit of our minds, and live in righteousness and true holiness; through Jesus Christ our Lord, who now liveth and reigneth with thee in the unity of the Holy Spirit, one God, for ever and ever. *Amen.*

THE PSALMS	18:1–7
	16:9–12

THE LESSONS	Jeremiah 17:7–8
	Roman 6:3–11
	Mark 10:35–45

PROPER PREFACE OF LENT, OR OF BAPTISM

8. THE COMMEMORATION OF ALL FAITHFUL DEPARTED

THE COLLECT

ETERNAL LORD GOD, by whom all souls are held in life: Give, we pray, to your whole Church in paradise and on earth, your light and your peace; and grant that we, following the good examples of those who have served you here and are now at rest, may at the last enter with them into your unending joy; through Jesus Christ our Lord, who lives and reigns with you in the unity of the Holy Spirit, one God, now and ever. *Amen.*

O ETERNAL LORD GOD, who holdest all souls in life: Give, we beseech thee, to thy whole Church in paradise and on earth, thy light and thy peace; and grant that we, following the good examples of those who have served thee here and are now at rest, may at the last enter with them into thine unending joy; through Jesus Christ our Lord, who liveth and reigneth with thee in the unity of the Holy Spirit, one God, now and ever. *Amen.*

THE PSALMS	36:5–10
	103:15–22
THE LESSONS	Isaiah 25:6–9,
	or Wisdom 3:1–9
	1 Corinthians 15:50–58
	John 11:21–27

PROPER PREFACE OF THE COMMEMORATION OF THE DEAD

At the discretion of the Priest, and when appropriate, any of the Collects, Psalms, and Lessons appointed in the office for the Burial of the Dead may be used in place of those given above.

9. OF THE REIGN OF CHRIST

THE COLLECT

ALMIGHTY AND EVERLASTING GOD, whose will it is to restore all things in your well-beloved Son, the King of kings and Lord of lords: Mercifully grant that the peoples of the earth, divided and enslaved by sin, may be freed and brought together under his most gracious rule, who lives and reigns with you and the Holy Spirit, one God, now and for ever. *Amen.*

ALMIGHTY AND EVERLASTING GOD, who didst will to restore all things in thy well-beloved Son, the King of kings, and Lord of lords: Mercifully grant that the peoples of the earth, divided and enslaved by sin, may be freed and brought together under his most gracious rule, who liveth and reigneth with thee and the Holy Spirit, one God, now and for ever. *Amen.*

THE PSALMS	99:1–5
	21:1–6
THE LESSONS	Daniel 7:13–14
	Colossians 1:12–20
	John 18:33–37

PROPER PREFACE OF ASCENSION

10. ON THE ANNIVERSARY OF THE DEDICATION OF A CHURCH

THE COLLECT

ALMIGHTY GOD, to whose glory we celebrate the dedication of this house of prayer: We give you thanks for the fellowship of those who have used it; and we pray that all who seek you here may find you, and be filled with your joy and peace; through Jesus Christ our Lord, who lives and reigns with you in the unity of the Holy Spirit, one God, now and for ever. *Amen.*

ALMIGHTY GOD, to whose glory we celebrate the dedication of this house of prayer: We give thee thanks for the fellowship of those who have used it; and we pray that all who seek thee here may find thee, and be filled with thy joy and peace; through Jesus Christ our Lord, who liveth and reigneth with thee in the unity of the Holy Spirit, one God, now and for ever. *Amen.*

THE PSALMS   122
                  84:1–7

THE LESSONS   1 Kings 8:22–30
                  1 Peter 2:1–9
                  Matthew 21:12–16

PROPER PREFACE OF TRINITY SUNDAY

11. FOR A CHURCH CONVENTION

THE COLLECT

ALMIGHTY AND EVERLASTING FATHER, who gave us the Holy Spirit to abide with us for ever: Bless, we pray, with his grace and presence the Bishops and other Clergy, and the Laity here assembled in your Name; that your Church, being preserved in true faith and godly discipline, may fulfill all the mind of him who loves it and gave himself for it, your Son our Savior Jesus Christ, who lives and reigns with you and the Holy Spirit, one God, now and ever. *Amen.*

ALMIGHTY AND EVERLASTING FATHER, who hast given us the Holy Spirit to abide with us for ever: Bless, we beseech thee, with his grace and presence the Bishops and other Clergy, and the Laity here assembled in thy Name; that thy Church, being preserved in true faith and godly discipline, may fulfill all the mind of him who loves it and gave himself for it, thy Son our Savior Jesus Christ, who liveth and reigneth with thee and the same Spirit, one God, now and ever. *Amen.*

THE PSALMS   146
                            125

THE LESSONS   Isaiah 55
                            2 Corinthians 4:1–10
                            John 15:1–8

PROPER PREFACE OF PENTECOST, OR OF THE SEASON

622

12. FOR EDUCATION

THE COLLECT

ALMIGHTY GOD, the fountain of all wisdom: Enlighten by your Holy Spirit those who teach and those who learn, that, rejoicing in the knowledge of your truth, they may worship and serve you from generation to generation; through Jesus Christ our Lord, who lives and reigns with you in the unity of the Holy Spirit, one God, now and for ever. *Amen.*

ALMIGHTY GOD, the fountain of all wisdom: Enlighten by thy Holy Spirit those who teach and those who learn, that, rejoicing in the knowledge of thy truth, they may worship and serve thee from generation to generation; through Jesus Christ our Lord, who liveth and reigneth with thee in the unity of the same Spirit, one God, now and for ever. *Amen.*

THE PSALMS   78:1–8
               25:3–9

THE LESSONS   Deuteronomy 6:4–9, 20–25
               2 Timothy 3:14—4:5
               Matthew 11:25–30

PROPER PREFACE OF THE SEASON

623

13. FOR THE MINISTRY

Ember Days

The following propers are used as appropriate to times and occasions.

The traditional days of Ordination, or Ember Days, are the Wednesdays, Fridays, and Saturdays after the Third Sunday in Advent, the First Sunday in Lent, the Day of Pentecost, and Holy Cross Day.

I

Especially suitable at the time of Ordination.

THE COLLECT

ALMIGHTY GOD, the giver of all good gifts, who of your divine providence appointed various Orders in your Church: Give your grace, we humbly pray, to all who are *now* called to any office and ministration for your people; and so replenish them with the truth of your doctrine, and endue them with holiness of life, that they may faithfully serve before you to the glory of your great Name, and to the benefit of your holy Church; through Jesus Christ our Lord, who lives and reigns with you in the unity of the Holy Spirit, one God, now and ever. *Amen.*

ALMIGHTY GOD, the giver of all good gifts, who of thy divine providence hast appointed various Orders in thy Church: Give thy grace, we humbly beseech thee, to all who are *now* called to any office and ministration for thy people; and so replenish them with the truth of thy doctrine, and endue them with holiness of life, that they may faithfully serve before thee to the glory of thy great Name, and to the benefit of thy holy Church; through Jesus Christ our Lord, who liveth and reigneth with thee in the unity of the Holy Spirit, one God, now and ever. *Amen.*

THE PSALMS   132:8–18
              27:1–7

THE LESSONS   Numbers 11:16–17, 24–29
              1 Corinthians 3:5–11
              John 4:31–38

PROPER PREFACE OF APOSTLES

13. FOR THE MINISTRY

II

Especially suitable at times of prayer for the increase of ministries in the Church.

THE COLLECT

ALMIGHTY GOD, whose Son entrusted to the hands of men the ministry of reconciliation: Inspire by your Holy Spirit the hearts and minds of many to give themselves to this ministry, that all mankind may be drawn to your blessed kingdom; through Jesus Christ your Son our Lord, who lives and reigns with you and the Holy Spirit, one God, now and for ever. *Amen.*

ALMIGHTY GOD, whose Son hath entrusted to the hands of men and ministry of reconciliation: Inspire by thy Holy Spirit the hearts and minds of many to give themselves to this ministry, that all mankind may be drawn to thy blessed kingdom; through Jesus Christ thy Son our Lord, who liveth and reigneth with thee and the same Spirit, one God, now and for ever. *Amen.*

THE PSALMS   61
                           63:1–9

THE LESSONS   1 Samuel 3:1–10
                           Ephesians 4:11–16
                           Matthew 9:35–38

PROPER PREFACE OF THE SEASON

13. FOR THE MINISTRY

III

Especially suitable for all Christians in their vocation and ministry.

THE COLLECT

ALMIGHTY AND EVERLASTING GOD, by whose Spirit the whole company of your faithful people is governed and sanctified: Receive our prayers which we now offer before you for all members of your holy Church, that in their vocation and ministry they may truly and devoutly serve you, to the glory of your Name; through our Lord and Savior Jesus Christ, who lives and reigns with you in the unity of the Holy Spirit, one God, now and ever. *Amen.*

ALMIGHTY AND EVERLASTING GOD, by whose Spirit the whole body of the Church is governed and sanctified: Receive our supplications and prayers, which we offer before thee for all members of thy holy Church, that every member of the same, in his vocation and ministry, may truly and godly serve thee; through our Lord and Savior Jesus Christ, who liveth and reigneth with thee in the unity of the Holy Spirit, one God, now and ever. *Amen.*

THE PSALMS   15
                  112:1–9

THE LESSONS   Exodus 19:3–8
                  1 Peter 4:7–11
                  Matthew 16:24–27

PROPER PREFACE OF BAPTISM, OR THE SEASON

14. FOR THE MISSION OF THE CHURCH

I

THE COLLECT

O GOD, who made of one blood all nations of men to dwell on the face of the whole earth, and sent your blessed Son to preach peace to those who are far and to those who are near: Grant that all men everywhere may seek after you and find you; bring the nations into your fold, pour out your Spirit upon all mankind, and hasten your kingdom; through Jesus Christ your Son our Lord, who lives and reigns with you and the Holy Spirit, one God, now and for ever. *Amen.*

O GOD, who hast made of one blood all nations of men to dwell on the face of the whole earth, and didst send thy blessed Son to preach peace to those who are far off and to those who are nigh: Grant that all men everywhere may seek after thee and find thee; bring the nations into thy fold, pour out thy Spirit upon all mankind, and hasten thy kingdom; through Jesus Christ thy Son our Lord, who liveth and reigneth with thee and the Holy Spirit, one God, now and for ever. *Amen.*

THE PSALMS 96
66:1–7

THE LESSONS

Isaiah 2:2–4		Isaiah 49:5–13
Ephesians 2:13–22	*or*	Ephesians 3:1–12
Luke 10:1–9		Matthew 28:16–20

PROPER PREFACE OF THE SEASON, OR OF APOSTLES

14. FOR THE MISSION OF THE CHURCH

II

THE COLLECT

O GOD of all nations of the earth: Remember the multitudes who have been created in your image, but have not known the redeeming work of our Savior Jesus Christ; and grant that, by the prayers and labors of your holy Church, they may be delivered from unbelief, and brought to worship you, through him who is the resurrection and the life of all men, your Son Jesus Christ our Lord, who lives and reigns with you and the Holy Spirit, one God, now and ever. *Amen.*

O GOD of all the nations of the earth: Remember the multitudes who have been created in thine image, but have not known the redeeming work of our Savior Jesus Christ; and grant that, by the prayers and labors of thy holy Church, they may be delivered from unbelief, and brought to worship thee, through him who is the resurrection and the life of all men, the same thy Son Jesus Christ our Lord, who liveth and reigneth with thee and the Holy Spirit, one God, now and ever. *Amen.*

THE PSALMS   96
       66:1–7

THE LESSONS

  Isaiah 2:2–4   Isaiah 49:5–13
  Ephesians 2:13–22 *or* Ephesians 3:1–12
  Luke 10:1–9   Matthew 28:16–20

PROPER PREFACE OF THE SEASON, OR OF APOSTLES

15. FOR THE NATION

The proper for Independence Day (page 588) may be used in place of the following:

THE COLLECT

LORD GOD ALMIGHTY, who made all the peoples of the earth for your glory, and summon all nations to serve in freedom and peace: Grant to the people of our country a zeal for righteousness, and the strength of self-control, that we may exercise our liberty in justice and compassion; through Jesus Christ our Lord, who lives and reigns with you and the Holy Spirit, one God, in glory everlasting. *Amen.*

LORD GOD ALMIGHTY, who hast made all nations of the earth for thy glory, to serve thee in freedom and peace: Grant to the people of our country a zeal for righteousness, and the strength of self-control, that we may exercise our liberty in accordance with thy gracious will; through Jesus Christ our Lord, who liveth and reigneth with thee and the Holy Spirit, one God, in glory everlasting. *Amen.*

THE PSALMS	67
	47

THE LESSONS	Isaiah 26:1–8
	Romans 13:1–10
	Mark 12:13–17

PROPER PREFACE OF TRINITY SUNDAY

16. FOR PEACE

THE COLLECT

ALMIGHTY GOD, from whom all thoughts of truth and peace proceed: Kindle in the hearts of all men the true love of peace; and guide with your pure and peaceable wisdom those who take counsel for the nations of the earth, that in tranquillity your kingdom may go forward, until the earth is filled with the knowledge of your love; through Jesus Christ our Lord, who lives and reigns with you in the unity of the Holy Spirit, one God, now and ever. *Amen.*

ALMIGHTY GOD, from whom all thoughts of truth and peace proceed: Kindle, we pray thee, in the hearts of all men the true love of peace; and guide with thy pure and peaceable wisdom those who take counsel for the nations of the earth, that in tranquillity thy kingdom may go forward, until the earth is filled with the knowledge of thy love; through Jesus Christ our Lord, who liveth and reigneth with thee in the unity of the Holy Spirit, one God, now and ever. *Amen.*

THE PSALMS   85:7–13
                   119:161–168

THE LESSONS   Micah 4:1–5
                   Ephesians 2:13–18
                   John 16:23–33

PROPER PREFACE OF THE SEASON

631

17. FOR ROGATION DAYS

The following propers may be used at any time, as appropriate.

The traditional Rogation Days occur on the Monday, Tuesday, and Wednesday before Ascension Day.

I

For fruitful seasons

THE COLLECT

ALMIGHTY GOD, Lord of heaven and earth: We humbly pray that your gracious providence may give and preserve to our use the harvests of the land and sea, and may prosper all who labor to gather them; that we, who are constantly receiving your bounty, may always give thanks to you, the giver of all good things; through Jesus Christ our Lord. *Amen.*

ALMIGHTY GOD, Lord of heaven and earth: We humbly pray that thy gracious providence may give and preserve to our use the harvests of the land and sea, and may prosper all who labor to gather them; that we, who constantly receive from thy bounty, may always give thanks to thee, the giver of all good things; through Jesus Christ our Lord. *Amen.*

THE PSALMS   147:5–11
               144:9–15

THE LESSONS   Ezekiel 34:25–31
               1 Corinthians 3:6–9
               Luke 11:5–13

PROPER PREFACE OF THE SEASON

17. ROGATION DAYS

II

For commerce and industry

THE COLLECT

O GOD, our Creator, from whom all men receive their appointed work on earth: Give your blessing, we pray, to those who are engaged in commerce and industry, that, receiving the due reward of their labors, they may supply the needs of men in humble and unselfish service; through Jesus Christ our Lord. *Amen.*

O GOD, our Creator, from whom all men receive their appointed work on earth: Give thy blessing, we beseech thee, to those who are engaged in commerce and industry, that, receiving the due reward of their labors, they may supply the needs of men in humble and unselfish service; through Jesus Christ our Lord. *Amen.*

THE PSALMS	107:1–9
	107:21–32

THE LESSONS	Acts 20:32–35
	Romans 12:9–18
	Matthew 6:19–24

PROPER PREFACE OF THE SEASON

17. ROGATION DAYS

III

For stewardship of creation

THE COLLECT

ALMIGHTY FATHER, whose hand is open to fill all things living with plenteousness: Make us ever thankful for your great goodness; and grant that we, remembering the account which we must one day give, may be faithful stewards of your bounty; through Jesus Christ our Lord. *Amen.*

ALMIGHTY FATHER, whose hand is open to fill all things living with plenteousness: Make us ever thankful for thy great goodness; and grant that we, remembering the account which we must one day give, may be faithful stewards of thy bounty; through Jesus Christ our Lord. *Amen.*

THE PSALMS   24:1–6
104:1, 13–15, 23–31

THE LESSONS   Job 38:1–18
1 Timothy 6:7–10, 17–19
Luke 12:16–31

PROPER PREFACE OF THE SEASON

18. FOR THE SICK

The Collect

HEAVENLY FATHER, Giver of all life and health: Comfort and strengthen by your healing power your sick *servants* for whom our prayers are offered, and bless those who minister to *them;* that *they* may have confidence and peace in your loving care; through Jesus Christ our Lord. *Amen.*

HEAVENLY FATHER, Giver of all life and health: Comfort and strengthen by thy healing power thy sick *servants* for whom our prayers are offered, and bless those who minister to *them;* that *they* may have confidence and peace in thy loving care; through Jesus Christ our Lord. *Amen.*

| The Psalms | 3 |
| | 13 |

The Lessons	2 Kings 20:1–5
	James 5:13–16
	Mark 2:1–12

Proper Preface of the Season

The Minister may at his discretion select other collects, psalms, and lessons from the Ministration to the Sick.

19. FOR SOCIAL JUSTICE

THE COLLECT

ALMIGHTY GOD, who created man in your own image: Grant us grace fearlessly to contend against evil, and to make no peace with oppression; and, that we may reverently use our freedom, help us to employ it in the maintenance of justice among men and nations, to the glory of your holy Name; through Jesus Christ our Lord, who lives and reigns with you and the Holy Spirit, one God, now and for ever. *Amen.*

ALMIGHTY GOD, who hast created man in thine own image: Grant us grace fearlessly to contend against evil, and to make no peace with oppression; and, that we may reverently use our freedom, help us to employ it in the maintenance of justice among men and nations, to the glory of thy holy Name; through Jesus Christ our Lord, who liveth and reigneth with thee and the Holy Spirit, one God, now and for ever. *Amen.*

THE PSALMS	72:1–4, 12–14
	75
THE LESSONS	Isaiah 42:1–8
	James 2:5–9, 12–17
	Matthew 10:32–42

PROPER PREFACE OF THE SEASON

20. FOR SOCIAL SERVICE

THE COLLECT

HEAVENLY FATHER, whose blessed Son came not to be served but to serve: Bless all, we pray, who, following in his steps, give themselves to the service of their fellow men; that with wisdom, patience, and courage, they may minister in his Name to the suffering, the friendless, and the needy; for the love of him who laid down his life for us, your Son our Savior Jesus Christ. *Amen.*

HEAVENLY FATHER, whose blessed Son came not to be ministered unto but to minister: Bless all, we pray thee, who, following in his steps, give themselves to the service of their fellow men; that with wisdom, patience, and courage, they may minister in his Name to the suffering, the friendless, and the needy; for the love of him who laid down his life for us, thy Son our Savior Jesus Christ. *Amen.*

THE PSALMS   146
                   22:23–28

THE LESSONS   Zechariah 8:3–12, 16–17
                   1 Peter 4:7–11
                   Mark 10:42–52

PROPER PREFACE OF THE SEASON

21. FOR THE UNITY OF THE CHURCH

The Collect

ALMIGHTY FATHER, whose blessed Son before his passion prayed for his disciples that they might be one, even as you and he are one: Grant that, bound together in love and obedience to you, your Church may be united in one body by the one Spirit; that the world may believe in him whom you have sent, your Son our Lord Jesus Christ, who lives and reigns with you in the unity of the Holy Spirit, one God, now and ever. *Amen.*

ALMIGHTY FATHER, whose blessed Son before his passion prayed for his disciples that they might be one, even as thou and he are one: Grant that, bound together in love and in obedience to thee, thy Church may be united in one body by the one Spirit; that the world may believe in him whom thou hast sent, thy Son our Lord Jesus Christ, who liveth and reigneth with thee in the unity of the Holy Spirit, one God, now and ever. *Amen.*

THE PSALMS   122
                    87

THE LESSONS   Isaiah 35
                    Ephesians 4:1–6
                    John 17:15–23

PROPER PREFACE OF BAPTISM, OR OF TRINITY SUNDAY

22. FOR VOCATION IN DAILY WORK

THE COLLECT

ALMIGHTY GOD, heavenly Father, whose glory and handiwork are shown forth in the heavens and in the earth: Deliver us, we pray, in our several occupations from selfish love of riches, that we may do the work which you give us, with singleness of heart as your servants, and to the benefit of our fellow men; for the sake of him who came among us as one that serves, your Son Jesus Christ our Lord. *Amen.*

ALMIGHTY GOD, heavenly Father, who showest forth thy glory and handiwork in the heavens and in the earth: Deliver us, we beseech thee, in our several occupations from selfish love of riches, that we may do the work which thou givest us, with singleness of heart as thy servants, and to the benefit of our fellow men; for the sake of him who came among us as one that serveth, thy Son Jesus Christ our Lord. *Amen.*

THE PSALMS   1
                  8

THE LESSONS   Ecclesiastes 3:1, 9–13
                   1 Peter 2:11–17
                   Matthew 6:19–24

PROPER PREFACE OF THE SEASON